Dani_l Simpson's amazing book should be read by everyone who is interested in how the human side of this world really works - which means EVERYONE! He uses humor as Shakespeare did - to lighten the load of a heavy, dark, and important story.
John Perkins, author of the bestselling *Confessions of an Economic Hitman*

A Rough Guide to the Dark Side is a funny, angry and insightful indictment of modern media practice. Daniel Simpson shows us a remarkably dangerous world shaped by the fantasies of the elite and journalists who have embraced subservient fear, savage cost-cutting and institutional laziness. Simpson's writing demonstrates that we not only deserve better journalism, but that it's still out there: observing, investigating and informing with humanity and passion.
A.L. Kennedy, writer and comedian; author of the *Costa Prize-winning Day*

The archetypal innocent abroad, Daniel Simpson thought he could help the locals. He dropped out of journalism to run a music festival in Serbia, imagining himself a jaundiced man of the world. But his project became a study in modern corruption, with a learning curve so steep it was more like a suicide's screaming spiral. Witty and compassionate, yet merciless on himself, he tells a story that's a constant pleasure to read.
Michela Wrong, author of *It's Our Turn to Eat. The Story of a Kenyan Whistleblower*

D0302531

A Rough Guide
To The Dark Side

A Rough Guide To The Dark Side

Daniel Simpson

WITHDRAWN

zero
books

Winchester, UK
Washington, USA

INVERCLYDE LIBRARIES

First published by Zero Books, 2012
Zero Books is an imprint of John Hunt Publishing Ltd., Laurel House, Station Approach,
Alresford, Hants, SO24 9JH, UK
office1@jhpbooks.net
www.johnhuntpublishing.com

For distributor details and how to order please visit the 'Ordering' section on our website.

Text copyright: Daniel Simpson 2011

ISBN: 978 1 78099 307 2

All rights reserved. Except for brief quotations in critical articles or reviews, no part of this
book may be reproduced in any manner without prior written permission from the publishers.

The rights of Daniel Simpson as author have been asserted in accordance with the Copyright,
Designs and Patents Act 1988.

A CIP catalogue record for this book is available from the British Library.

Design: Stuart Davies

Printed and bound by CPI Group (UK) Ltd, Croydon, CR0 4YY

We operate a distinctive and ethical publishing philosophy in all
areas of our business, from our global network of authors to
production and worldwide distribution.

CONTENTS

For Guy

Author's note

I hope this isn't fiction, or one-sided. I've tried to record the truth as I perceived it, but no reporter's work can be objective. In keeping with media convention, some facts are more factual than others, and a few of the details are blurred to protect the guilty. One or two walk-on characters are composites, and occasional quotations are doctored, for clarity. As Rudyard Kipling emphasized: 'The most remarkable stories are, of course, those which do not appear - for obvious reasons.' He was also a stoner.

London, September 11, 2011

'I imagine that every historian is similarly affected when he begins to record the events of some period and wishes to portray them sincerely. Where is the center of events, the common standpoint around which they revolve and which gives them cohesion? In order that something like cohesion, something like causality, that some kind of meaning might be revealed and that it can in some way be told, the historian must invent units, a hero, a nation, an idea, and he must allow to happen to this invented unit what has in reality happened to the nameless.'
Hermann Hesse

'The bigger you build the bonfire, the more darkness is revealed.'
Terence McKenna

ZERO

I never really meant to join the underworld. I fell in. Fate proved far more powerful than me.

If our story began with a word, that word was lost, and the world appeared to have lost it more than me. I'd been asking people why for most of my life, but it struck me that this question might be pointless. The one that mattered more was how to change things. And I'd struggled with that for a while before meeting my partner.

Back then I didn't see him in those terms. Our earliest encounters came at random; or so I'd assumed as a skeptical journalist. I felt streetwise when I first set foot in Serbia. In a way, I was sure I'd seen it all before: another country stewing in self-pity, fiercely independent in character, while pimping itself around foreigners for cash. From afar, this sounded rather like a turn-off, with none of the furtive thrills of Balkan wars. The cartoon villains who started them were long gone, and they'd left behind a miserable pariah state. Who cared if it was festering in woe?

To my amazement, I found that I did. This was largely down to my partner's sense of purpose, and the visions it awakened in us both. Music had revolutionary potential, he said. Young Serbs could be the masters of their destiny, provided they organized ways to come together. The forces that oppressed them would be sidestepped.

There were so many reasons to think he had the answer. Being safe might not be one, but that didn't bother me. Although it was clear we'd face risks, they mostly seemed trivial. I was hot off the achievement conveyor belt from Cambridge, with boundless expectations for the future. I'd grown accustomed to getting my way if I put my mind to it, and was convinced that if I only kept talking, I'd summon the words to persuade other people of anything.

But nothing's quite that simple in the Balkans. My partner said we'd need a cunning plan. And for the past few weeks, he'd supplied them in abundance, while puncturing my ignorant assumptions. Despite this affront to my pride, I felt inspired.

'You know, most stories are like parody of history,' he'd said one evening, plying us both with savage shots of firewater, in a bar at the foot of a tower block in Belgrade. 'What you tell me is grotesque hallucination. No one here believe those lies of West. Speak Serbian, fuck it, so whole world understands you.'

Although I didn't always understand him, G made sense. Most of what I was paid to write was bunk, especially the bits from politicians. As my partner said, they routinely spouted fiction. Serbia wasn't a nation in transition, as most of my articles implied. It was stuck in a rut and it needed urgent help. But since there wasn't a hope of any such thing arriving, our only option left was to intervene: we'd have to hijack its election for a president, and engineer the outcome that we wanted.

G wasn't the kind of guy you'd want to say no to. And whatever it was he came up with, he sounded for real. His English had a confident authority, with the captivating ring of a pie-eyed piper. It rattled out in blasts of manic brass, which bludgeoned you into surround-sound submission. He'd strut across the city like a battery bunny, while I trotted willingly to heel. Yet despite this perpetual performance, he seemed sincere. 'I don't give a *fuck*!' he'd exclaim, because he did. Though he was patently absurd, I couldn't help liking him. His recklessness was infectious, like his laughter.

When the bar had started spinning, he leaned closer. 'This place became laboratory for future,' he explained, gesticulating vaguely round the room. 'For centuries Balkans was battleground of empires, so now we show to world whole different model.'

What was there to say, except why not? G appeared to know what he was doing. Though he must have been twenty years older than me, he looked ageless. Beneath the greying mop atop his head, the expression on his face was like a baby's, gurgling with unencumbered energy. He walked tall with his shoulders braced back, and he chortled through my ethical detachment. He appeared to believe almost anything was possible, and talked as if we'd already seen it was.

The morning of truth was upon us before I'd thought twice. There was nothing to fear, he assured me, as we zeroed in on our mission's first objective. Everything would be fine if we kept it casual. I couldn't help agreeing. Reporters aren't meant to be actively political. But I hadn't felt professional for months, and the October sun glossed over my objectivity. G slowed to a halt at my side, shielding his gaze with the morning's unread tabloid, and together we surveyed the square in which we found ourselves. Revived by autumn gold, its statue to a footnote of history gleamed with majesty.

I've always loved this time of year the most, perhaps because it's when I was born. The crisp bright light felt fresh with possibility, and the academic promise of renewal. I thought back to an afternoon just two years earlier, when I'd watched what looked like a televised revolution, beamed live to my sofa in Zurich from Belgrade. In those days, it wasn't a place I'd thought of visiting, and like most of the rest of the world I'd soon switched off. But now I was here, I was learning I'd been wrong.

Slouching on a bench, I let my partner's words blow over with the breeze. Beyond the gravel park that yawned before us, oppressive walls of tenements receded. Their rusting terrace irons oozed faded charm. It mightn't be the prettiest of cities, but Belgrade wasn't so dreadful, I decided, as long as you were squinting through shades. I lifted mine to my head and turned to G, who'd clutched two horny thumbs towards his lips, palms cupped as if to imitate an owl. Instead, he inhaled throatily, until a joint between his little fingers buckled. A murky cloud of dope smoke masked his face. Exhaling like a laryngitic dragon, he flicked the spliff to the ground and pronounced it kicked.

'Whoa, that shit is strong,' he boomed through the haze. 'I gotta be careful.'

Having already smoked myself senseless, I concurred. Although our rendezvous was nigh, we both sat still. The birds around my head cheeped frail excuses. That building didn't look like a party headquarters. Its entrance was a residential stairwell. The sole distinguishing feature was a patchwork of plaques. But I knew one belonged to our quarry, whose logo was as clunking as its name: G17 Plus hadn't fired up the public, and a chorus of foreign endorsements hadn't helped. At his final rally, their candidate was egged. Now he was facing defeat in a run-off for president, against a populist with next to no charisma.

This was where we came in. Plan B was disguised as an interview with *The New York Times*, the most self-regarding paper on the planet. As cover for meddling outsiders, it was perfect. I was their correspondent in the region, and my interest would by nature sound tangential: the office up for grabs possessed no power.

Such was the zombie state of Yugoslavia, which staggered on in name if nothing else. At the start of the 1990s, it had six theoretically Communist republics. Now, in 2002, just two survived: Serbia, which attacked its neighbors in the name of 'brotherhood and unity', and Montenegro, which demanded independence. When it broke away like Slovenia, Croatia, Macedonia and Bosnia, Yugoslavia would formally be dead. And at that point, the Serbian president would call the shots again, as he did when he was Slobodan Milosevic, who'd presided over crimes against humanity, before promoting himself to run the union he'd destroyed.

By the time I arrived in the city, he'd been sent to The Hague, deported to rant at a trial for coordinating genocide. Though some Serbs watched proceedings on TV, most preferred *Sex and the City*. Pigsty politicians made them queasy. All the mouths in

4

the trough talked democratic platitudes, yet no one seemed to benefit but gangsters, the wartime elite who became the nouveau riche. Popular anger had wilted into boredom. Voters were so downcast they stayed at home. Barely 50 percent, the legal minimum, turned out for the first round. The second looked a cert to be annulled.

We had to get our act together fast, before we got too twisted to care much either. As a properly accredited reporter, I had to convey some semblance of chasing the story. Against the better judgment of nausea, I stood up. 'Come on,' I urged my partner, who was puffing out his cheeks while walking in circles. 'Let's get to work.'

G strode ahead, bolt upright in a suit of bilious check, which appeared to be trying to emulate Highland tweeds. An impish grin topped off his gaudy aura, eyes glinting like costume gems in a Serbian moon face. G's burly frame clattered through the doorway as if he owned the place.

'We have appointment with Mr Labus,' he beamed at the receptionist, and any colleagues within earshot down the corridor. 'He is expecting us.'

I trudged demurely behind, unused to such a forthright translator. My regular assistant barely spoke when spoken to, which suited me just fine as an idle hack. But it wasn't what was called for today. An androgynous aide in jeans burst out of an antechamber, and told us in jaunty English to step inside. I'd scarcely lit a cigarette when the target joined us.

One thing was clear from the start: he wasn't a statesman. Bearded like an unassuming uncle, Miroljub Labus was patently a wonk. He'd have been happier drafting someone else's budget. That looked like his lot in opposition. But when Milosevic was toppled in 2000, people like Labus got chronic delusions of grandeur. Having formed their 'democratic' coalition, they duly gridlocked government with infighting. While Serbia stagnated in recession, politicians mostly jockeyed for position. And stalemate suited most of them but Labus, which was why all his allies backed his bid for president. If no one bothered to vote, he'd be the fall guy.

Our interview got straight to the point. 'How are you going to rouse the electorate?' I asked, after navigating awkward small talk about harvests.

For all its metropolitan pretensions, Serbia was at heart a land of peasants. Politically, they split themselves quite neatly. A third still drooled over warlords and heirs to Milosevic. To them, Labus was a stooge of Western enemies, effectively an agent of The Empire. If they voted at all, they'd back his conservative rival, who also had a third of people's support. That left the Labus bloc of 'reformers'. The Western media labeled them 'pro-Western', which meant 'those least unlikely to do as they're told.' Though marginally less numerous than the others, their ranks included a wily prime minister, who used Milosevic's laws to cling to power. This made him as widely reviled as the former tyrant, and that gave Labus little hope of winning.

Not that he'd admit it to a journalist. 'Serbia is one big family that is voting for its future.' The contender smiled at us, as if addressing cameras. 'I am sure that it will make the best choice.'

'Perhaps,' I said.

'I started with nothing and received almost one million votes. This is a great success for me.'

'Perhaps,' I repeated. It was barely more than a quarter of the total, which was little more than half of what he needed. If Labus refused to see the problem, how could we solve it?

'What about the young?' I asked. 'They've all lost interest.'

For years, they'd been the vanguard of resistance, exposing the old regime's self-serving lies. Their parents were either jaded or co-opted, but younger people weren't so easily cowed. Activism became a rite of passage, until they saw how little they'd achieved. Democracy was rich in televised insults, but a poor source of hard currency, or work visas. Serbs with big ambitions tried to emigrate. Their country's outcast status ruled out the only goal that most people shared: joining the European Union tomorrow. Labus knew in theory how to get them there. He was the closest thing in Serbia to a blueprint from Brussels. But he didn't know how to persuade disgruntled youngsters.

'You're their natural candidate,' I said. 'Can't you offer them something they believe in? Otherwise they'll carry on ignoring you.'

He didn't have a talking point for that. Nor did he mind much. We all sipped fizzy mineral water in silence. I opened a folder, and pulled out a sheaf of papers.

'We can help you,' G translated, as I pushed the printed bundle across the table. Labus looked baffled. My partner tried English. 'You know, this gentleman did wrote first positive story I read about our country in Western media.'

The dossier stayed unopened where I'd placed it.

'Presidential Campaign Phase II,' its cover announced. 'In which Miroljub Labus invites the young people of Serbia to a free party on October 5, in front of the Federal Parliament, to celebrate the second anniversary of the day Milosevic was driven out.'

I'd finished the text around dawn, after staying up all night. The concept was simple. A few weeks beforehand in England, a quarter of a million people had swamped a beach. They'd gone to hear a balding man spin records. Though he'd done the same thing for years, he seemed unique. Fatboy Slim was a festival personified: funk, soul and disco rolled into one, as big a hit on adverts as in nightclubs. If only we could bring him out to Serbia, he'd probably pull an even bigger crowd. Serbs wished the outside world would treat them normally, but no one remotely famous ever toured there. The last big act to visit was The Prodigy, who flouted Western sanctions in the war years. In return they'd been given the keys to Belgrade. Simply by virtue of being there, they were legends. Local counter-culture didn't have much to shout about.

Of course, rocking the vote was a dismal cliché. And it might not change the country in itself. But what if it woke people up and got them active? That sort of movement builds momentum. Serbs were desperate for any kind of kicks. A fortnight earlier, they'd won the basketball world championship. A hundred and fifty thousand went on the rampage, smashing up cafes and shops in celebration. Surely there were better things to do. And who'd say no to a big free gig on Saturday? I reclined in my chair while my partner got into details.

We had seventy-two hours left to make the show happen. That was more than enough. G had already met the DJ's agent. A few calls and we'd have everything sewn up: TV promos, radio hype, and megaphone salvos fired from flatbed trucks. Posters could be pasted overnight, and the streets would be littered with flyers that afternoon. We'd rig up the stage the next day, if someone got a permit from the police. All Labus had to do was address the nation. We'd written his lines, and could film him within hours. The networks would screen our tape on constant loop. It was breaking news.

On and on G went, jabbing at the paperwork for emphasis. 'We have wasted time here because of what we've been through,' he read from the speech. 'But it is not too late. Now is the time for change. We need to be united again to make it happen.'

Cut to some footage of protests in 2000, then whack up a banging soundtrack, and wait for the hordes of punters to descend. Labus could tell them to vote if they liked the show.

'What have you got to lose?' our pitch concluded. 'Do you have any better ideas?'

Well? Do you? The candidate glanced from one of us to the other, then down at my *New York Times* business card.

'It's really very simple,' I said. 'If you give us fifty grand, we'll get you elected.'

LIMBO

In hindsight, our adventure sounds misguided. Although G made life more fun, it felt surreal, and the closer we grew, the stranger he became. But he was also undeniably exciting. His example would constantly tempt me to do as I pleased, the opposite of what editors required. Suppressing my opinions in print only made me outspoken. I'd talk about ideas without daring to act. Though I didn't like following orders, I lacked convictions, and an outlet to express them. Suddenly, I felt challenged to take a stand. It was like being brought back to life from a highbrow coma.

From the first conversation we shared, G had seemed eager to impress me. Initially, this roused my mistrust. But it didn't take him long to win me over. He reminded me of myself, only much less self-conscious. He was earnestly romantic and irreverent, an idealist with a wicked sense of humor. And best of all he seemed entirely fearless. Around me, this combination worked like rocket fuel. I felt sure I was on the cusp of liberation.

When we met at the start of the summer, I was floundering. The job that had brought me to Serbia unsettled me, even more than my efforts to stay straight enough to do it. I didn't see how I could do it especially well. My employers had minimal interest in the Balkans. This meant there was nothing to send them most of the time, apart from a few hundred words of 'nothing changed'. But I had to pitch ideas to prove my worth. In the absence of news, they liked cultural features best. So I scratched around to find one that inspired me. And when I did, it couldn't have been a stronger tonic.

Everyone I asked said 'go to EXIT'. It was an event that had morphed out of protests against Milosevic. Designed to radicalize students on the quiet, it began as a series of concerts in 2000, which ran for 100 days in a provincial square, and ended in calls for the president to kill himself. A year later, EXIT honored his demise, by occupying a fortress on the Danube. Stages were wedged between grassy moats and turrets, and for nine balmy evenings in July, the music played from dusk until well after dawn. The afternoon heat was far too hot for dancing, and Serbs preferred to party through the night, regardless of whether they had work to do in the morning. By its second incarnation, in 2002, EXIT drew tens of thousands every day, among them a token handful of foreigners. One was a *New York Times* reporter. Me.

When I interviewed the festival's youthful founders, G had sat in on our colloquy and yawned. He seemed to have the manner of a shyster. Attired in ostentatious clashing fabrics, he spoke with all the focus of a Catherine wheel that was spinning off its nail. His sole contribution of note was to declare that he was 'man in charge of program'. This brought to mind *The Great Rock and Roll Swindle*, and Malcolm McLaren's insistence that he was the Sex Pistols.

The duo I'd come to hear from sounded sharper. Like me, they were both in their 20s, but they'd hit upon a more uplifting lifestyle. 'We want to do what we enjoy,' one said, 'and gather hundreds, thousands of creative, capable people around us who think like we do and try to have an impact on society.'

These words were disconcertingly impressive. They also seemed true. They were ordering police around the fortress. From a lookout on the sunbaked veranda, which crawled with A-list visitors most evenings, the organizers of EXIT scanned their domain. As a setting for a festival it was perfect, with a sunken DJ amphitheater out back, where thousands stomped and gurned their way to sunrise. By day, it looked a little like a tourist trap, which is what it might have been had there been any tourists.

A radio crackled on the table between the Guarana cans, and a girl barely out of her teens skipped up in hot pants, asking where she could find supplies of vodka. Her job was to pander to performers. Others her age were lugging racks of kit.

The brasher of the two youths beside me swelled with pride. His cherubic cheeks gushed unaccented English. 'We're showing people that what looks impossible can be achieved,' he said. 'So anyone who claims change is impossible here has a concrete example of that not being true.'

Corporate logos tempered his idealism, but our Stella Artois parasols kept the rays off, and I guzzled down the product feeling grateful. My hosts didn't seem too fussed about who they worked with.

'Part of our aim,' said the serious one, 'is to show you can cooperate with local authorities and still achieve what you want.'

The chubby chap even spouted half-baked Zen. 'Our motto is: If not you, who?' he said. 'If not now, when?' They'd sold me at once on selling them wholeheartedly.

Their festival's name was its history, as in 'EXIT out of the ten years of madness'. But it was hard to escape the bombast of their rhetoric, which remixed Milosevic's with 'civil society' newspeak. Apart from a sublime setting for excess, their event was said to be 'one of the greatest marketing campaigns in the country'. Lashing on the 'third sector' jargon, they promised it would 'establish a new discourse for the young people from the whole region', while 'promoting positive democratic values' and 'becoming an unavoidable part of the transition mechanism.' If they didn't get rich off music, politics beckoned.

From the ramparts behind where we sat, a vast red banner was dangled at Novi Sad, urging citizens to heed what was brewing in the ruins. 'SERBIA ARE YOU READY FOR THE FUTURE?' it screamed in English, a strong political statement in itself. They'd spurned Serbian to distance EXIT from nationalism, and the decade of dark bellicosity it spawned.

The river below held reminders of the Nineties. It lapped at the carcass of a bridge that was bombed by NATO three summers earlier, ostensibly to drive Serbian troops from Kosovo, while pursuing a broader goal of regime change. This had climaxed in the downfall of Milosevic, and the story behind that was murkier than the waters.

EXIT was born as a spin-off of U.S. policy. A substantial amount of its money still came from America, which was why *The New York Times* had shown an interest. Uncle Sam was investing in Serbian political futures, by funding influential student activists.

Being bombed didn't make most Serbs big fans of The West, or keener on giving up Kosovo to Albanians. But some people blamed their leader for getting them blitzed, as well as having bankrupted the country. American planners raced to take advantage. Dollars were funneled to a youth group called Otpor, which had sprung up to mount resistance to Milosevic. Its cadres had a flair for self-promotion, and their stenciled fist graffiti surfaced everywhere. The U.S. Army trained them how to take beatings, which police supplied without much provocation. Crackdowns were widely reported, by alternative media financed from Washington, enlisting more young people in the cause. To round off their plan, the Americans helped unite the opposition, and enticed them to field a joint challenger to Milosevic. When the strongman lost an election but wouldn't stand down, the capital's streets were filled with young protesters. The army defied an order to send in tanks, and chose instead to recognize his rivals. The machinery of oppression had switched sides, because the old regime's tyrannical boss was 'finished', precisely as Otpor's signature slogan forecast.

It was textbook non-violent direct action, and the U.S. aimed to repeat it far and wide, ideally across the former Soviet Union. Serbs could teach Georgians to oust a leader backed by Russia. Despite misgivings about American imperialism, several of Otpor's alumni spread the word, briefing youth groups from the Balkans to Belarus.

They weren't the only ones still on the payroll. EXIT got almost $200,000, from some of America's shadier three-letter agencies. The Office for Transition Initiatives was part of the Agency for International Development. And like the National Endowment for Democracy, and its IRI and NDI subsidiaries, it did in public what the CIA does secretly: interfere in other countries' politics. The OTI even put out a bragging press release. 'The revolution is over,' this missive decreed. 'The evolution now rests in the hands of the youth!'

Whatever else EXIT achieved, it helped me evolve, providing me with a personalized 'transition mechanism'. Once accredited, I decamped to the press hotel, and embarked on a weeklong stint of immersion reporting, sozzling myself insensate every evening, and dancing like an amphetamine-powered windmill.

Why should I stew all summer in Belgrade, in an apartment that doubled as my office, struggling to follow complexities few readers cared about? Far better to be a strategic hour's drive north, on hand in case anything newsworthy happened, but too far gone to worry much about it. As long as I kept my phone on, who'd even notice?

Come the final morning of EXIT, I was woozy. When a figure approached backstage, I could barely see him. Through the muted hues of daybreak and lights on the gantry, to say nothing of all the chemicals in my bloodstream, I could have sworn his head was a ball of flaming gas. He had a hypnotic air about him, as if smiling through me. Grabbing my arm, he began gabbling at my ear.

When the amplified break-beat subsided, I heard it was G, the self-styled master of ceremonies. He suggested taking a walk behind a tent. In the shadows, he looked the measure of his swagger. There was none of the usual Serbian machismo. If anything, he seemed a bit effeminate. His face had the sheen of a barmaid at Oktoberfest, and his trousers were cut from stripy curtain chintz. His hair sat clumped round his ears as a pair of muffs. Yet something about this appearance stopped me laughing. His every movement flowed, swift and precise. And his eyes shone wide from effervescent depths, as if glimmering with esoteric insight.

'Yeah man,' he announced, by way of greeting. 'You having good time then, or *what*?' When I'd met him before, he'd sounded barely lucid. But now he seemed to be singing out his words, which took the edge off their Kalashnikov delivery, and addressed you as if you were all you'd like to be. Some gesture of respect appeared in order, but before I could think what it was, he'd steamrollered on.

'You know, this show it was born in my shop in a Shepherd's Bush,' he said, cackling wildly in the direction of the stage. This contradicted everything I'd been told. But rather than start with an argument, I sought common ground.

'So you used to live in England too?' I said. Though employed by an American paper, I was born there.

'Man, I spent my best times in London,' G sighed. 'I was travelling to city for years since I was kid. We organize whole project from my store.'

I stared at him, no less confused.

'That place was pretty much everything but business,' he laughed. 'First floor it was juice bar, kinda coffee shop selling ice cream and smoothies. Basement was illegal social club. All day were coming Rastas and Crusties. You know like poets, buffoons and socially devastated people. So one of these guys did bring me up to Glastonbury. I'm telling you experience blew my mind. It was beautiful night, yeah, clear with stars quite visible, and he brought me up to Tor there on the hill, and he said long time ago those Pagans practice rituals here, until day that hill was repossessed by Christians. So he told me I should disregard monastery, right, just to lay straight down, open eyes and desire something beautiful. And I did wish I wanna do festival. Like this.'

He motioned at the throng. Backlit by the first shards of sunlight, twenty thousand faces bounced around. The front row heaved with adolescent beauties, with a dress code of crop tops and boob tubes. From the apron, MC Dynamite ogled their contents, raising a glass of lager in salute. Behind, Roni Size dropped grinding drum and bass, undeterred by continual threats to shut down the system. When security intervened to bundle them off, they decamped to another stage by the fortress entrance, where they remained until they'd almost missed their flight. Eventually, someone stuck them in a taxi, and sent them home to play in sweaty rooms.

'These guys, they my lifeline man,' G said. They'd headlined the previous year too, and like all the other performers he'd imported, they'd gone back to Britain dazzled by their reception. 'Here, the people act like they are superstars. You know, I call them and they came because of those times.'

Except we both knew it wasn't quite like that really. All week, I'd been told the line-up sounded stale, with too many acts that had already played before. A constant gripe was the lack of foreign bands. The DJs could just about stretch to a blowout weekend: Darren Emerson, Derrick Carter and LTJ Bukem. But nine nights had spread them too thinly, especially over a dozen different stages, including a cinema and theatre. For all that the crowds were in raptures, the consensus seemed to be that EXIT had peaked.

G's response was dismissive. 'Round here people totally confused,' he scoffed. 'Serbs think because they value themselves that everyone else is gonna treat them special.'

The first year, mere existence was a triumph. With the end of international isolation, people would have paid to hear buskers from abroad. But EXIT didn't know anyone who'd send some. This was where G came in. He had contacts who'd helped him run parties in England. And when he returned to Belgrade in 2000, he'd gone looking for student activists he'd heard about. They had the local manpower for a festival, and he had access to artists and their agents. On a budget too tight for names most

Serbs had heard of, they scraped together the makings of a bill: Finley Quaye, Tony Allen and Banco de Gaia. It went down a storm. Yet twelve months on, disillusionment was rife. G put this down to an ingrained national mania.

'You realize not much changed here man,' he said. 'I came from London like ten days after end of the Milosevic, and it was one of my worst experiences in this country.'

He'd gone to a football match, he explained, between the Belgrade rivals Partizan and Red Star. It erupted in a riot on the pitch. Rockets were fired at the stands. Players and the visiting coach were beaten. The fixture was scrapped in three minutes.

G put a hand on my shoulder and stared at me hard. 'It was *weird*,' he said. 'Somehow in that game I knew whole saga about revolution is not genuine, and this violence is just going to transfer.'

He started laughing. 'You know, here lotta people still have same bullshit attitude. But fuck it, we take kids with guns and get them looking you in the eye man and smiling. That's what festival can do, hey. It's beautiful.'

I nodded, none too sure what he was getting at.

'Now question is how we take things to next level,' he said.

I tried to sound agreeably non-committal. 'It's not easy, I guess.'

'Exactly, my friend,' he said. 'People here don't wanna *work*. We should show to them what is real transformation, not to change just heads on the Godzilla, or build up some new monster here for masters. I sometimes think was better with Milosevic. At least there was a talk about alternative. Now it seems they all go back to sleep. You know, all these Serbs and Croats they were same. People used to say about Yugoslavia that it had head in Russia and a stomach in America. Now Serbs have the head in fourteenth century and their ass in twenty-first. They get fucked by world while thinking they do fucking.'

He'd lost me, but my mind was drifting anyway. From his

pocket, he'd pulled a blob of black hashish.

'You wanna make joint?' he asked, proffering his palm. 'S'aright man, no one gonna trouble themselves back here.'

I picked up the piece and held it to my nose. It smelled rich, and crumbled easily when heated. It mightn't be the cream of the Himalayas, but it had to beat the local rope-grade weed, which was all I'd been offered since moving to Belgrade. That stuff swelled the skull like a vodka espresso, and wore off just as roughly shortly after. I'd left it alone. Being hired by *The New York Times* was my big break, and I was anxious to exploit it to the full. It was only a matter of weeks since I'd joined, and I was trying to ape the paper's sober style. G's hash was different. It reminded me of a life I'd been denying myself. I knocked up fast, and lugged back three deep tokes.

'Not bad,' I said, and it wasn't, even through the accumulated booze fug. 'Where did you get it?'

Dumb question, I thought, the moment I asked.

The reply was as unexpected as his smile.

'I'll introduce you,' he beamed.

We were friends.

There was only one intruder on my stupor: the Serbian prime minister.

When I first arrived in Belgrade two months earlier, I'd tried to meet some senior politicians. As the newly appointed *Times* correspondent, I'd assumed they'd want to talk to American bigwigs. But no one obliged. Instead, I had to call an American, who was embedded in the government advising on public relations. Having helped me get accredited for EXIT, she also got me summoned back to Belgrade, for an hour-long chat with the premier, Zoran Djindjic. Unfortunately, I knew nothing much about him, except that he'd led an opposition party, but hadn't been popular enough to get himself elected, so the Americans built a coalition round him. Once in power, it quickly splintered, when Djindjic overruled his partners to extradite Milosevic.

That was the last time Serbs made worldwide headlines. Nowadays, Balkan affairs were news in brief. It was nine months since the September 11 attacks, and the *Times* was full of fighting talk and terrorists, regaling itself in American hyperbole. My dry reports on stagnation were 'overheld' for weeks, waiting for a stray 'shelf' or 'gutter' among the jewelry ads. I generally looked for reasons not to write them, and most of the time my editors approved. Quite what I was going to ask Djindjic was a mystery.

I briefly indulged the notion of snorting speed, which appeared to be the festival drug of choice, but a dullard sense of duty overcame me. I sweated through the interview in German, which Djindjic spoke far better than me, but nothing he said sounded worthy of a story. Short of declaring war, or deporting investors, it was hard to see how he'd make *The New York Times*. So I buried my notes in a drawer and drove back to EXIT.

Everyone's priorities felt warped, my own included. Americans might not care about the Balkans, but foreigners had been meddling there for centuries, mostly without consulting the inhabitants. And the *Times* didn't have much space for their point of view, except as a colorful sound bite now and then. My task was not to ask what people thought, but to explain how Western planners thought they should.

As Djindjic had complained: 'It is unfair.' Foreign powers behaved like Americans abroad, repeating their orders loudly and slowly, as if hoping they might yet sink in, while persistently ignoring why they wouldn't.

'Most world leaders are very realistic at home but very moralistic when dealing with us,' he'd explained. He was always being told to arrest more war criminals, but no one offered incentives for him to do so, which might have persuaded Serbs to go along with it. Instead, most people thought they were being victimized. So Djindjic agreed that they were, to keep his job. The most wanted men had protection from the army. Confronting them alone was political suicide.

Serbia couldn't change overnight, Djindjic had said. 'To say now we will determine who was guilty in Bosnia, Croatia and Kosovo, it's too much. It's more important for me that society recovers internally so that what happened can't be repeated.'

It took Germans a generation to confront Nazi guilt, he stressed, and 'in Germany they did it under occupation, but we are not under occupation and we also didn't murder six million Jews'. No: just tens of thousands of Muslims in Bosnia and Kosovo. But even so he clearly had a point, though it wasn't one my bosses would have printed.

News comes packaged in narratives for convenience, and most of these are defined by the powers that be, which set the agenda by announcing what they're doing. Reporters simply write down what they say, and explain what it means from official points of view, to put the information 'into context'. Government spin is therefore background fact, but to draw one's own conclusions would be biased, which was how the U.S. was rebranded 'the international community'. Other perspectives were published, of course, but only if you labeled them as partisan. I couldn't frame the news the way I saw it, and certainly not with comments from a Serb. They'd have to appear as a line in a broader story, which would need to reflect American assumptions. And if I didn't write it that way, editors would. I soon gave up trying. So much for hoary journalistic clichés, like the *Times* editorial code of conduct, which urged staff to report 'without fear or favor'. Toeing the line was less hassle on the whole.

Initially I'd meant to be more rigorous. My shelves were stacked with books I planned to read, until I realized my assignment. Covering the Balkans for *The New York Times* consisted of monitoring whether The Serbs had agreed they were Bad Guys. Trying to explain why they hadn't, or how 'we' made the opposite more likely, was tantamount to 'understanding' suicide bombers. And in the fog of War On Terror, this wasn't on, especially not at a paper boasting 'All The News That's Fit To Print.'

My boss, the foreign editor Roger Cohen, had started his job on what he called 'this solemn date': September 11, 2001. The response to being attacked defined his remit. While Americans asked each other 'why do they hate us?' the *Times* had asked the White House who'd get bombed. A year on from The Crime That Changed Everything, Cohen sent a memo to reporters. 'To judge by the President's plans,' he confided, 'the first half of next year may be busy.'

Well, that was one way to describe the invasion of Iraq. He wasn't finished. Declaring himself 'in awe of the commitment and dedication of everyone to ensuring and sharpening our excellence,' Cohen urged us to 'celebrate life' by 'chronicling its every nuance and its every possibility'. Except, of course, for those that might derail 'the President's plans', because war is stuff that happens when he says so. Since journalists are obsessed with what's going to happen, they fixate on What Powerful People Plan To Do. And if no other powerful people obstruct them, then why should the press? Our task would be to chronicle the cavalcade.

Not from the Balkans, however. There, my directions marched me backwards, to dredge up Roger Cohen's recent past. He'd covered the Bosnian war in the 1990s, and called it 'as morally indelible to my generation of correspondents as Vietnam,' only this time he thought Americans were the Good Guys; at least once they intervened to bomb the Serbs. He'd also written a book, which strove 'to consider Yugoslavia's destruction through families broken asunder, for this was a war of intimate betrayals.' I hadn't read it. Reviewers praised his 'forceful, elegant prose.' I found it flowery.

When he hired me, Cohen promised: 'Your scope to write

about whatever you wish would be broad.' In practice, this meant: 'Tell the same old story at regular intervals.' Once a month, the desk demanded war porn, and dispatched me to dredge up brutal recollections. I begged Bosnians to peel off their scabs so I'd look good in print.

'A lot of this is about picking the right situation,' a veteran editor suggested, recalling Balkan gore with abhorrent glee. 'A place of hideous atrocities, of course, but also a place where people had been quite friendly before the war.' That was 'loaded with dramatic possibilities,' he said, such as: 'what do they say to their neighbors, who at least stood aside, if they didn't actually participate, when the nasty stuff was going on?'

This was what *The New York Times* excelled at: overwrought reportage in hindsight. One guy specialized in resurrecting the Khmer Rouge. Survivors recalled its savagery at length, but there wasn't the space to mention American carpet-bombing, or how it wiped out hundreds of thousands of Cambodians, and helped bring Pol Pot to power to till his Killing Fields. These stories taught a simplified morality, beseeching readers to yell 'Never Again!' without examining 'our' role in the process. They had style, if you liked cod literary flair. But there wasn't much substance behind the 'vividness and immediacy' that Cohen prized, in his regular email eulogies to 'wrenching issues', and 'every expression of the mystery of the human heart'. This sort of stuff left me cold. I was hopeless at it.

According to more illustrious reporters, witnessing a conflict is a privilege. In the words of Kurt Schork, who died doing it: 'every day I see the grace and dignity of ordinary people trying to survive under extraordinary circumstances.' I just asked them to cry into my notebook. It was seven years since fighting stopped in Bosnia, and still the tears would pour forth on cue. A quarter of people lived as refugees.

I kept being asked if their country could be salvaged. But a peace deal struck by Americans had divided it, handing Serbs the bits they'd already won at gunpoint. The two halves of Bosnia were separate, and only pretended they weren't because they were occupied, by tens of thousands of well-armed foreign troops. It was preferable to combat, for the moment, but it didn't help most Bosnians move on.

'My life has no meaning,' sobbed one woman whose son had been murdered by Serbs at Srebrenica. 'It would have been better if they'd killed me.' Another scoffed when I apologized for intruding. 'You can't upset me,' she sniffed in her poky flat. 'I've been through everything, apart from having my throat slit.'

The bereaved mostly languished alone, and rarely gathered together except to mourn. Their ceaseless grieving started to depress me. I wondered if they'd ever see beyond it, or would they carry on and wail themselves to death? And if so, would the next generation seek revenge?

I found answers when somebody lent me the Bhagavad Gita. 'For all things born in truth must die, and out of death in truth comes life,' it advised. 'Face to face with what must be, cease thou from sorrow.'

The situation couldn't be clearer. I had to stop wallowing in Bosnia, at once.

After EXIT, I spent several weeks with G, whose protégés had vanished for a holiday. Our days were spent pleasantly stoned in my apartment, where I was technically at work. It didn't take long to find a common goal: both of us needed something new to do, and music mixed G's expertise with my frustrations. Together we'd hit on the plan to hustle Labus. If a DJ could get him elected, we'd be able to finance even bigger projects. Unless something gave people hope, Serbia seemed to be set for another lost decade, and I didn't fancy hanging round to watch.

Amazingly, the candidate hadn't said no. To be fair, he didn't actually say yes, but he sent us to see his campaign manager, an activist whom G knew from EXIT. This aide agreed to get us police permission. That took care of immediate concerns.

Whether Labus could raise fifty grand was a technicality. First we had to book Fatboy Slim. To buy ourselves more time to find the cash, G said we could fax him lots of paperwork. We'd drown him in logistical information. As long as he promised to come, we'd get a sponsor. All we had to do was seal the deal.

G had made it sound so straightforward. But when he handed me his address book, I felt scared. Thankfully, he passed a joint as well. I tipped back the chair in my office, plunking my feet on the desk as I inhaled.

'Now begins most serious part of action,' my partner said. 'Agents man, they know what they are doing. No way they want you talking straight with artists. And they control here very strongly what come on territories. I was in Russia man, I'm telling you, it's worse. Always they assume you with a mafia. For Moscow, they want fifty thousand just for DJ. Like Carl Cox, you know, for one guy like that.'

Bands could make this figure sound a bargain. Assuming they'd come, they'd be wary of trusting local equipment. 'For EXIT, they wanted Red Hot Chili Peppers,' G said. 'For that you have to pay half million dollars, and fly whole stage from California.'

A famous DJ wouldn't play for free. Superclubs had been spoiling them for years. Raves had been commercialized and branded, long before the police had shut down warehouse parties, and opened up new outlets for the licensed trade. In Britain, five-figure fees became the norm. By the millennium, a backlash had begun. To keep the money flowing as they wanted, agents had to open different markets. And that meant dictating terms to the likes of us. Either we booked all the acts they couldn't sell for much at home, or we'd have to pay outrageous sums for the rest.

There wasn't any way around this. We needed a household name, with presence and a crowd-pleasing sound. I could only think of one who'd fit the bill. Better known to his mum as Quentin Cook, he'd played drums in a band at school, hip-hop records at college and bass for The Housemartins. After a number one hit as Beats International, he'd knocked out acid jazz and house mixes, until he finally found his calling looping grooves, while he pranced behind the decks in lurid shirts, and brandished bottles of spirits at his fans. Since he named himself Fatboy Slim, he'd been huge.

I'd already picked out the backing track for an advert, with Labus dissing his rivals to the bass line. It was blasting out of my stereo as we spoke: *'They just know what they know, but they don't know what is what, they just strut... what the fuck?'* 'Bosh!' I clapped as the depth-charge beat kicked in, spilling ash across the keyboard of my laptop. 'How could that fail?'

G dragged me back to practicalities. 'You know he is controlled by David Levy?'

My partner's eyes lit up. Mine went blank. 'That guy is serious man, I'm telling you,' he said. 'Serious asshole.'

'David Levy.' I repeated, nonplussed.

'He's kinda pissed at me right now, but I am working on that. I think he appreciate more that message you can give.'

Of all the contacts bulging from G's leather book, they'd whittled themselves down to one before we'd started. Everything depended on calling a stranger. I'd been doing that professionally for years, but had never felt much at stake except my pride. This time, feeling foolish was the least of it.

I wandered onto the balcony for air. Along with a large black Jeep, my flat was one of the perks of working for the *Times*. While living off expenses and banking my salary, I was furnished with four vast rooms, a Jacuzzi bath and two roof terraces. This one looked out on the Sava, and across to the concrete turrets of New Belgrade. Though the capital's name meant 'white city', these Soviet-era monoliths were dark, sprawling upwards like a clutch of middle fingers.

I turned to see G in the doorway. 'You wanna make call?' he said, holding out my handset. I punched in the number he dictated, gagging on nerves. A male voice replied with disdain.

'Hello,' I said. 'Is that David Levy?'

'Who's this?'

'I'm calling from Belgrade. I work for *The New York Times*. We're organizing something massive here this weekend and, well... I know time's tight, but we were hoping...'

'David's at lunch.'

'Oh.' It was past four o'clock.

'What's it regarding?'

My nerve had faltered. 'Perhaps it's better if we write to him.'

'As you prefer.' He hung up first.

G was striding round the office, twitching edgily. 'Why you don't make joint,' he said, 'we relax a little.'

'You roll,' I said, grabbing the keyboard. 'I'll write.'

Firing up Eudora, I typed the subject line 'S.O.S.' then let rip. 'Dear David, I need to book a big name with a big sound for an event that could make history.'

The email adopted a tone of pseudo-deference. 'I apologize for the ridiculously short notice, but I hope you might be able to help,' it fawned suggestively. 'Do you know anyone who might be available? I assume Fatboy Slim is busy, but you never know. If he were free and willing to talk about it, I'd love to try.'

I glanced for some reassurance from my partner. He smirked impenetrably. I hit send, and pasted the text into a new window. Fearing overkill, I downgraded the message to 'URGENT'.

'What about that other guy you mentioned?' I asked.

A flick through his pocket book later, and we were hassling someone called 'Jack at EC1'. He'd also never said yes to G's approaches, though he might in response to this: 'I assume a Chemical Brothers DJ set would be out of the question...'

Another few turns of the page yielded Primary Talent.

'Eileen Mulligan,' G laughed. 'Welcome to my fan club!'

She got the same shameless spiel. 'The only way we can pull this off in the way we need to is to have a really big name with a big sound to move the crowd. Something like a Basement Jaxx DJ set. Pretty unlikely I know, but you can always ask. Money is not tight, but we can't afford crazy prices.'

Again, I tweaked the text to start anew. 'Who else is there?' I asked. 'Let's just send this out to everyone we can think of.'

The rest of the day unfolded in a blur. We trawled around the Internet for contacts, and honed our patter with help from a friendly agent, who claimed to be a mate of Groove Armada's. He told us to cut out the hype and stick to business. Keep it simple, he said, and prove we weren't the novices we appeared.

Subsequent emails oozed geeky nous. Among the technical specs that inundated readers, there were stage dimensions, speaker outputs, PA wattages, light fixture racks and every knob-twiddling detail I could paste; from an old EXIT invoice of G's.

A few people even replied. 'One of the DJs I represent would LOVE to do this,' said a booker called Martje. 'His name is Phil Kieran, he is an amazing DJ. He travelled all through Eastern Europe.' I'd never heard of him.

Someone else suggested Alex from The Orb, but told us he was unsure of the doctor's whereabouts. So was I, having once tripped out for days to his *Huge Ever Growing Pulsating Brain That Rules From The Centre Of The Ultraworld (Live Mix Mk 10).*

Another agency tried it on up front. 'The Biggest DJ I could offer you for this would be Junior Sanchez,' their salesman wrote. 'He would need a business ticket from NYC and a fee of $10k.' He wouldn't be getting either from us.

Twenty-four hours later, it was over. David Levy put us in our place.

'I don't open unsolicited attachments,' he'd replied, ignoring the text of my message. 'It is unlikely any of our clients will be available.' What's more, '95% of my djs are fully booked thru until spring 2003. hope that helps for now.' Though he'd signed off with some corporate 'kind regards', he might as well have told us 'kiss my ring'.

We weren't exactly deluged with alternatives. Without Fatboy Slim, or fifty grand, all we had to trade on was our words. And I couldn't see how to talk them into anything. My enthusiasm melted into gloom. But I couldn't stay down for long with G around. He'd put a new complexion on the city, revealing what I'd longed for in my solitude.

As a one-man foreign bureau, I felt isolated. There weren't any colleagues to befriend, and my translator seemed as uninspired as me. Though we met most days for a chat, we knew no one cared in New York. Provided I batted back emails, I could have filed nothing for weeks before they registered. Most Western correspondents had departed. Those that remained I avoided, for fear of talking shop. It was hard to take the media business seriously, but I was trapped inside its golden cage of privilege. I hoped my prestigious job would open doors, which made me feel a lousy hypocrite. My partner hauled me from this funk. He'd introduced me to artists and musicians, and taken me to hidden bars and parties, where we talked about reviving Belgrade's past.

To restore our spirits, G proposed a nightcap. We set out for the Globetrotter's Club, an ironically named relic of the Nineties, when embargos barred Serbs from travelling abroad. In the Cold War era, things were very different. Unlike the Soviet bloc, which it abandoned, Yugoslavia let its citizens have passports. Their standard of living was high, and subsidized by the West for snubbing Moscow. Ideas and technology flowed readily, along with European visitors. Yugoslavs didn't slobber over Levis. Their punk bands got reviewed in the *NME*. But when the rest of Eastern Europe opened up, the Balkans closed and fell apart. Wars replaced the tourists with refugees. Escapist kitsch and thugs took center stage. Only radio helped sustain alternative culture.

G had spent much of this period in New York. He'd moved there in the late 1980s, and got by selling salvaged furniture for cash. He paid his way through film school doing removals, and wound up shooting straight-to-video movies, with a sideline in exporting CDs. When all of these ventures palled, he left for London. By the time he got back to his birthplace, it felt foreign.

'You know Belgrade is freaky city,' he said, steering us left down a street of taverns and kebab stalls. 'It has been lot of history here, a lot of forces, lot of energies, for centuries. Some good, plenty *bad*.'

I felt inclined to agree. We were suddenly being attacked by a band of gypsies. It had burst out of nowhere to serenade a couple, who'd been strutting down the cobbles on our shoulders. We turned to see a nymphet kick off her heels. She started jiving to the flugelhorns and trumpets. *PAH-pa-papa-pah-pa-papa, OOM-pa-papa-oom-pa-papa, PAH-PAH-pa-BWAAAH-pa-PAH!* A gap-toothed loon in a waistcoat bawled them on. This menagerie clattered towards us prancing and parping. G whisked me out of their path and into a doorway. Then he marched us to the club's enchanted basement.

The face control on the door kept flatheads at bay: you had to speak decent English to get in. Inside, the décor was baroque, with none of the chrome-plated logos of trendier bars. Its curios and bric-a-brac looked homely, not rejects from the nearest Irish theme pub. All of the armchairs were threadbare, and one was invariably home to the resident cat, which looked equal parts contented and lugubrious. It felt like a time capsule.

I could have stayed for hours, but G had other plans. After brandies with beer on the side, we stumbled back up to the street to order *pljeskavica*, a discus slab of pork, beef and lamb, spiced and served with onion in a bap. It would 'aggravate' the gut to handle booze, my partner said. Reeling, I savored the grease as it ran down my chin.

We followed this up with a trip to a bar called Idiot. Again, we didn't stay there very long. I'd barely had time to steady myself with gin, and we were off to a nameless dive on the edge of a building site. It was tucked away at the bottom of a cul-de-sac, somewhere off the endless central boulevard. You rapped at a metal gate to be buzzed into rubble. A light shone from a room containing a fridge. Sinister hip-hop rumbled from some speakers. There weren't any staff or customers in evidence. I was told it might get busy nearer dawn. We helped ourselves to beer, and left some dinars on the mantelpiece. Then we wandered outside to relax on a concrete Ping-Pong table.

My brain felt tamed to pliant mush, but I couldn't shake an underlying panic. What if *The New York Times* heard what we'd done? I'd been ready for that if the Labus plan succeeded, but failing hadn't really crossed my mind. Now the potential consequences frightened me. Was my job worth putting at risk for a few cheap thrills?

G's voice snapped me out of this hysteria. 'What you thinking?'

'Oh, nothing much.' I hunched further forward, rolling a joint.

He grinned. 'My friend, you have a sensitive perception. I think you can trust it more, like Eastern wise men said. You know, feel ocean in veins and wear a crown of stars. Most important thing is keep a backbone strong.'

My smile was wiped away by the sound of the Nokia tune. And the number on the screen was even worse: +11111111111, the *Times* foreign hotline. At one in the morning, that meant trouble. In New York, it was close to deadline time. It was also when they'd share new ideas. Whatever I did, I had to take their calls. A reporter is always on duty. If he isn't, then there's someone else who wants to be. My relationship with my editors was dysfunctional. The more unenthused I felt by their requests, the likelier I was to agree, and the less I'd feel like working in the morning. Reluctantly, I answered, knotting up.

'Hello? Yes... Sure,' I told the desk. 'Uh-huh... Right... Absolutely.'

'What they want?' My partner grinned when we were done.

'The usual.' I grimaced. 'Old war stories.'

'Oh man...'

'A Bosnian Serb pleaded guilty to get less jail time,' I said. 'So they want to know if others will as well. Like it would mean something.'

The New York Times saw war crimes trials as therapy, a way of bringing closure to the region. They didn't care that prosecutions were politicized, and timed to suit the needs of Western policy. What mattered was whether criminals confessed. Truth would lead to reconciliation. And if it didn't, the fault lay squarely with the culprits. In reality, the process made things worse. People's views were polarized more sharply, and no one seemed to focus on the facts. Everyone felt cheated by the courts. Aggressors had the sense that they were victimized, while victims were denied a sense of justice. But questioning any of this would be out of the question.

'They want a story from Bosnia tomorrow,' I said. 'They're annoyed I haven't gone there already. I'll have to leave at dawn if I'm going to make it.'

G shrugged. 'You be back soon, right?'

'Yes of course. But I'd rather stay here. If we were going ahead with Labus, then of course I would have done.'

My partner laughed. 'Don't you worry yourself too much about that. We have plenty time. Whole thing we try with Labus was just dummy run.'

As so often the case with G, I felt I'd missed something, like the throw that flips the queen in three-card monte. But I also got a rush of adrenaline. 'How do you mean?'

'You heard what Labus was saying, right?' I shook my head. Though I'd been taking weekly lessons since I got there, my Serbian skills left much to be desired.

'Well, you can take it from me that idiot don't know nothing,' G said. 'He told me how you expect politicians on stage in such short notice. And I said we don't want *any* politicians on a stage. And then he was happy. Hey, what can we do?'

I shrugged. He carried on.

'There is appetite now for actions in this city, and we did show to people here that we are ready. This is place for festival, not provinces. Big change can only happen in Belgrade. City did send me signal, man, I'm telling you. Those people wanna *help*.'

I nodded, unsure what to say.

'Now is not the time for backing up,' G continued. 'Madonna soon can come here flashing beaver. She would be perfect too for Serbs, but we don't care about that. You know, music can be catalyzing focus, to break the people's stupid habits. We give to them direct, on level of soul.'

I felt bewildered. 'Sorry?'

'Festival,' he repeated. 'In Belgrade, next summer.'

'But what about EXIT?'

His eyebrows narrowed. 'Why you wanna talk about EXIT all of sudden?'

'Well, aren't you going to be working with them next year?'

My partner looked rattled. 'I don't think they do another festival. They lost whole lotta money there this time. Last I hear they in Spain, still regrouping. Maybe they scared they wind up in a jail. I don't see them try to build things up.'

'Yes, but...' Protest was pointless. G's face was glowing through the darkness.

'Listen Daniel,' he said, looming closer. 'You know your name means prophet, right? You show to me already you read signs here. I appreciate very highly what we doing. Most people these days like wah-wah-wah, whole fucking time. I had sensation once in subway in New York, I was going to work, like any other day, and everyone in car seemed like they speaking in a voice of someone else. I had the feeling these are not human beings.

These are images, pre-recorded from TV. Here it is same. Most people live like machines man. They sleeping and they need to wake up fast.'

I was struggling myself. The hash and booze had knocked me sideways.

'I think it could be good if you meet mayor,' G said. 'They should understand what is that we can do for them. With city behind us, sponsors release money quickly, so we prepare. I'm gonna show you one location when you come. I been last week already man, is beautiful. All trees around, like Hyde Park.'

'Sounds great,' I whispered. 'But I should probably get moving. I have to drive to Sarajevo in a few hours.'

My vision blurred. In an instant, we were standing on the boulevard.

'What I'm gonna do,' G was saying, 'is I'm gonna put you into cab, if you don't mind.'

He was waving indiscriminately at traffic.

'Yeah, that's great...'

'I tell driver he should bring you straight to *Prag*. And he will probably take you right to Czech Republic... For two thousand euros they will drive man. Maybe ten with heroin... No, *Prag Hotel*, you know, that one by your place... The cab drivers do that here, man. They drive wherever you want to go.'

As he babbled, a beat-up Mercedes pulled alongside us. G opened the passenger door and I fell in.

'*Narodnog Fronta!*' he barked through the window. Then he turned to me, frothing with excitement. 'You know what means name of your street? A People's Front, like Partisan Yugoslavia. I think is sign. Relax my friend, I'm gonna call you on weekend, see what's cooking. Now you take care, and be good!'

With a crunch of dilapidated gearbox, we sped off.

LUST

Our project soon advanced on my return. But if we really meant business, we'd have to find some partners. You can't run a festival alone, least of all in Serbia. You need cash up front and connections with officials, long before you can start booking bands, or trying to cover the bills by selling tickets.

We couldn't afford to hire staff, and we didn't have offices. But we needed a corporate shell to sign our contracts, and it would help to have a place for meeting sponsors. I didn't know where to find either, or where to begin trying to network with Serbs. G brushed objections aside. An organization could be improvised, he said: we'd simply borrow someone else's. His first idea was a government department.

The Institute for Cultural Development Research had a dozen state employees, and a basement bar. We arrived there in a lashing autumn thunderstorm. Our contact led us to a table in the corner by a radiator. Steam rose up from our clothing as we thawed. A girl at the counter was summoned to ply us with caffeine. Rolling her eyes, she dropped her magazine. Tobacco-tinted walls closed in on the drabness.

'Let me tell you,' G said, at no one in particular, 'you need about twenny-five thousand euros to make this place *modern*.'

Our hostess bristled. She was already well acquainted with my partner, but seemed to feel uncertain how to deal with him. She twirled at brunette ringlets with a forefinger, above a cardigan even redder than her lipstick.

'You have a list with questions?' she sneered, almost sweetly, speaking English for my benefit. 'Would you like to know about crisis in marriage, human rights? If you didn't know, we all have the right on culture. United Nations gave us...'

'Rights on a culture,' G interrupted. 'Good. All I need to know is if offices are empty, and is it possible to have them, for like something similar what you guys do.' His eyes were sparkling. 'And I could probably get them, you know.'

'And what do you see...' she stammered, 'where... where do you see this Institute in that?'

'As somebody who can help us,' he replied. 'We can offer program to you, but I need to know who is in charge here.'

She stared at us as if we were half-wits. 'Director!'

G snarled like a hungry terrier with lockjaw. 'Director,' he said. 'Who is that? What's the name?'

'She's not here at the moment.'

'All right, we're gonna prepare meeting with her, we tell you what we're up to and we prepare the meeting, let's say Friday.' He paused. 'Is she conservative, or like liberal, or what?'

'Rigid,' the woman said. 'And frustrated.'

'She's *what*?' My partner recoiled.

'Rigid and frustrated,' she nodded. 'You can manage her.'

'I can *manage* her?' G sounded disconcerted. 'What you mean I can manage her?'

Raising an eyebrow, she leaned towards him. 'You can *handle* her.'

'Whoa!' His face screwed up. 'Like what way? What I have to do to her?'

'It's up to you.'

G held up one hand. 'Listen, we are good guys, don't worry. Just tell me, we need to know who we are dealing with, if she is the person who is positive, who wants to *do* something about this institution, because you have like sign on door saying...'

'Yes, generally yes.'

'That's all I need to know. I don't care where she... er, basically we can help you a lot.'

She switched to Serbian. 'Can we earn money on this?'

My partner repeated the words in translation. 'I mean institution,' she said, reverting to English.

'Your *institution*?' G was appalled. 'We gonna drag some funds and help you, but you need to work. We can take over this place and give you better salaries.'

This made her giggle. 'Pah!' she said. 'It's OK with me!'

'Ultimately, that's not excluded,' G laughed back. 'But we need job done, you know. We need a lot of good people.'

Her cigarette smoldered in the ashtray between us. 'We have good people,' she said, 'but we also have lot of projects.'

'OK, we go through these projects and tell... er... advise to Ministry of Culture that these are losers' projects. And so you quit them and concentrate on other projects. And we have a means to actually back up our beliefs with people who are powerful, I would say, but people who are smart. OK?'

She was indignant. 'You know what is main mission of this institute?' she said. 'It is taking part in creating the cultural policy in Serbia.'

'That's what we do too,' G beamed, 'but with performances. It's not like we gonna call Guggenheim Museum and say, OK, can you send exhibition of Kandinsky, you know, to Belgrade because we need it. We can't pay it, but we need it. No! What we gonna do, we gonna incorporate more alternative styles that young people living with. More like taking them off drugs and stuff like that, so that's culture, you know.'

She looked bemused. He carried on. 'When you have somebody coming and telling, oh, we want Max Ernst exhibition in Museum of Modern Art in New Belgrade, and meantime kids are like shooting each other with machine guns, then what's the use of having a Max Ernst?'

'OK, OK,' she surrendered. 'And you say you need people for that, for what kind of job exactly?'

'All kind of jobs,' G said. 'With marketing, research, and communications, going to radios, TVs, going to Cacak, Kraljevo, all these nowhere towns, talking to people who might become incorporated. We need contacts with local communities. With the people who are believing, not with cronies and idiots, you know

I mean?'

'No,' she said. 'You cannot find it here. This is a quite healthy surroundings in this institute.'

'That's what we are looking for!' G said. 'So far anywhere I was going wasn't very healthy. Institutions around here, I mean.'

She made another attempt to trawl for details. 'So if you need some research, we make project. And I can bring this project here, and we will see, in written form.'

G waved her away. 'We need to talk to the head, on Friday potentially.'

'No.' She shook her head. 'She is coming back next week.'

My partner would be in London by then, for some meetings with agents.

'Maybe Daniel can talk to her?' he said.

They both looked at me uncertainly. I'd barely opened my mouth except to smoke.

'OK,' she said. I nodded, feeling none too sure myself of my capabilities.

She turned back to G, and touched him on the knee. 'How are you?' she whispered, in Serbian. He drained what remained of his coffee and slammed down the cup.

'Busy,' he said, reaching for his coat.

We never met her boss.

The next step was to hone a proper sales pitch. We withdrew to G's apartment in the suburbs, a relatively recent construction, like most of the city. Belgrade was largely rebuilt after World War II, when both the Nazis and the Allies bombed it to rubble. The Communist response was strictly functional.

My partner's home was a dingy single room. Above the double bed that almost filled it, a blowpipe hung from telescopic sights. Aside from a sliver of window, the rest of the walls were all shelves, stacked with records, CDs, comics, films and books. In the flame of a candle, titles danced before me: *Soft Subversions*,

Evolutionary Agents and the *Chapel of Extreme Experience*. I grabbed a tome at random and scanned its cover. A blurb proclaimed it: 'Wholesome in a bizarre way.'

From his seat on the edge of the mattress, G waved at the bookcase. 'Right there is like hundred grand of Western products. It may be good venture for some doped out criminal to buy and open shop. He can clean his dirty money and expose himself as modern European. I would be glad to take from him half that if he want... S'aright man, I don't see that as plan. We use those texts to help with our ideas.'

I pulled out a folding chair and sat down opposite. He grinned. 'You know, wherever we find our money for this business, people here will say that you are spy?'

That didn't surprise me. 'They already do,' I said. 'Journalists are automatic suspects. The British ambassador has a theory. He says if you aren't called a spy in the Balkans, it probably means you're doing nothing useful.'

'That guy is playing clever game,' G said. 'I think we should meet him. I hear he is music lover.'

'Why not?' There were plenty of reasons, of course, but they could wait. It was hard enough to meet him as a reporter. 'I think we'd need a clear proposal. Then we could ask for help with something specific.'

G shook his head. 'We just need general statement of support, like how we partner up on cultural exchanges. People should see we international festival, not typical Serbian roasted pig on stick.'

I wasn't so sure. 'Wouldn't it be best to look less British?' My homeland's reputation wasn't great. Tony Blair once said that bombing Belgrade would 'save thousands of innocent men, women and children' in Kosovo. Even if it did, NATO killed hundreds of civilians. Depending on whose figures you believed, they could have been up to a tenth of total war deaths. No one I met shared NATO's moral clarity, which masked its more strategic motivations. Even dissidents don't welcome being bombed. Serbs could spot a plot where none existed. Regarding themselves as perpetual victims of history, many thought foreign powers were out to get them.

'I don't give a fuck,' my partner said. 'Much of best music in my life come from your country. Young ones of today they should appreciate. I think you find that many do.'

'Yes, but are they the ones whose minds we need to change?'

Serbia's identity was warped. Though the nation's myths said unity would save them, Serbs conspired again and again to undermine each other, and cited this as proof they'd been betrayed. That led them to seek protection from a strongman, who undermined them more in defense of unity. As a recipe for victimhood, it was devastating. And worryingly, it fed on basic facts, like the horrors of World War II, when Croats killed countless Serbs in concentration camps, before Marshall Tito stifled ethnic grievances. For the next forty years, they festered on in private, apart from occasional bursts of drunken mewling, to the usual Balkan drone of a one-stringed harp.

Belgrade has been sacked and plundered two dozen times. It's been the capital since the Turks invaded Kosovo, where they crushed the medieval Serbian kingdom. This defeat still ranks as the nation's finest hour. Although the Ottomans won, their sultan was slain, along with the Serbian sovereign and most of his nobles. Poets hailed their refusal to surrender, calling it stoic acceptance of God's will. Thus was the greatness of Serbia defined: defending lost causes in the mud, while enshrining a field in Kosovo as New Israel.

This cataclysm struck on June 28, 1389. Six hundred years thereafter, to the day, Slobodan Milosevic returned to the spot. Addressing several hundred thousand Serbs, he warned that new 'armed battles' with neighbors 'cannot be excluded.' Four wars later, he was sent to stand trial in The Hague, on June 28. This was also the date of the Treaty of Versailles, which ended World

War I with crippling sanctions, which in turn fuelled Adolf Hitler's rise to power. And the War To End All Wars began the same day, when a Serb shot dead the heir to the Austrian throne, unleashing violence that ended in Auschwitz and Hiroshima.

As dates go, June 28 was quite a big one. To Serbs, it was *Vidovdan*, the saint's day of Vitus. And in June 2003, it would fall on a Saturday. When better to schedule national catharsis? We could call the event constructive 'ethnic cleansing', a way of reclaiming Serbia from its past. It named itself: St Vitus Dance, a miracle cure 'characterized by rapid, irregular, aimless, involuntary movements,' as the Internet put it.

For once, G was warier than me. 'That day is red flag for most primitive forces in this country,' he cautioned. 'There would be serious risk they turn it into riot. Round here the people are experts at creating problems. Solving them is not top priority.'

'So you think we shouldn't do it?'

He smiled. 'I didn't say that. This is here land of paradox. Anything is possible, and all can be impossible. You know that guy what shot Franz Ferdinand in Sarajevo? You know what he said on his trial? He said whatever state we live in must be *free*. People need connection to that spirit. Everyone has inside him wolf and lamb, and dancing helps us balance out those forces. Festival can unite Balkan brothers. Music brings down borders man, I'm telling you.'

I'd never exactly lacked for ambition, and opportunities to indulge it once seemed limitless. But I'd hit a mirrored ceiling in the media, and what I witnessed through the looking glass repulsed me.

It started at Reuters, where I was trained as a foreign correspondent after college. I imagined I'd be reporting on injustices, from conflict to natural disasters. But they packed me off to Frankfurt to cover the stock market, then on to Zurich for more of the same. At no point did they offer me a choice. When I complained, in 2001, I was sent to Romania, where half the Reuters staff had just been fired. I'd barely had time to move in when my fortunes changed. I was asked to help cover a war in Macedonia.

Having landed in the Balkans by chance, I had to learn fast. My first question was 'where the fuck's Macedonia?' closely followed by 'why are these idiots fighting?' The republic had left Yugoslavia without a shot fired, but now its Albanian minority had rebelled. Western envoys rushed to intervene, containing the rebels by giving them what they wanted: control of land adjoining Kosovo. NATO's spokesman called this a 'dishonorable score draw.' I agreed with him that something wasn't right. He'd covered the Kosovo war for the BBC, where he talked the NATO line so well they hired him.

There were so many questions to ask, but the news map changed. On September 11, the Balkans disappeared, along with its corps of major league reporters. Most of them went to Afghanistan, expecting to see Osama bin Laden's 'head on a platter', as Dick Cheney commanded. This exodus got me hired by *The New York Times*. They called me up and asked me to apply. My stories from Macedonia had impressed them, or at least been copy-pasted into print. They'd be granting me the same creative license. Reuters and other agencies are wholesalers. When TV anchors tell you something's breaking, they're reading it straight off the news wires they subscribe to. Reuters would handle the daily grind of newsgathering, while I told American readers what to think. How could I refuse?

I naïvely assumed my prospects must be bright. Most journalists are egotists at heart: never mind the story, look who's telling it! You're only as good as you make yourself look. The best can sound authoritative when clueless. As a guy from Sky News once confided: 'we're glorified gossips.' What distinguished *The New York Times* was its choice of gossip partners.

In the words of the editor, Howell Raines, 'it misses the point to say that the *Times* is an "elite" publication. It is the indispensable newsletter of the United States' political, diplomatic, governmental, academic, and professional communities, and the main link between those communities and their counterparts around the world.'

This meant jump to heel and take dictation. And ideally become their friends and learn to think like them. When George W. Bush said 'you are either with us or with the terrorists', *Times* reporters opened up their notebooks. To prove they weren't liberally biased against his government, they hyped its most egregious propaganda, unbalanced by the facts that contradicted it. The worst of these offenders was Judith Miller, who ran 'scoops' on Saddam Hussein's purported arsenal, via a feedback loop of spooks and Iraqi front groups. Smeared across the front page of the *Times*, this confection of phony factoids spread like herpes.

'Iraq has stepped up its quest for nuclear weapons', one story claimed. According to 'officials' Miller spoke to, 'the first sign of a "smoking gun" [...] may be a mushroom cloud'. These officials promptly seized on their own creation. 'It's now public,' Cheney thundered on a talk show, while Bush made 'mushroom cloud' a ghoulish catchphrase.

Way down the production line of the fantasy factory, Americans in the Balkans told a different story: Serbs were selling 'weapons of mass destruction'. I was informed that a Serb-run company had been caught shipping plane parts to Baghdad. This annoyed the U.S., which had been bombing Iraqi defenses for a decade. But there was no sign of 'much broader military collaboration', as alleged by 'officials', nor of missiles or unmanned aerial vehicles, or any means of delivering chemical weapons. For the record, I filed an article that said as much. Miller immediately emailed me, concerned.

'Great story today,' she wrote, without conviction, 'but apparently there is more.' According to her unnamed informants, 'what they have already sold is an advance UAV that is capable of carrying "hundreds of klg. of material": — chem, bio, nuclear...'

In breathless typos, she asked 'what the U.S. is doing about it beyond just issuing demarches? And what assurances they have gotten from the Serbs? Also, are the other Yugoslav entities also involved in this trade. Longer term, if you could ask about LIbya...I hear the sales also involve UAV technology — and nuclear related components... I know you won't want to discuss LIbya over a phone...but I don't think we can wait a week for the Iraqi stuff...can you make some calls on that for us?'

Er, calls to whom exactly?

'The most credible of the theories doing the rounds here,' I replied, 'is that the Serbs were helping the Iraqis to convert their fleet of decrepit Mig-21s into planes that could be put in the air without pilots to become flying bombs.' However, since each of these would need a turbojet and guidance system, 'there'd be no need to have a rusting Soviet plane wrapped around it.'

That did not impress her in the slightest. 'We should keep pursuing it,' she said. 'I'm told there is more.' Perhaps there was. It never surfaced.

The rank hypocrisy disgusted me. I was told to hold Serbs to account for supporting warmongers, while the *Times* helped enable the invasion of Iraq. Worse still, this was carbon copied from Milosevic: attack in the name of defense, in the face of imaginary threats, with manufactured enemies and evidence. Little wonder Americans called it 'shock and awe.'

The Serbian sort had more straightforward aims: to seize the land where Serbs lived as minorities in Croatia and Bosnia, by killing or expelling all their neighbors. None of Yugoslavia's republics was ethnically pure, and as they broke apart minorities were pawns. Most of them proved easy to incite, by playing on earlier crimes against their kin, like Americans conned into thinking that Iraq was somehow involved in 9/11.

When Serbs ran amok at the start of the 1990s, America and Europe left them to it. Stuck in a Cold War mindset, they approved of Communist monoliths imploding. If republics declared independence, they were recognized. But minorities couldn't break away as well. This fanned the flames of the problem, reviving hatreds blamed by the West for all the fighting. Meanwhile, Serbs and Croats carved up Bosnia, butchering its Muslims as they went. United Nations troops were sent to police 'ceasefires', but lacked the power to impose them. Force was inconsistently applied, until Bill Clinton needed something new to boast about, whereupon NATO air strikes froze the conflict.

By then, 100,000 had been killed. All future interventions formed a pattern: each one addressed the failures of the last. So, Serbia was bombed for crushing separatists in Kosovo, to prevent a repeat of atrocities in Bosnia. And Macedonia was told to cave into Albanian rebels, because NATO hadn't disarmed their Kosovo allies, for fear of having to fight them in the process. And this was where things really got confusing.

Albanian and Serbian nationalists fed off each other: they sought the same land. For decades, they'd looked certain to collide, long before Milosevic made it happen. But the World Police didn't try to broker compromise. When the Kosovo Liberation Army surfaced, America said it was 'without any questions, a terrorist group.' Yet a year after that, NATO helped it take power, because Balkan wars had threatened Western interests, which revolved round promoting business in the region. Helping was an afterthought at best. But *The New York Times* was a cradle of true believers. As one of its editors bleated, 'the West has put so much energy into teaching people to care.'

The ungrateful sods weren't following the script. KLA goons had taken charge of Kosovo, attacking what remained of its Serbs, and managing a trafficking economy. And Bosnia was a

neo-colonial wreck. Its four million people had three presidents -
one Serb, one Muslim, one Croat - plus dozens of multi-ethnic
government ministers. An international viceroy outranked all of
them. Unless they obeyed his edicts, he'd overrule them, in the
name of fostering regional democracy. No matter how sincere his
delusions, he couldn't save the natives from themselves: they'd
just re-elected the parties that started the war.

'Nation building' in the Balkans was sold as a blueprint. Yet if
all the ethnic groups remained at odds, it was hard to imagine
Iraq had a rosier outlook. Would Sunni and Shia ignore their
vicious history, or Kurds befriend the Arabs who oppressed
them, to satisfy the West's demand they should?

None of this stopped the *Times* taking leaps of faith. A report
on Afghanistan warned that it 'may come as a shock to
Americans' to learn that the 'entire war on terror' was 'an exercise
in imperialism'. But it stressed that this 'doesn't stop being
necessary just because it becomes politically incorrect.' Besides, it
was 'the kind of imperialism you get in a human rights era', not
the kind that controls strategic oil and gas reserves. So America
would reconcile 'imperial power and self-determination', by
'sticking around for a while', for the good of the locals. And that
was how the Great Game continued.

When bugles sounded to take up the White Man's Burden, the
Times would declare that 'distant war and genocide could not be
ignored', and the Pentagon would morph to the armed wing of
Human Rights Watch. Since Saddam Hussein was self-evidently
a Bad Guy, deposing him trumped asking what came next. Why
even try? The Emperor couldn't possibly be naked. He'd be
covered in credulous prose till he threw in the towel.

If success meant selling out, I'd rather fail. But I couldn't see
how to achieve that with the *Times*, because I wanted their
approval more than anything.

The alternative was to make some news myself. Though I'd have told almost anyone anything for money, that didn't mean I didn't believe our hype. I was ready to test it on corporate crusaders at Davos, who flock there every winter for a ski junket. Their World Economic Forum liked to talk about development. If I got myself accredited as a journalist, I could strut its Alpine corridors preaching like Bono.

Surely *someone* rich could spare a paltry million? George Soros might even call it Doing Good. The proposal I'd drafted was simple. 'WAKE UP!' it proclaimed in bold capitals. 'Ever wondered why billions of dollars of Western aid have achieved so little in the Balkans? None of the conventional agencies active in this region know how to change the way people think. But we do and we want your help.'

It was time to stop the self-congratulation. 'The white-jeep brigade have done all they can here. The absence of conflict is not the same thing as progress. Every country in the Balkans now has a democratic government. They all want to join the European Union. But none of them has a hope unless their societies change quickly. And nobody seems to have a strategy for making that fantasy a reality. Except us.'

Ours would be a different kind of trip: an intervention in the mind. G glanced up from reading the text, in a restaurant beloved of diplomats near my flat. Handing it back, he squeezed out a grin. His face looked like he liked licking nettles.

'Pretty good,' he said, tucking into his chocolate pancake. 'Maybe you should show to Serbian government. You can ask few thousand euro as adviser.'

The prime minister's office was right outside the window. Beyond it stood the remnants of the Defense Ministry, which thrust its jagged brickwork at the sunset. Like the rest of the damage wrought by NATO bombing, it was left as a public alibi for impotence, pinning the country's problems on outsiders. This wasn't a helpful form of shock therapy, any more than those on offer from the International Monetary Fund. A festival was a less destructive catalyst. If we raised sufficient money, we'd run several. They'd operate as entrepreneurial boot camps, training our employees on the job, to help them access grants from foreign donors. In time, they'd repeat the process by themselves.

Within a few years, young Serbs could run an empire. There'd be concert venues, CD pressing plants, design studios, web development hubs; whatever people wanted to create. They could undercut Western European prices, and multimedia work could be outsourced. Shops full of pirate CDs bore ample tribute to their artistry. But they also deterred investment in new music. Only the most commercial acts survived. We could build a more sustainable model. All we lacked was seed money.

G was clear that this ought to be our priority. 'We need to start approaching soon to sponsors,' he said. 'This is the place where you have to invest and kinda stick around for a while, until it starts coming back. But it's gonna happen man, it's going in right direction. It's still not very, you know, like secure, but we gotta start somewhere. We should make now presentation of our project. Stage I can get five thousand, plus PA and backline, then security, salaries, medias, program all needs budgeting. Whoever wanna cover, we expose them. We can make Pepsi fest if they pay us, I say fuck it.'

That didn't sound appealing to me. But when I said as much, my partner burst out laughing. 'If you have million dollars, say me word,' he said. 'Already agents offer Massive Attack.'

It was the first time I'd heard him name names. I felt excited. 'How much would they cost?'

He shrugged. 'Like hundred grand, one fifty maybe.'

'Fuck.'

He pushed his plate aside. 'Yeah man, we know this game is rigged.'

'So why don't we book someone huge who'd attract investors?'

'Like how you mean?' G's forehead scrunched up.

'Well, imagine we put Pink Floyd back together...'

He butted in. 'And why we would wanna do that?'

'I'm just saying...'

G was dismissive. 'You know they try to get Rolling Stones here for next year? I have information price for that would be at least one million. I don't see many sponsors run to give them. We need to associate more with young, progressive and cultured market on territories, know what I mean?'

I did, but I was stumped on how to start. Thankfully, the waitress had distracted me. If girls from Ukraine knocked The Beatles out, perhaps they should have visited the Balkans. Everyday women in cafes could have been models. They flashed cheekbones at passers by as if they knew it. Our server's lithe arms stretched out across the table, her caramel eyes holding mine as she cleared the plates. I longed to sidle round and cup her buttocks. I looked away, afraid she'd notice my intentions.

'I see you like her,' G winked, once she'd departed.

I uneasily doubled the tip I'd left on the table. 'Who wouldn't?' I said.

'Why you don't just grab her cunt?'

'You *what*?' It was sometimes hard to tell if G was serious.

'If she wants to play, she will like that.'

'And if she doesn't?' I felt strangely repressed.

'I think you will know.'

His logic was unanswerably obscene. I was tempted to test it at once, but my phone interrupted. I answered anxiously. It was an ex-girlfriend, or to be accurate, not quite. After living in eight different cities in the past four years, I'd developed an aversion to attachments. At the same time, I couldn't let go. I felt too lonely. So I juggled foreign women from Belgrade. I kept my distance so they wouldn't get ideas. This girl lived in Romania. She said she thought I saw her to escape.

'I just interviewed minister for economy,' she frothed in my ear. She was a journalist. 'There is a scandal because she flew to

Taiwan in first class.'

'Mm.' I rolled my eyes and held up a finger at G. He nodded back.

'She asked me isn't it normal to want nice things? I said my grandmother doesn't have such things and she worked forty years. Now she is struggling with hundred dollars pension every month. And you know what this stupid woman told me? Well, young lady, maybe you should help your grandmother with some money.'

I mumbled disapproval.

'Is something wrong?' she asked.

'I'm just in a meeting.'

'You're always busy.' Her dejected tone unnerved me. She'd told me once that a friend said I was dangerous. Then she'd laughed, and called me a big baby.

'I've got to go,' I said. 'I'll speak to you later.'

G smiled as I hung up. 'What you think she wants from you? Like passport?'

'She's good to me,' I ventured, feeling even more unsettled than before.

'I bet!' My partner chuckled. 'Women here they do that, to control you. You think she understands you?'

I feared she might. She certainly seemed to feel sorry for me, which made me sorrier for myself. I felt guilty that I wasn't what she wanted. 'No,' I said, without conviction.

'My friend, we gonna find you one sweet Serbian girl,' G said. 'Like sensitive one, you will see. Maybe she is watching you tonight.'

It was time to unleash our patter on the public. G had arranged for fifteen minutes of fame on a late-night chat show. A friend of his was a friend of the presenter's, who invited the three of us on to discuss what we liked.

My only experience of the limelight was at college, where I

played myself as the lead in *Look Back In Anger*. 'Nobody thinks, nobody cares,' I railed as Jimmy Porter. 'No beliefs, no convictions and no enthusiasm.' A critic said my Angry Young Man had wildly 'stamped and snarled around the stage, giving the uneasy feeling that at any moment he might massacre the rest of the cast and start laying about the audience.' This wouldn't go down well on Serbian TV. Fortunately, G had other plans.

'You will be presented as worldwide expert for youth situations,' he said. 'Idea is to put on urgent level that something has to be done here with youth capital.'

Our appearance would give us a videotape to show sponsors, and potential foreign backers in the 'donor community'. So I'd come to ham it up like Tony Blair, First Fig Leaf to the Almighty. When the lights went up I waffled at the cameras.

'Young people in this region understand the way the world works but they don't necessarily understand how democracy works.' I mean. Look. You know. 'They don't necessarily realize that it's a flawed system. There is only one choice really - how to make it work for you.'

G squirmed on the armchair beside me in orange jeans. When asked to speak, he mumbled at his sweatshirt. I cut back in and chuntered on in freestyle.

'Young people here were better organized, more long-term in their vision and more politically motivated than young people in any of the countries I've lived in before I came here, and in two years that's gone. People in this country have gone to sleep and I don't understand why. It's time to change that. It's time they woke up!'

The host of *Level 23* smiled indulgently. His show was billed as an antidote to 'fake exclusivity and elitism', with guests who were 'exquisite, even unknown'. The set consisted of heavy black drapes, four chairs, and a wooden table.

G had spent the past two hours preparing me, smoking up 'a great ambassador to some psychedelic nation from other psychedelic nation.' The training went straight to my head, and left him gibbering. He looked like falling asleep at any moment.

'Propose not a concrete utopia, but an abstraction,' he'd urged, quoting from favorite scriptures on his shelves. 'One decisive evening, people will look at each other and say enough! To hell with work, to hell with boredom! Let's put an end to it! And everyone will then step into the eternal festival and the creation of situations.'

Why not? It worked for me. 'There are actually some viable alternatives for young people,' I said. 'Service industries, creative industries are the industries of the future.'

Hypnagogic visions danced before me: of screaming satellite boxes hacked to get six hundred channels; T-shirts boasting 'I'm not just perfect, I'm Serb too', and postcards of Mickey Mouse getting buggered by a warlord, beneath the caption 'Fuck the USA!' Another design showed an American Stealth bomber, which was downed by Serbs in 1999. 'Sorry,' it said. 'We didn't know it was invisible.'

I told viewers 'people here could really benefit. They speak foreign languages. They are very Internet literate. They are very technologically well educated. All they need is to re-establish more contact with the outside world. And it seems to me that this music business is a way of doing that.'

To finish, I took a swipe at local pride. 'I don't see a happy society for young people to stay in. I don't even see a fun society for me to live in. EXIT is great but there's only one a year. I want to go out every Friday and Saturday night and have a good time. Who's going to do that for me? I need somebody in Serbia to do that. I can't go to London, it's too expensive.'

Cue insufferable chortle to camera, and cut.

The final piece of the jigsaw was commitment. Whatever we choose in life, we're bound to lose: we can't have it all. And the thought of being a loser was alarming, so I tried to avoid decisions if I could, preferring instead to let them take me, while blaming other people for the outcomes. Without deciding to, I'd gone native in the head.

Nonetheless, I felt unsure about my guide. I'd been drawn to G because he reminded me of someone. We'd also met a festival, one year earlier. It was two hundred times as vast as the EXIT fortress, on the banks of the River Ganges in India.

The Kumbh Mela was like a medieval carnival, a sprawl of tents and fires and strange attractions. On the most auspicious dawn in 144 years, millions of Hindu pilgrims came to swim. I joined them, fried on ecstasy, which I got off some aging hippies I'd encountered. These leather-tanned Europeans were as old as my parents, but that was where the parallels had ceased. Some of them lived itinerantly as *sadhus*, among sects of naked yogis smeared with ash, who regarded smoking dope as a kind of sacrament. Getting stoned with these ghostly statues felt transcendent. Everyone's presence expanded into harmony. I returned to Europe spiritually high.

I was eager to share the magic I'd experienced, but whenever I tried to express it, all words failed me. A festival seemed a way of reconnecting with that energy. But how to ensure it manifested purely? I needed inspiration from an expert.

Like the others I'd run into at the Mela, M had been visiting India for decades. He'd been dressed in a lime green vest when we met, with clashing fluorescent crescents on his loincloth. When he spoke, he peered down his nose through half-moon spectacles. Although he'd been guzzling drugs for as long as I'd lived, he sounded more coherent than I felt, and he shone with an oddly vital radiance, as if he'd somehow cracked the key to staying young, despite having lost his hair and half his teeth.

He and his friends were Goa pioneers. They'd staged parties on the beach since the 1970s. At the outset, these featured psychedelic bands, but DJs proved much better in the long run. They kept the dancers going for days on end, and played whatever sounds might hit the spot: electro, funk and disco; *Qawwali* for Afghans fleeing the war; The Cure. When vinyl warped in the heat, they switched to tapes. Then they chopped them up and spliced them into loops.

As M liked to say of these creations: 'Trance is the name the music we played got when it started to be made by people who had been to Goa. Before it was acid, garage, house, techno, and so on. For us, it is a danceable music that you can listen to as well, especially under the influence. And no words, since words are very specific to the one who hears them, but not very trustable for passing on emotions.'

This made it tough to seek advice. I'd have to go wherever he was playing. So I flew to a dusty town in northern Spain, and ventured into the mountains with a hire car. The sun was setting when I reached the scene of the party, in a clearing up a dirt track by a cliff. About a hundred heads had made the journey. The dance floor rumbled with pinecones, to a squelching beat like tent pegs hitting concrete. Luminous spirals shimmered in the trees, framed by white muslin sheets. Away from the action, M had rigged up a tarp, beneath which several friends hunched round a fire. As I sat, he plucked a bottle from his shoulder bag. The moment I was scared of had arrived.

'Acid is like your father, but mescaline's your mother,' M said dramatically. His vial was full of the latter, in synthesized replication of the peyote cactus. 'They both want to teach the same lesson, only one is just a *little* more severe.'

I didn't need reminding. The last LSD I took had shocked me rigid. Maybe I shouldn't have swallowed it for kicks. In my teens, I thought a trip was cracking value. You could blow your mind for the price of a four-pack of lager. At first, I found the hairy stuff hilarious. I got off on watching skin breathe in the mirror. But that was before the night I munched too much. The Fear had stalked my thinking ever since. I spiraled round in search of reassurance, but secretly feared I'd never think straight again. I was aghast. What of my precious sense of being *clever*? 'Help!' I screamed in silence. Save me from me! But no one could. Anxiety was an extra thud of pulse.

Obsessed with the damage I'd done, I tried denying it. And that only made the poison pound much harder. Feel bad; tell self off for it; feel worse. I went to see a doctor. He pooh-poohed it. Self-diagnoses gripped my rotting innards: toxic psychosis and irritable bowel syndrome, savaging the flesh like barbed wire ticks. Eventually, I found a way to cope. To prove I hadn't lost it completely, I'd push myself on to more demanding feats, and numb all the pain in my soul with strong hashish.

Acid hadn't brought me enlightenment. Instead of transcending ego, I'd just bruised mine. Hey, I'm not mental, OK? Look at my achievements, damn you! But who's you, and why am I arguing with me? Around the infernal identity twist we go again...

I wasn't like the others at the party. They liked their perceptual filters being stripped, to see that every thing was everything. Conceptually, I thought I understood. But I couldn't let go. The loss of my sense of self hurt too much. Instead of enjoying the unity of consciousness, I clung to the razor-edged shards in which it shattered.

For the past ten years, I'd steered well clear of acid, and anything else that sounded vaguely similar, but now I somehow felt obliged. M was already doling out the grains. 'It's like reality,' he said, as he reached round the group. 'We take or leave.'

Attempts to mount resistance got me nowhere. 'I have to work on Monday.' I said, before embarrassment kicked in. 'Not that that's a reason for anything, of course.'

I looked at the dose in my palm. Was it strong? Compared to what? I didn't ask. I ate some with a flourish, and spilled the rest. Or so I thought, until I feared I'd been too obvious. An accusing globule glistened on my thumb. Snickering, I slurped it down and shivered. Whatever happened next, I'd lost control.

The hours of darkness melted in the flames. When M took off for the dance floor with his DAT player, I felt far too mentally jellified to follow. It was oddly reassuring.

'Why worry?' asked a voice in my chest. It sounded like G. 'Why not risk everything, be free?' To the strains of M's tunes from afar, I decided I'd try talking to his friends.

I turned to a DJ from England. 'What sort of music do you play?'

He looked up from the joint he was packing with one hand. I felt emboldened. 'Like faster stuff, or more downbeat? Or both?'

His eyes narrowed slowly. 'Are you asking if I plan my sets in advance?'

That was enough. He'd begun to liquefy as dots. To steady myself, I staggered to my feet, and stumbled into the under-growth to piss. Some time later, I realized I'd been there a while. Everything was suddenly translucent. The veins in leaves were limbs of living light, and the rocks had all crumbled to dust and rearranged themselves. There was nothing to do but witness nature's glory.

Around dawn, I returned to the fire to find M stoking embers. Everyone else had vanished in the meantime. I'd never get a better opportunity, but all my thoughts got jumbled when I spoke.

I blurted out the question on my mind. 'What's the secret?'

M held my gaze for half a minute. He said not a word.

I tried again. 'I mean what's the answer.'

I paused. 'Like how do you do it?'

His head tilted slightly to the left.

'You know,' I said, 'to make people positive. How do I make a party work like yours?'

He started smiling. 'A good party always loses money,' he said.

This wasn't the sort of endorsement I'd been after.

He tried again. 'You know, you don't always get what you want.' He started laughing. 'But sometimes you can find what you need.'

I despaired: I feared I'd never really find it. So I blundered on as before, skirting the subject. 'Is that what you learned from Goa?'

His face lit up. 'You know, what we were doing was kind of an experiment,' he said. 'We tried to break down barriers, with open hearts and minds not politics and whatnot. We really thought we'd change society. The CIA was watching us of course. And they let us have as much as acid as we wanted. We were guinea pigs.'

'Really?' I kept a straight face, though the urge to laugh was intense.

'Sure! They were testing acid on Americans for years. They wanted to use it to control people.' He chuckled heartily. 'But it didn't give results like they expected.'

'So what were the results of your experiment?'

'Ah, you know people showed their limitations,' he said. 'We hoped we were making a paradise, but we recreated most of the usual fuckups.'

'So it wasn't the CIA that fucked things up?' I was only half joking.

'*Well,*' M grinned, 'in a *way*, we're all the agents of central intelligence.'

We were back on topic. 'If that's the case, then what does it want us to do?'

'Now there's a question,' he said. 'I thought that *maybe* the anti-globalization people might start something, but now I don't know.'

Neither did I. As far as I could tell, no one knew. It was obvious what to oppose, but not how to change it. Though I found M's example inspiring, his generation's failures weighed on mine. Activism struck me as a lifestyle statement, a self-indulgent howl to match Thom Yorke's: *'I wish it was the Sixties, I wish I could be happy, I wish, I wish, I wish that something would happen.'*

With G, I meant to see that it did. My sanity hinged on it. The festival wasn't an end in itself, any more than politics with Labus. I had a higher goal in mind. My guiding star was as lofty as Allen Ginsberg's, 'burning for the ancient heavenly connection to the starry dynamo,' like all the 'angelheaded hipsters' since the beatniks. I still wasn't sure how to give this vision form, but everything conceivable was possible. And this conclusion stood to reason, because it didn't, which was the point. Or so I thought as I collapsed in fits of giggles.

When I'd pulled myself together again, a Dutchman's face was wobbling above me. I'd last seen him several hours earlier, when I turned down a glass of his potent acid punch. His ruddy features bulged through whirling eyes, and the matted curls on top were drenched with sweat. Wheezing hard, he lowered his ursine bulk.

'Hey, hey,' he said, planting a hand on one of my shoulders, for balance. 'I think now maybe we *relax*. It is OK? Ja, ja, I think it is *OK*. So, I was hearing that you're going to make a party, *hoor*? And I want to say I think it's good you do something. Some of us need very much to do. I think you are one. For me, I think it's better I don't do. You know, not doing can be harder work than doing.'

He erupted in rasping coughs, and squeezed my arm. 'Listen,' he said. 'I give you some advice. You use how you want. Life is an illusion, choose a nice one.'

GLUTTONY

It's impossible to have too much cannabis. That's part of its seductive appeal. You may not even think it's addictive, but the harder it gets to find the best, the more you stockpile, as the humblest Amsterdam day-tripper learns within hours. And once you get into the grip of a serious habit, you need enough of a stash to stay properly high.

Discovering what this means can be a challenge. The better coffee shop menus offer tasting notes, but they're worse than useless, unless you already know what they class as 'very strong stoned', and how it differs from a 'very strong high'. As for 'energetic', or 'incredible stoned', or the tantalizing 'experienced smokers only', well you'd just have to sample them all to be sure of the contrast, by which point you'll struggle to detect it. Hence the greened-out tourists hugging canal banks.

I longed for the 'intense clear high' of Himalayan *charas*, the essence of bliss I'd relished when in India. It's probably the finest hashish in the world, but it wasn't to be found in Belgrade. The closest I'd got was buying €300 worth of formula. Three lugs and I'd had to stub the first joint out. It left an aftertaste of bin-liners, with similarly asphyxiating side effects. Though it looked like what G brought to EXIT, something oily had been added to make it go further. My partner said he'd help me get my money back, but his tone deterred me. I'd inspected the piece before parting with the average monthly wage, so crying about it now served little purpose. Instead, I'd need to source the pukka product.

The obvious place to go was Amsterdam, but carting drugs through Schiphol sounded risky. The airport crawled with dogs and armed police, and on arrival you'd surely be scrutinized, even in Serbia. I'd rather try out somewhere lower key. And where could sound less threatening than Switzerland?

To my surprise when I'd been stationed there for Reuters, the

Swiss seemed almost as tolerant as the Dutch. Perhaps it was a Calvinist thing: if they assumed they were predestined for salvation, they didn't mind letting the damned do their worst. Bags of weed were sold as 'potpourri', and smuggled hash was easily bought in bulk. The difficult bit, of course, was how to import it.

It was M who first explained the technique. 'Of course, the gay guys have it easier,' he'd winked. Anatomically, a hundred grams was feasible. It merely had to be molded into a bullet. Fifty might be comfier to start with. Wrapped in cling film and condoms, that would barely be the size of a couple of film canisters. 'All you need is Vaseline,' M advised. 'And first you smoke a joint and take a shit. Really it's no big deal. Dress well, keep calm and smile when you walk through the customs.'

So I bought a ticket to Zurich, told the *Times* I'd scheduled an interview in the transit lounge, and flew off on expenses to pack my backside.

As befits a banking citadel, the city hides its treasures with bland facades. Its vaults of gold are stashed beneath a giant duty free mall, stretching from the station to the lake. K's underground store was more discreet, tucked away on a tramline to the suburbs. And unlike Zurich's glut of walk-in humidors, its doors didn't look like they'd opened in years. Apart from some yellowing books, the shelves were bare. A till-side rack of incense gathered dust. The smeared glass window shouted: 'Go away!'

Finding the place unlocked was a thrill in itself. A bell tinkled as I stepped across the threshold, and a shower of ribbons stirred behind the counter. A spritely figure burst forth, looking even more like a caveman than I recalled. Though his hair grew down his back and his beard was wild, it was largely to do with the primate pose he struck.

'Hi, hi!' he beckoned, arms dangling like the scoops on a JCB. 'Ja, come!'

K had never told me much about himself. I just knew he was

hardcore. He'd printed lighters with his address and hours of business. If he recognized you, he'd let you in the shop. Otherwise, its contents told their own story. A hefty minimum charge kept skate kids at bay, and the only people I'd met there were full-on dope fiends.

He led me out the back to his *sanctum sanctorum*: a poky kitchenette across the hall. A squat wooden table filled up half the room, leaving paths to the sink and a worktop, which was stacked with pendulous sheaves of marijuana. Ganesh loomed from a drape in tie-dyed form, bestowing elephant-headed blessings on proceedings. Two figures sat hunched by the door, inhaling deeply. The one in the pinstriped suit raised a hand. The other doffed his grey woolen cap, murmuring greetings in the local singsong German. K stuck to English.

'Sit,' he said, pulling out a stool. The guy in the cap passed a joint. Squatting on his throne beside the worktop, K was rolling another twice the size. 'Outdoor,' he said, crushing heaps of pungent buds. 'Full biological, *gell*.' When he'd finished, he held the reefer to his forehead, recited an incantation and sparked up. After three deep breaths, he hacked out fits of coughs, mutating into a chant concluding 'Yes!'

The others kept chatting away by themselves, their dialect as baffling as baby talk. Odd phrases filtered through, like 'therapeutic ecstasy'. Noting my curiosity, K introduced us. 'He is *psycholog*,' he said, nodding vaguely at both. I asked if I'd understood their words correctly. Did therapists really give ecstasy to patients?

The guy in the suit replied in fluent American. 'We don't just give them pills and send them home. It's part of a process. They talk about their trauma and let go. If you face your inner conflicts, you find peace.'

'And that's legal here?' I asked. I was intrigued. 'It sounds like what people need in the Balkans.'

He smiled. 'Let's just say you can do it. Swiss labs run trials on many psychotropics. We help people see through the limits they made in their minds.'

'That sounds fantastic,' I said.

K's piercing eyes shot my way. 'If you are interested for *yourself*,' he said, 'I make guided psychedelic explorations. Beyond all time and space to world of spirits. No more fears. For hundred francs I sit with you, the full DMT experience. BOOM!'

I tried to disguise my terror at the prospect. What little I knew of this drug I'd gleaned from ambient music, and its samples sounded freaky in themselves. 'DMT is a mega-tonnage hallucinogen,' one of them cackled. 'It occurs naturally in the metabolism of every single one of us.' The pineal gland secretes it in our dreams, and it floods the brain at birth and death, or when smoked in the form of an extract from plants. In the Amazon, shamans boil their roots as tea. It's referred to as 'vine of the soul', and it administers a mind-expanding brain massage.

'Another time perhaps,' I said. 'I'm flying back to Belgrade this afternoon.'

K shook his head. 'Life today is always going faster. But psychedelics go deeper, to where mind is programmed. This is where we go for to make progress.'

While he spoke, he pulled a crate from under the counter. It was packed with zip lock bags containing cannabis. He had more than a dozen varieties, and of each there were hundreds of grams, with plenty more elsewhere if you required it.

'So,' he said. 'What can I offer you? Maybe coffee?'

The guy in the cap poured a shot from the pot on the hob. I downed it in one. He also passed a plate of lemony sponge cake. To taste buds parched by smoking potent grass, the fluffy slabs looked succulent and tempting.

'Please,' K gestured. 'We had already.'

While I scoffed a slice, he talked me through his wares. There were multiple grades and flavors of Moroccan, from sandy golden pollen to a gooey caramello; an exotic type of yellow

Lebanese; and five different Himalayan blacks, from Afghanistan, northern India and Nepal, which rhymed with PayPal. Each had its own distinctive characteristics.

'This one is fresh from the harvest.' K picked up a paperback slab of resin, and ripped it like a strongman tackling a phone book. Inside, the *charas* was textured like crystalline compost. Its earthy smell of spice was overpowering.

'Top quality.' He nodded. 'Instant nirvana.'

Prices were high by Dutch standards. But after due consideration, and more samples, I opted for a thousand-franc selection bag, clocking in at almost sixty grams.

It was time I got moving. But my legs had been transformed to sticks of licorice. My thoughts raced straight to the snack I'd just consumed.

No! It couldn't be. Could it? Really? I didn't know what I should think, let alone what I'd say. And what would they think if I went ahead and said it?

'Er...' I stammered, lurking by the doorway.

All three of them were staring at me keenly. My heart was pounding.

'Just a question,' I said, trying desperately to sound casual. 'Was that, um... was that a *normal* cake?'

'No, it was a *special* one!' K roared. 'From the mother of my daughter.'

I made my excuses and fled.

I started smoking dope when I was fifteen. In those days, I didn't care where it came from, which was handy when dealing with dealers in Newcastle. Who knew what oily poisons lurked in 'tack'? It was sold in tenner deals of flat-press 'slate' and 'rocky', and squidgy stuff they marketed as 'red seal'. But what was it really? If it left you leaden-headed, well, who cared? Genetically modified skunk was overpriced. If we couldn't get hash, we'd smoke bog-standard weed. In theory that was meant to be

Jamaican; I just knew it came wedged in packs of Regal King Size.

Indian *charas* was something else entirely. It never knocked me out; it woke me up. I felt so happy I was certain it was medicine. The higher I got, the more capable I felt. I was sure I could have done anything I chose. I just chose to do nothing.

This joy had first entered my life when Reuters hired me, and awarded their graduate trainees an advance on salary, to cover the cost of some suits and a London flat. With three months to spare before my start date, I blew mine on a retreat to the Himalayas, unaware of the charms that loitered in their foothills.

At the head of the Valley of Gods, away from busloads of Indian tourists ogling snow, there was a hamlet with few obvious attractions. But further up the slopes beyond its orchards, peasants rubbed a cash crop in their palms. A quiet day of graft could yield a *tola*: a ten-gram lump of belting hash. When Westerners arrived, they saw potential. Some threw away their passports and took to farming. Others sent tons of airfreight round the world. Together, they'd made a factory out of Eden. The plants grew by the roadside by themselves, but out of sight their crop was better tended, and bred to feed a foreign taste for 'cream'. The mark-up back in Europe was immense. But this slowly brought a darker side to business, with Indians fighting back for market share. The externalized costs of the trade could be counted in corpses, and another idyll tainted by materialism. None of that stopped me gorging on the product.

'Yes, YES!' its dodgy peddler would beam, wobbling a Saddam moustache above his doorstep. 'You coming sitting, yes!' This appeared to be phrased as a question. I liked the order. 'Yes, yes, you sitting smoking!'

For a month, I deferred to his wisdom with abandon, moving only to sit in the baths at a Shiva temple. Its chanting took on choral intensity, and appeared to be piped from deep between my ears. Wrinkling in hot water felt sublime. I trusted the world to provide, and it did, every day: a quarter of *charas* per head, without a thought.

The shop had more than anyone could want. Though primarily stocked with cobwebs and grime, more desirable wares were cached in a rusty fridge, and guarded by an opium-addled wraith. 'How much?' he'd leer at anyone summoned to see him. Then he'd thrust a plastic bag in your face, brimming with dark brown cylinders and discs. 'One kilo?' he'd start drooling. 'Very good!' In time, you could haggle him down to an ounce of scraps, and sling it when you found some better stuff. It cost ten bucks.

'Sitting smoking! Coming going! Yes!' Like the dreadlocked *sadhu* parked behind the counter, who was introduced as 'Babaji from Nehru Kund': he came one day to impart his sacred teachings. He sat there, and he smoked, and then he went.

My departure from Zurich was frantic. The tram was rammed, so I stood in the aisle, and fingered at the pieces in my pocket. Most of them stayed stubbornly misshapen. When a seat came free, I pulled out plastic wrap. Shielding my lap with a newspaper, I swaddled each lump and cradled them into a block, smoothing off the contours with more layers. Each successive sheet increased my pulse. I felt the eyes of gnomish burghers boring into me. But by the time we arrived at the station, I had a butt plug.

It looked frighteningly wide.

I didn't want to skimp on the cling film. It was hard to say which smell concerned me more, and I didn't fancy chancing it with either. In a toilet on the train to the airport, I double-bagged the bundle in condoms, and dipped it in Vaseline. The next bit wasn't easy, but once the tip was in, the rest slid up. I realized this could work the other way. The lubricant was squelching hard already, and the pellet inside my crack felt like a stone. It was much too late to fret about that now.

'I'm a foreign correspondent,' I thought, my head full of

sunshine.

Everything was fine until the gate, where bags were being screened a second time. This was how I learned of my mistake. I'd brought a wash bag, to look less conspicuous. Unfortunately, I forgot to check the contents.

'I'm sorry, but you can't take this with you.' The woman at the scanner was holding up my nail scissors.

'Why not?' I asked, predicting what she'd say.

'This is the rule.' The Swiss can sound more German than a German. But I'd got used to living in countries with flexible rules. When you've talked a Romanian policeman out of fining you, using lines like 'he's driving my car without a license because I'm wasted,' you can think you're undiplomatically immune.

'Can't you just pretend you didn't see them?' I said. 'If I wanted to put someone's eye out, I've got keys.'

'Excuse me.' A uniformed colleague intervened. 'Please come here.'

He gestured at a row of curtained search booths. Horrendous images danced across my forehead: of latex gloves, the pencil torch, and toilets with transparent u-bends. Adrenaline was thudding uncontrollably.

'No problem,' I heard myself say, 'I leave the scissors.'

He pointed out a cubicle. 'This way please.'

Time appeared to switch to freeze-frame playback. It reminded me of being sent to the headmaster. I felt queerly calm. It was far too late to change the situation. If it had to be jail, well better here in Switzerland than Serbia, where I'd surely be swarthily gang raped on arrival. The guy pulled shut the drape, and frisked me down.

In fewer than sixty seconds I was free.

The rest of the journey passed without event. In Belgrade, the airport was deserted. The customs officer's eyelids drooped like mine. Once home, I rushed straight to the toilet feeling nervous, but the package plopped into the bowl with a sigh of relief. Its outer layers had the faintest whiff of bum grease, but the fruity odor inside was fully cannabinoid. No hash I smoked had ever tasted finer.

I took to routing work trips via Zurich, on the grounds that there weren't any flights between Balkan capitals. Within a few months, I'd built up half a kilo. With my range of eighteen strains, I could have run a coffee shop. I had more personal priorities. I took to smoking joints like cigarettes, and swore to myself I'd never run out again.

Winter cast a pall on Belgrade. The wind blew down from Siberia, piling the Balkans with snowdrifts the height of parked cars. An all-pervading lassitude took hold, as stuffy as the smokiest *kafana*, where nights and the following days could disappear, on a diet of cannonball stodge and bottled piss, which was known to the locals generically as *rakija*.

Weeks before the weather turned hypothermic, the city's shroud of grey put London to shame. Smoking was my only source of light, and what delights it could provide! The pangs of the present dissolved into rapturous reverie, awakening a spirit of endurance. It helped me find the strength to reengage.

Inspiration comes from the strangest sources. As a Biblical clairvoyant had foretold: 'I, even I Daniel, had seen the vision, and sought for the meaning, then behold, there stood before me as the appearance of a man.'

But who was this freak apparition in my flat? Well, 'he came near where I stood: and when he came, I was afraid, and fell upon my face: but he said unto me, Understand, O son of man: for at the time of the end shall be the vision.'

His visionary babble spun me out at first. But wherever I turned, I heard the words repeating. And poets could read the writing on my wall; their voices deciphered it. 'You resemble, do you not,' mused Baudelaire, 'a fantastic novel that is being lived instead of being written.' He was blatantly a caner after my heart. 'You seem to live several men's lives in the space of an hour.'

Suddenly, it all seemed very clear. I needed to invent a new identity. That way I could interview myself, and talk us up in print to lure some sponsors. I set to work at once on laying a paper trail.

A few days later, *The New York Times* ran a letter, from a certain Raoul Djukanovic in Belgrade. His missive was headlined 'Nanny for the Balkans?' and it said what Daniel Simpson never could.

'The West may well be concerned about the stability of this volatile region, but its strategy for dealing with the threat is devoid of vision and divorced from reality,' the text harrumphed. 'Instead of patting each other on the back for keeping a lid on conflicts, Western officials should consider how they can become a catalyst for change in the Balkans by investing heavily in economic revival.'

This rant got printed faster than most of my stories, unhindered by its hint of fear and loathing: the author was a Balkanized version of Raoul Duke, the pseudonym of the volatile Hunter S. Thompson. As Doctor Gonzo's wingman once explained: 'When the going gets weird, the weird turn pro.'

I redesigned my business cards accordingly. Raoul became a 'Why Do They Hate Us Correspondent', employed by *The New Hawk Times* for special projects. His task was to test the media uncertainty principle, which holds that journalists can't be objective, because by writing about events they shape their outcome.

This innovation met with G's approval. 'If you are now Raoul,' he said, 'I wanna be archetype of Balkan refugee, like a Goran Needsavisavic of no man's land. Together we make Utopia in shithole.'

Our horizons had expanded quite dramatically. A one-off event on a Saturday was too small. G said serious festivals lasted a weekend, so we'd agreed to run from Thursday through to Sunday, with four different stages. And that meant lots of slots left to fill. I felt sure we needed names to make it work. Glastonbury could trade on reputation. Their tickets would sell whoever was on the bill. We wouldn't have the same luxury, and Serbian aspirations knew no bounds.

G refused to see this as a problem. 'What you wanna give to them?' he sneered. 'Like Coldplay, Britney Spears and U2? Youngs here they much more influenced by urban styles, like a hip-hop, break-beat, reggae, whole that fusion. I have in mind a stage of Bristol sound. You know scene they building up there since in Eighties. I get all those guys for just few thousand pounds. They wanna send to me full program, fifty artists. With Massive Attack together, that can kill it.'

'Sounds great,' I said. 'But who else are people going to recognize? They'll want to see someone famous every night.'

Bookings always touched a nerve with G. Of course there were bound to be limits to what we'd get, but if we had to go begging to agents, why not think big?

'Can't we try for R.E.M. or Radiohead?' I said.

My partner winced. 'Man, those guys they crying on a stage. We need more sound of positivity. I am thinking now one stage just for reggae. Lotta people here they would appreciate. Skies above this country cry for righteousness, and will come, you should believe.'

He stared at the mist through the window. We'd adjourned to a tower-top café, above the confluence of the Danube and the Sava, where Romans built the first of Belgrade's forts. Nowadays, the complex housed a war museum. Its overgrown maze of ramparts couldn't host a festival, but they afforded clearer sight lines to our target.

G's first suggested venue was no use. Though its glades were undeniably enchanting, they'd only hold some fifteen thousand people. Our aim was now to lure five times as many. Another idea was a park by a bombed-out skyscraper, but we heard it had just been earmarked for construction. That left an island in the Danube, which my partner called 'part nature reserve, part pleasure beach'. The season for both had ended weeks before, and crossings by boat were finished for the winter. But G said he'd find a way to get us over there. From the tower, we only saw a greenish hump.

'I tell you man, that island can be perfect,' he said. 'For centuries was frontier here of empires. On one side was Turks, other Austrians. Now it brings magical energies, like crossing to extraordinary world. You know that anarchistic space in Copenhagen, Christiania? We make here similar Interzone in Belgrade. People they will come here just to see that. We don't have to sell them with cheap names.'

G could be unnervingly inspiring. I sometimes felt he'd tapped my buried thoughts. When he winked, I even wondered if he'd planted them. Either way, I felt closer to my instincts.

'I've been thinking,' I said, abandoning all caution. 'Imagine if Serbia legalized soft drugs. They could call it learning lessons from The Hague. The Dutch have shown the benefits for years. People there don't even smoke all that much weed. Coffee shops are full of foreign tourists. Imagine if we ran one on a beach, in hot Balkan sunshine. This place would be crawling with Westerners and cash.'

My partner laughed. 'Many here would like that, sure. But mafias did make powerful friends for trade. This is the country where dealers hide in church. Police will put you to jail for smoking joint, while they give clearances for transit of the heroin. And most of the people whacked out still on tranquilizers. Memory chips on Balkans should be wiped man. You know, reset all fucked-up wartime connections.'

'Why don't we put acid in the water?' I said.

G shook his head. 'Radicals had that dream already years ago.

But I think chlorine can destroy it. And also you should bear in mind commandments.'

'Which ones?'

'Only two what count in age of molecules. Not to change the consciousness of others, and also not to stop them changing consciousness.'

'OK, then let's just offer them the option. I know where to get a jar of liquid acid...'

'Don't you worry yourself too much about all that,' G said. 'Already cultural program has that form. Plan is to make new summer of love in Belgrade, and I am pretty sure that island is predestined. You know what is name of that place?'

I glanced at the wooded shoreline in the distance. Before today, I'd barely even noticed it.

'No idea,' I said.

'They call it *Veliko Ratno Ostrvo*. Big War Island. Where Serbian heroes go to lick their wounds. What can be better location here for love-in?'

To establish ourselves, G said we'd need support. Our earliest port of call was City Hall, where the man who pulled the strings was not the mayor. He was an ally of the Serbian prime minister, and a player in his ruling Democratic Party. He was also big on communications.

'I am sole representative of Alcatel for all Balkans,' Nenad Bogdanovic announced, when asked if he could suggest potential sponsors. His office bore no trace of this affiliation. A plaque said he was President of the Executive Board of Belgrade.

G took this comment at face value. 'I think telecom could be logical partner,' he said. 'But what we want from city is protection.'

To me, this word had sinister implications, but it almost seemed synonymous with friendship. Such was the local obsession with undermining.

'We need help with police,' G ran down our list, 'with permits and garbage collection, and also with barriers for crowds and mobile toilets. If city will give us a paper with commitments, that can help. Investors wanna see all that been cleared.'

Bogdanovic was a funny looking figure. He seemed to have a neck that wasn't there. It skulked behind the jowls of a fatter man, only shrunken as if he'd been fasting in a sauna. The skin appeared to be dripping off his skull.

He rapped his desktop. 'First we need to know how Belgrade profits.'

This was our cue to talk about community, but plans for raising consciousness could wait. The finer details wouldn't help.

'We'll be showing tourists a different side to Serbia,' I said. 'A lot of them will want to move here and invest. This is going to be Europe's cutting edge, like Prague in the early Nineties. Creative minds and business grow together. If we give them incentives to come here, there's a massive market.'

G stepped in to translate with practicalities. 'We gonna have partnership with airlines through all Europe,' he said. 'City can make money from hotels, but will also be big opportunities in future.'

Bogdanovic nodded. 'And where are you planning for this festival?'

'We intend to go on island of a *war*,' G said. 'We can make a transformation back to paradise. It would be colony of artists here in city.'

The politician's fingers stroked his cheeks. He eyed us up and down before he spoke. 'You know, I think some investors already showed their interest there.'

'And more they going to come, that is for sure,' G said. 'We have like long-term plan to expand in all of Serbia. Maybe we also give grants, so others do their jobs well, and help the money to match with right people. It is good way to grow.'

Bogdanovic smiled. 'I think I understand you,' he said. 'Send me a proper list with what you need, and we can meet again next week to confirm.'

It sounded promising to me. But once we'd left, G laughed at my naivety.

'I don't trust that guy without a contract,' he said. 'Is harder here to be hypnotized than West. You just take look around and eyes explode. But hey that is potential source of wisdom. You hear what he was telling us on Alcatel? How you think they got contract on Belgrade telephones? Still is greedy game of all or nothing. Either you are colonel here or dead man. S'aright man, we not gonna play that shit. We make sure we don't give space for too much screw-ups.'

He looked exhausted. I proposed a restorative session on the hash pipe, but my partner had other things on his mind. 'I think I'm gonna rest a little, purify myself,' he said. 'We talk later yeah? Stay cool.'

Later, as the evening yawned ahead, I thought how much I depended on his presence. Without him, I was a drifting correspondent, too fearful to set myself a new direction. This wasn't to say that I feared being on my own. On the contrary, I knew I never was: I had *charas*. Alone with the world inside, even staring at the ceiling felt divine.

The only downside to getting so high all the time is uncertainty: like, what if everybody *knows*? However content I felt, there was always a paranoid sense I'd done something wrong, without recalling what it was. Staying at home seemed safer on the whole. But tonight I had a date I couldn't miss: the Belgrade foreign press corps Christmas party.

Journalists make irritating dinner guests. If they're not roaring off at tangents, trying to use you, they'll be assaulting you with other people's views, and embellishing all their anecdotes and exploits. Among themselves, they tend to start a pissing contest. So it wasn't with much relish that I went. I'd smoked myself half mute in preparation.

Our host was holding court when I arrived. He was twice my age, and no less disillusioned. This put me at ease. Everyone else's pleasantries unsettled me: couldn't they have the decency to hate themselves?

'Why don't we write what we say in the pub?' the elder statesman had enquired.

'We do,' said one of his guests, who didn't drink.

'Of course you don't,' I butted in, half-cocked, 'At Reuters they write what London wants to hear. You ask the local staff in your bureau.'

He wasn't impressed. 'We can't all write what we think and call it news.'

'No,' our host chuckled. 'We write what The Man thinks and call that news.'

Everyone felt impotent in Belgrade. The drive to invade Iraq had made us vulnerable. Our Balkan jobs could be cut to pay for war news. But tonight there was hope: people talked about embedding with Americans. Reinforcements were required at Central Command, to take dictation from the bellicose ranks of generals. I suggested trying a different tack at briefings: ask them if they checked out privates in the showers.

'You shouldn't have planted that question,' said one of the guests. 'It could slip out in public and end my brilliant career. But what a way to go!'

There weren't a lot of more attractive options. A photographer friend had become a human shield. It was the simplest way to obtain an Iraqi visa. Besides, if war couldn't be prevented, she said, we ought to document the suffering. This commitment made me think of going with her, until she revealed her boyfriend was as well.

Eventually, temptation overcame me. I rolled up a massive cone and passed it round. Hardly anyone smoked. The joint was back in my hand before I knew it.

The next thing I recall, I'd chucked a whitey. I felt the comforting clunk of cranium on plate. My breath was like Darth Vader down a stethoscope.

When I sat up again with a shudder, the flat was empty. Someone had put me to sleep on the sofa. I tried glancing at the time, but got lost in my watch. Its plastic strap was embossed with a 007 logo, complete with the words 'The World Is Not Enough.' Some drunken wisdom flashed around my brain. It was the last I remembered of the party.

'Tahiti people say,' a voice had boomed, 'either you eat life, or life eat you.'

I collapsed on the couch.

Over Christmas, in my absence, G made a breakthrough. Two men had been promised a lease on Big War Island. And he'd talked them into talking about a partnership. We were waiting to meet in a restaurant by the Danube, on the fringes of a suburb called Zemun. This was once a separate town under Austrian rule. Its pretty green knoll was flecked with terracotta roof tiles, but it was otherwise as grim as the rest of Serbia. A chief of police had recently been shot there. Not that Zemun's ambience betrayed as much. From our riverside seats, it looked sleepier than us.

G swigged a fresh glass of blueberry juice, ignoring his own advice to stick to brandy. He'd ordered us the special mixed grill, a gut-busting paean to the abattoir, with fried rolls of pork on the side, stuffed with cheese, cream, ham, pickles and spices. Serbia was rich in organic vegetables, mainly because its farmers couldn't afford chemicals. But vegetarians struggled in its taverns. You couldn't just say to a waiter 'I don't eat meat.' You'd have to tell him this meant ham and chicken, and unless you expressly stressed otherwise, it would usually be assumed you'd want some fish.

Though I wasn't at all averse to feasts of meat, the Serbian version went down rather heavily, like a buffet at casinos in Las Vegas, removing the need to consume again that day. Gassy water helped to ease the cramps, and settled the belly to take on extra booze, which would soon get you reaching for more of the lardy fare. Merely thinking about this diet made me nauseous.

My partner's brain was fizzing with ideas. 'You know, I looked to registrate utopia dot com, but someone got idea already. We still can take as Serbian name, with "j". U-TOP-I-JA. It means like me inside a cannon. I guess clowns were fired from those things long time ago. I think is perfect for oasis here in mud.'

I gulped at my chaser of beer and let G talk. It often seemed easier.

'You know, I heard joke what sum up muddy drunken mindset,' he said. 'Bin Laden was planning attack on Eiffel Tower, so he find three volunteers: one Irish guy, one Spanish and one Serb. Each did come to sell his plan to boss. Irishman says OK, for million dollars I fly one plane in tower. So bin Laden ask why he needed all that cash. He said that he has wife and kids to pay for. Then Spanish guy says he'll do, but for two million. Why two? Well, one for wife and one for girlfriend. Finally comes Serb and asks three million. *What*? Bin Laden says, why now *three* million? Simple, says that Serbian guy. One for me, one for you, and one for stupid Irish kamikaze.'

He sniggered out the punch line. Both made me smile. 'Not many people do much for free,' I said.

'That's true my friend, but how much do we *need*? Wise men say we should learn to live with nothing. You know, not even begging, just what come to you. I was thinking now we need to be quite clever. People here don't value what is free. It is important that we charge to them fair price, so we promote like more sustainable kinda business. We can pay to ourselves small salary, and reinvest profits to build up more for future, with orientation for stronger social actions.'

'I think you're right.'

Serbian commerce was certainly shady: as in other Balkan countries, the state had parceled assets out to *biznis* men, who'd got rich on the back of sanctions in the wars. These mafia types worked closely with officials. Some were licensed money-changers, selling Deutschmarks that people used to buy black market food. Others got enlisted in the fighting, ignoring the enmities they leeched off. The Yugoslav army command was in Belgrade, so Serbs had a surfeit of guns, which they bartered for petrol. Their suppliers were Croats, Albanians and Bosnians, who in turn armed kin to keep the conflicts raging. These gangs built up a regional cartel, whose network had expanded in peacetime, sending drugs and immigrants west, along with prostitutes and bootleg cigarettes. The profits were split between crooks and their government backers.

G said we could set a good example. 'Would be big change if we just start by paying tax. When I last went to taxation office, they look on me as extraterrestrial. Security guy told me taxes are for poor people. With hundred euros salary, you pay. But rich only pay their cut on dirty business. Some day they should legalize payola, like as tax. Then we professional enough to present ourselves as civilized.'

For now, politicians got death threats unless they took bribes. And the ministers who did just told each other to stop. 'It is time,' one said, 'for those who are still in the pay of various businessmen to decide who really pays their salary.' *The New York Times* had deemed this too dull to print. G agreed. We could tell a better story, he said, by 'putting money in the pocket without monopolizing.'

I didn't object. I could barely see straight.

Suddenly, G stood and waved at the doorway. It seemed our prospective partners had arrived. Swiveling, I saw them soar above me. Both wore black leather jackets. The thin one was a dandy in a trench coat, with pointy two-tone brogues and oval shades. His look was *Mambo No. 5* meets *The Matrix*. G introduced him as A, and his friend as B. Neither spoke much English. My partner had to interpret almost everything.

'*Sta kaze?*' A kept asking. He sucked his cheeks and his nose flipped up at the ceiling. It meant 'what's that dozy foreigner trying to say?'

B's monotone was slightly more expressive, but his tongue lolled out of his mouth while he composed it. Tanned and robust, with a shoulder-length bob, he resembled the Indian chief from *One Flew Over the Cuckoo's Nest*, only crossbred with Dougal off *Magic Roundabout*. Both he and his mate carried under-arm man bags, which to me suggested cash or hidden handguns.

G didn't shirk from bossing them about. Though promoters as well, they lacked his depth of experience. He'd suggested a trial collaboration, in the form of a New Year all-nighter in Belgrade. He'd organize some DJs from abroad, if they took care of a venue and the tickets. When they'd proved themselves, we'd talk about a festival.

These terms had been accepted on the spot. Then B pulled out a dossier of papers, which he said had been 'approved' by Zemun council. This body controlled the beach on Big War Island, where they proposed to hold the debut 'Lido Festival'. Like *Sziget*, upstream in Hungary, the event would take its name from the planned location.

They mellowed as they shared their ideas, and my woeful attempts to speak Serbian made them laugh. We toasted each other at length between platefuls of meat, and A lit my cigarettes with his pocket flamethrower, which roared from its plastic shell like a Bunsen burner.

According to the document they'd drafted, a festival would 'engage 2,540 technicians and 1,450 people in various services,' and 'at least 300,000 visitors are expected.'

When I questioned some of these statements, B said: 'Yes!'

'*Naravno,*' his partner agreed. Why, of course! 'We will be biggest and best on all of South East Europe.'

Hall Fourteen at Belgrade Congress Center looked like an aircraft hangar. It was also treacherously cold. Our so-called 'People's Party' couldn't heat a corner of it.

As celebrations go, it seemed disastrous. Barely fifteen hundred people came to party, which was roughly a tenth of what we'd hoped. There'd been talk of selling tickets for a euro, but our partners had ditched that idea to raise their take. At ten times the price, only affluent poseurs showed up. The selection of tech-house DJs guaranteed it.

If nothing else, the light show was impressive. Lasers played their way around the hall, bouncing off people's fake designer clothes. A bank of outsized screens flanked the centerpiece bar. At the projectionist's whim, they flipped between snowboard and surf films. I pulled up a chair to gawp idly. G sat beside me, wearing a bobble hat. A long night loomed.

'S'aright man,' my partner smiled. 'We see already what we need.'

'All I can see is a flop,' I said. 'They can't even work the fucking heating.'

I zipped my Arctic parka to the chin.

'Hey, nothing is perfect,' G said, 'for sure not in this town. But I have confirmation now that they are serious. We have here party.'

A few dozen people hunkered by the bar. Several were shivering.

'I see those guys aren't frightened of work,' G said. 'They put this thing together in two weeks. OK, it would be better we make money, but I don't plan to give to them control of that. We need connections in Zemun. You and me we handle all promotions. You think they can talk to agents or to medias? That's why they have that promise on a paper. Together we can make it proper festival. Like real one with spirit of ecstasy, not date for all these lovers of bad tablets.'

Others didn't seem so convinced. G had flown in several

friends from London, whom he hoped to enlist in our quest to find sponsors and artists. They huddled together quietly, and got drunk. One of them laid out endless lines of coke. E's potential input wasn't clarified. When I asked him, he said he did 'specialist imports and exports'.

'I think he can help,' G whispered later. 'With equipment.'

I queried if E was here on business or for pleasure. 'Business,' he replied, staring me out. 'Always business.' Then he laughed and slapped my thigh. 'But I like to have fun.'

He rolled up a banknote and hoofed back two fat rails.

Accessing Big War Island proved to be easy. B and A took G to see the council, and said he was the man who created EXIT. Five minutes later, a deal had been arranged. We got exclusive rights to run bars at the Lido beach, and permission to use the fields that stretched behind it. Our lease on the land ran all summer, and could be extended, subject to mutual satisfaction. As supporters of the mayor's conservative party, our local partners autographed the paperwork. And if they were friends of ours, he said, we were welcome.

The following day, we went to inspect our fief. A fishing boat was chartered on the Danube, and we chugged across icy waters to the island. It was shin-deep in snow. B's head was swathed in a fleecy balaclava. The temperature was roughly minus ten. It was hard to imagine a hundred thousand revelers, but G was convinced the site had space to hold them. The beach was perfectly suited to his reggae stage, and the scrub nearby could be cleared to house a dance pit. A vast open meadow sprawled beyond. Our biggest stage would occupy the far end, and a DJ collective from Bristol could take the other. All that remained to be done was to level the land.

'Now that we have island we have festival,' G said. 'Only option here is to be big. And believe me it is better that way, or Serbs will doubt that action gonna happen.'

It seemed the moment to establish my credentials. G's contribution was obvious, but I wasn't sure my role had been explained. I turned to our partners.

'Did you ever see that movie *Field of Dreams*?' I asked. 'A guy turned his farm into a baseball ground, because a voice had told him to build it and people would come. In the real world, we have to sell the dream to build.'

'*Cekaj, cekaj,*' A twitched. Hang on a minute, eh? '*Sta kaze?*'

G translated freely, along the lines of: 'He is gonna handle all those medias.' Listening to them did wonders for my Serbian.

'If we want to raise money fast, we need a good story,' I said. 'I think we could even get help from the European Union. What we're doing is a project for development, on the fault line between East and West. It could have a big impact.'

Again G relayed the gist, and B's response. 'He said they have connection in Brussels. Apparently she looks positive on Serbs.'

I nodded, but I had ideas of my own. I'd spent too long in my salaried role as a human tape recorder, reporting the world as it looked to politicians. I didn't intend to stay mute, or bow to anyone. I wanted to *say* something, *do* something; *be* someone.

'I'm going to ask the EU to sponsor us,' I said. 'I can interview their senior officials, and tell them I'm a friend of Raoul Djukanovic.'

B and A looked flummoxed.

'His name is on the brochure I'm preparing,' I said.

Their foreheads furrowed. G smiled and told our partners not to worry.

'Raoul has right idea,' he said. 'This place become a twilight zone of Europe. For West to establish itself here, they should provide. They still have lot to offer, like help for infrastructure. If we can melt with Eastern spirit, will be great. Sometimes occupator comes to bring some progress. Only question is whether he is just.'

Fortune would favor our boldness. I felt sure of it.

AVARICE

The Balkans didn't exist two hundred years ago. The name only really caught on in the nineteenth century, when Europe's Great Powers stroked their whiskers over The Eastern Question: who'd control the crumbling Ottoman Empire?

As Turkish occupation forces left, and new nations mushroomed in their wake, the Western mind regarded them as savages. Cartographers started marking the 'Balkan' peninsula (from the Turkish for its 'wooded mountain' range), which was understood to mean lawless and aggressive. They might as well have marveled 'here be dragons'.

This ignored how Great Power meddling stirred up nationalism, inciting some of the fiercer bouts of bloodletting, from the turn of the 20th century to World War II. And that ensured the label stuck for good. The region simply wasn't European. While other ex-Communist countries queued to join Europe's premier diplomatic clubs, in return for providing markets to exploit, war-torn Yugoslav territories were barred.

Bureaucratic wall-charts put it graphically. The continent's states were mostly colored brightly, denoting members of the European Union, and applicants. But a hole gaped wide at the bottom, opposite Italy. If you lived in the bowels of the West, then your shit was your problem.

This seemed unfair. America spent a fortune reviving Europe 50 years back. And the EU's founders thought they'd invented a force for peace. But their heirs betrayed this dream in Yugoslavia. They might have made fights over borders seem irrelevant, had they doled out bundles of Deutschmarks, or fast-track membership. Instead, they hit the Balkans with embargos, fuelling inflation more extreme than in Weimar Germany. While gangsters got rich, most normal people suffered. Bribing them all to be friends would have worked out cheaper.

If billions could be splurged on building Spanish motorways, and salvaging Greece and Portugal from dictatorships, why not share a pittance with some Serbs? My desk was cluttered with studies that implied as much.

'The challenges facing the Balkans,' some German researchers had concluded, 'are not categorically different from those which the European Union has been dealing with in its own territory for many years. However, as it stands, the promise offered by Europe to the region is curiously insubstantial.'

Smarter statecraft was vital, said an aide to Tony Blair. 'Western governments need a much broader and more creative idea of what public diplomacy is and what it can do,' he'd urged, while his peers were concocting reports on Iraqi weapons. 'The challenge is to move from supplying information to capturing the imagination.'

The Greeks seemed ready. They were eager to invest in their non-Turkish neighbors, and freebies from Brussels would help improve returns. Having just taken up the EU's rotating presidency, Greece had vowed to 'keep the Balkans high on its agenda.' It said that 'a powerful message must be sent to governments and peoples in the area, reasserting EU support for their European vocation.'

Where better to do this than Belgrade, the fulcrum of regional instability?

G agreed that these omens augured well. We'd spent a morning culling quotes in my apartment. With some artwork jazzing them up, they'd sound persuasive. A designer was laying them out in a glossy pamphlet, and he'd promised to send us some proofs before the weekend. For now, we were on my terrace, smoking heavily.

The street below led downhill to the station, through a market selling little but root vegetables. Gypsy traders hawked bras in the underpass opposite, where kiosks retailed everything but contraband, at least in the window. Their hardcore porn was displayed beside the tabloids. The shops up the slope went steadily upmarket, overshadowed by advertisements for 'Megatrend', and a state-run overpriced grocery chain called 'C Market'. Staples like butter cost more than they did in London.

'This is here capital of wannabes,' G said. 'But next few years they will be crucial. We should avoid saying Western-style democracy is working. They cannot hide they are on down slide. Unability to deal with honesty will ruin them. If West want end of history, they can have it. Myself, I wanna learn more from ancient East. My old scar is itching me. In desert, what I hear I was intrigued. The wind there it takes you away and you arrive back on a start position all over again. I wanna spend quality time man. Save money, and like maybe slowly die there, if I can predict when I'm gonna die...'

He passed the joint and I took a grateful lug. His morbid conversation made me edgy.

'You should know I'm not scared of death,' my partner said. 'I think she was my friend for while and still is. We have mutual trust. Everybody dies man, sooner or later. It is only now a question how we take it. You know, one day I'm gonna buy boat and sail away far from Uncle Sam and Union Jack, and also two-head Serbian eagle. Maybe I sail directly into vortex. But first I wanna bring here something good. Fuck it, if EU pay, we change island name on Europa. All those idiots wanna do is plant their flag, and pray that no one gonna snap it. They can use for propaganda how they want.'

'Now you're talking,' I said. 'We have to give them something they can work with.'

So far, they'd kept themselves at cattle-prod length, wagging fingers at Serbs in the hope this might transform them. Meanwhile, entrepreneurs fenced inferior Western imports, like tawdry high street knock-offs from last season.

The Greeks aspired to something more inspiring: a summit to promote the case of Balkan laggards, at the end of their EU presidency in June. Apart from Slovenia, the richest ex-Yugoslav republic, none of the rest had a hope of being admitted any time soon. In the interim, they were told to band together. And we could help to catalyze this process.

Our strategy was titled 'Regional Development', and it was dripping with commercial ballyhoo. 'More than 50 million people live in the Balkans,' our brochure explained. 'This is now Europe's biggest emerging market. Ten years ago, adventurous investors took a gamble on transition in Hungary, Poland and the Czech Republic. They were handsomely rewarded. Along with much of the rest of the former Eastern bloc, these countries will join the European Union next year and their people have started to prosper. The same thing can happen here.'

It could all be launched with a fanfare from Big War Island, with events the year after in Croatia and Bosnia, and further afield in Romania and Bulgaria, to capitalize on economies of scale. We'd seek 'synergies between entertainment businesses and tourism', and 'support the growth of similar events and related industries throughout the Balkans,' so as 'to offer disenchanted young people something tangible to get excited about.'

Europe still denied them simple perks: they needed visas if they planned to travel west, which were hard to obtain and alarmingly expensive. One simple change could make a massive difference. If travel restrictions were eased, airlines would try to cash in with cheaper flights, and tourists might be enticed to visit Serbia. This was the sort of investment we were after. But we'd need effective branding to attract it. And G was convinced that this word had a sinister undertone.

'Don't be silly,' I told him. 'Everything's branded nowadays. Even that Dada art you're always on about.'

His reply was scathing. 'I think you missed whole point of what they saying. You wanna buy my artist shit in can? For you, my friend, best price. Hundred grand.'

I ignored him. 'We need a name that sells our image.'

'And image should be *essence*,' he said, 'not gap between a fantasy and real.'

That ruled out UTOPIJA at once. To trigger some better ideas, we'd listed concepts we intended to embody: energy, exchange, switch, direction, focus, love, respect, progressive, positive, urban, roots, streetwise, security, righteousness, dedication, commitment, perspective, beacon, destiny, magnet, inspiration, and so on. And so on. Realistic names still proved elusive.

'How hard can it be?' I said. 'It just needs to sound clear.'

Like EXIT, in other words: a verb that was also a noun with punchy symbolism. So not MOVE, GROOVE, YES, FLY, CORE, MORE, or any of our other weak ideas. It would have to work in Serbian and English, which sort of accounted for shockers such as MOTOR, ELIXIR, VOODOO, SPARK and PORTAL, and maybe SKREAM. The rest were dire. GO evoked Saturday morning kids' TV, and efforts to woo Greek donors were feeble too. EROS, DIONYSUS and HERMES sounded like strip joints.

The designer helped us crack it with an image. When we gave him our list of words as inspiration, he drew a hard-boiled egg chopped in half. He told us this captured 'the sound, the wave, the island, the river...' and the spirit of a name we'd almost ditched: ECHO.

If you stared for a while, you could see he was onto something. The logo had ripples of energy, and looked like what you'd see inside a bell. In the middle was a clapper, or the festival, reverberating out beyond its borders. It summed up everything. Even the font of the text had struck a chord. It was called Univers, and came in vibrant saffron.

ECHO's very emptiness was its power. Anyone could project a meaning into it. It was also comprehensible to Serbs, who spelled it *'eho'*. With the 'c', it formed an acronym: for the European Community Humanitarian Office, which paid out aid money. It also had a link to Greek mythology. Echo was a nymph torn to shreds for spurning Pan, or silenced for distracting Hera from

Zeus's philandering, depending on the fable. All that survived of her voice was its imitative qualities, which she'd used to try seducing Narcissus, a youth who fell in love with his own reflection. But he wasn't so keen on his words repeating back at him. He jilted Echo, who withered away, while Narcissus wept himself to death, having failed to embrace his image in a fountain.

Everyone's an echo, in a way. Our parents give us names and DNA, and surroundings leave their imprints on our minds, before we've even learned to speak a word. With all this compounding confusion, it's a wonder that anyone feels they're individual. We might as well be everything combined. Only one thing troubled me slightly: ECHO sounded like EXIT.

I'd tried to airbrush their existence from our prospectus, but we needed to liven it up with scenes of crowds, and I had high-resolution photos of EXIT 02. Some quotes from *The New York Times* appeared as well. Stripped of all its references to names, one said: 'changing the world with a music festival seems a lofty ambition. But the zeal and professionalism of the organizers has secured them influential backing.'

Reuters taught trainees to 'cheat and steal'. This maxim allowed you to plagiarize from colleagues, lifting lines from their stories to speed up news production. The principle had broader applications. Most writers borrow ideas from somewhere else, however they disguise their inspiration. And we weren't exactly lying about our roots. G was presented as 'the production manager of EXIT', which he had been. We were merely implying that EXIT had mutated, into ECHO.

'Now that more people are eager to see for themselves what life in this region is really like,' our sales pitch said, 'it is time to bring them to the Serbian capital and a unique inner-city location.'

The ECHO festival: what wasn't to like? Absolutely nothing, G maintained.

'Don't forget that EXIT sucks as name,' he said. 'It sends precisely opposite message to realism. Point is not to escape but to advance.'

Our spiel continued by quoting clips from the UK music press, none of which named the festival they raved about.

'It was like DJ-ing the main stage at Glastonbury,' said Grooverider. 'Everything was going off in there. Off the hook, man. I've never seen anything like it.'

Or as *Seven* magazine salivated: 'The strong British contingent of DJs assembled onstage is nothing if not completely stunned. Acid house, it appears, is alive and well and hiding out in the former Yugoslavia. Maybe it's time to rethink next year's summer holiday destination.'

Muzik put it most simply: 'The crowds are mad for it.'

So were we. We just needed a patron.

'Who do I call to speak to Europe?' Henry Kissinger is reputed to have asked. Only he didn't really, because America liked to divide and rule its allies. That didn't stop the European fantasists. After overseeing the bombing of Belgrade, in his capacity as Secretary General of NATO, Javier Solana became the first High Representative for the Common Foreign and Security Policy of the European Union.

I'd met him on a mission to Macedonia, where I became the proud recipient of his mobile number. Not that he ever answered it, however, and not that I'd have learned much if he did. He bumbled clichés in a heavy Spanish accent.

'You're very pessimistic,' he'd once told me, pumping my arm on a staircase outside peace talks. It seemed entirely fitting under the circumstances. NATO had just bussed some rebels from a frontline drug-running town, which Macedonia's army had failed to destroy. Having killed their own special forces in the process, the Macedonians begged NATO to help them save face, by escorting Albanian gunmen to safety. But when footage of this convoy was broadcast on TV, a crowd of Macedonian rioters stormed parliament, shooting into the sky and beating up journalists, who were clearly Western stooges; like Albanians.

The time had come to question who used whom. Solana was visiting Belgrade, on his latest diplomatic frequent flyer stunt. And I'd been summoned to the airport to hear all about it, before the envoy departed for Brussels in his Learjet.

He was late. Dollops of snow decked the tarmac outside, while I chain-smoked for an hour in the VIP lounge, my nerves jangling harder by the minute. Our brochure was still being typeset, so all I had to hand were A4 printouts. No pictures, no color, no logo; just page after page of droning text.

Finally, the man himself arrived, tailed by a trio of aides with twitching clipboards. As we sat, I was told we'd only have five minutes.

'Mr Solana,' I said, soft-pedaling regardless. Rushing wasn't the way to get an answer. 'Congratulations on forming the new state union.'

He'd come to fake a replacement Yugoslavia. To be known for three years as 'Serbia and Montenegro', this entity would postpone Montenegrin independence, and thus stop Kosovo demanding instant freedom, along with the Serbs in Bosnia, and all the rest of the usual Balkan bullshit. Solana grinned and spouted some himself.

'So what happens next?' I said. 'When can these countries expect to be EU members?'

'We have to be realistic,' he said. 'Important progress has been achieved. The regional picture has improved. The European perspective will consolidate the reform process.'

'But don't they need some proof the EU's serious?' I said. 'Why not offer them a date?'

He stared as if I was wasting precious time. Did *The New York Times* not want exclusive quotes? 'There is hard work ahead,' he said.

He wasn't wrong there. The EU was Eastern Europe's favorite sugar daddy, until they learned what it required. To join, they had to adopt the EU's laws, which ran to eighty thousand pages, listing values that members flouted when it suited them. This regime might be less oppressive than the Communists, but many people felt robbed by a new elite, who ordered privatizations and government spending cutbacks, while dictating rates for heating oil and pensions. Liberal economics meant higher prices, and better returns for investors than mere citizens.

I tried again. 'How could you give them a sign it's worth the effort?'

Solana glanced at his assistants. 'The Western Balkans are a big priority,' he said. 'We are working very closely with the Greek Presidency.'

'I'm glad to hear it.' I pulled out my papers. 'This plan could help to change the EU's policy, in line with the latest Greek ideas.'

Solana left the document untouched. His palms stayed resolutely on his thighs, as if I were trying to get him to wear an al-Qaeda tiepin. I pressed on regardless.

'Many young people in Serbia want to emigrate. They need to see there's a future for them here. For a small investment, half a million at most, you could send them a sign. It would start here with a festival in Belgrade, but...'

An aide stepped in and stopped the interview. Solana darted straight for the exit.

'I'll give the details to your colleague,' I called at his heels, foisting my folder on the minion, together with Raoul Djukanovic's business card. 'Please,' I said, as he bolted with his boss. 'Pass it on, even if you can't make him read it.'

I was left to face an archetypal Eurocrat, sporting a crimson shade of corduroy rarely spotted north of the Alps. 'Good for you,' he drawled in soupy English. 'You realize of course that Solana hasn't a *sou*?'

'Sorry?'

'It's never been his job to dish it out.' He extended his hand and introduced himself, as the EU's resident delegate in Belgrade. Another Western diplomat I'd ignored. 'I'm an opera man myself. But I always think there's room to promote more culture.'

'And who might have some money for that sort of thing?' I asked.

'Come to my office and we'll talk. You need to scope out the right DG to ask.'

The Directorate General for External Relations seemed ideal. I departed the following evening for Brussels, armed with a PDF file of our brochure. The real thing was still in production. On arrival at the Hotel Dorint, I ordered color printouts on expenses.

To justify the trip, I'd found an alibi: an interview with the president of Croatia, who'd come to talk about starting talks on EU membership. Compared to Serbs, the Croats got off lightly. The past wouldn't get in the way of their application, even though their 'patriotic war' of independence had included what prosecutors called a 'joint criminal enterprise' in Bosnia, and a massive forced expulsion backed by America.

Although my chat with their head of state was inconclusive, he named all the people he'd met on his flesh-pressing visit. Apparently, only three bureaucrats dealt with the Balkans. I spent the next few days attempting to recruit them.

They weren't encouraging. 'You only get money out of the EU if you start a war,' said a man who told Solana what to say, 'or you're already a candidate for membership.' He told me to try the External Relations Commissioner directly.

I wrote an email from my *New York Times* account. 'I would not be bothering you,' I said, 'if I did not believe strongly in the merits of this project and the potential it offers the European Union.' Funding ECHO would 'generate far more positive publicity for the EU's engagement in the Balkans than any other initiative I can think of.'

The man in question didn't reply, and his secretary hung up when I tried to call.

Someone else said there was unclaimed cash in a fund called Culture 2000, but the date for filing grant forms had passed. I asked 'if there may be some other way to access funding'. But Brussels doesn't function like the Balkans. A flunky replied: 'I'm afraid the deadlines are legally binding and there's no way round them.'

My only remaining option was the Greeks. I flew on to Athens, where I interviewed the foreign minister, who told me most of his EU partners were being short sighted. Serbia would remain on a blacklist until it arrested Ratko Mladic, the general who besieged Sarajevo, and oversaw a massacre at Srebrenica. The minister said there were other things to think about.

'We have to give politicians something they can sell,' one of his advisers stressed. 'The more reassuring Europe is, the easier it will be to deal with war crimes issues and other problems.' On cue, I asked for half a million euros. The aide agreed to help me meet some businessmen. No one coughed up.

I retired to the gloomy bar of the St George Hotel, where I drank myself under a stool, and fell asleep. The morning after, revived by a joint, I bashed out a turgid feature on my trip. Groping to account for the travel, it analyzed the EU's lack of interest.

'Five Balkan presidents are meeting next month to develop a common negotiating position,' I wrote, 'but with European attention focused on Iraq, major policy changes are unlikely.'

Really? How *interesting*. An editor cut my article to shreds.

Unhindered by the absence of funding, our program was taking fairly rapid shape. G had paid friendly agents small advances, and three of the four different stages were confirmed, with further fees deferred until the summer.

The promoter of The Dub Club in London was sending reggae artists. For hip-hop, progressive house and drum and bass, we'd arranged to import a stage from a Bristol festival. There was talk of them bringing out Banksy to spray graffiti. And to satisfy those whose tastes were more urbane, Nuphonic Records had booked an eclectic mix of DJs, blending techno and house with salsa, funk and soul.

That just left the expensive acts for the main stage. For those, we'd have to speak to bigger agents. But at least we now had handiwork to show them. Our brochure almost sounded the part. 'Mobile toilets, dressing rooms and a private bar for performers and their guests will be situated behind each stage,' it boasted. 'Power, up to 600 KW, will be supplied by army generators.'

We hadn't exactly agreed this with the military, but G said our local partners could arrange it, along with a long pontoon bridge to the island. Like commanders of Serbia's fearsome special forces, they were men of their murky milieu in Zemun.

'Is not always pretty,' G told me, 'but we have to work with world the way it is.'

News from our surroundings was unnerving. The police had raided a shopping mall near the island and dug up an arms cache, plus heroin worth at least a million euros. The mafia's venomous tentacles kept growing. Aided by lax enforcement of the law, they were importing a third of Europe's cocaine. The prime minister made no bones about their power. He'd depended on gangland help to overthrow Milosevic. Zemun's bosses were mostly wartime paramilitaries, who'd been trained by the secret police and had friends in the army. They also had helicopters, armor and artillery, and stood accused of dozens of murders. And this was just one suburb of Belgrade.

When I asked how things had got so out of hand, G started laughing. 'All institutions are destroyed except police,' he said. 'They are the ones controlling drugs and arms, and every other trade on territories. To believe that one or other politician who turned in past fifteen years around here is better or worse than rest, you would have to be idiot. Real powers are almighty police and so-called intelligence. They decide which friend is gonna profit, and West now wash whole scam as new democracy.'

The government had incentives to comply. Few other people brought in foreign currency, and mafia money was laundered in Belgrade, or squandered in cafés and restaurants, and on real estate. Some of the richest Serbs lived abroad, but still sent local leaders tokens of gratitude, and visited now and then to check on business.

We found raising cash much harder work. Embassies were friendly, to start with. The Swiss said they'd fix up meetings with Nestle and Swatch. Neither took place. Direct approaches didn't fare much better. Whether at Microsoft, or Nivea or Samsung, the managers were always out of reach. We could only sip coffee with underlings, who appeared to hope we'd bribe them to support us. Most big multinationals worked like Coke, with a distant hub controlling Balkan marketing. British Airways made their regional plans in London. British American Tobacco said the same.

G suggested trying our luck in England. A friend of his there ran a firm that did corporate promotions. If we prepared a presentation pack for sponsors, he'd send it on to some of his trusted contacts. It seemed better than hoping for miracles in Serbia.

My partner agreed. 'I am sick of shave-head pit bulls roaming Belgrade. Last week I confront a scum in brand new Mercedes, what was pushing pedestrians off the road. He jumped on me thinking that middle age *chika* will be easy bite. We exchange few punches and he left. Well, he could pull the gun and shoot me, but I had to react. My legs are not fast any more and kicks are not strong like before. But still was good enough for degenerate to back up. He had attitude like world should owe him living, same as all these morons we been meeting. At least in London fools have budget.'

Living abroad had left me feeling rootless. Britain now seemed as alien as anywhere. With every trip, it grew a bit more plastic, shrink-wrapped in an inflated sense of self. London's empty trendiness disheartened me. I hated how it made me feel exposed, as if missing out on everything I lacked. I was glad we'd only be staying overnight.

On arrival, we retreated to a bedsit that G's friend had lent us. I set about skinning up right away. I'd already shat out my stash in the toilets at Heathrow.

G apparently found this amusing. 'You know that is behavior of an addict?'

I passed him the joint. 'Yeah, well you don't seem to be objecting.'

He flipped on the TV, which flickered with bellicose pictures of Colin Powell. That morning's *New York Times* said he'd made a 'powerful' and 'sober, factual case' for war. Apparently, his speech would persuade 'even the skeptics' to invade Iraq. An email from the night editor called the Secretary of State's recital 'a tour de force'. He told all staff to 'press for any subtle shifts that may soon become evident in attitudes' in foreign governments, 'once they read the speech and look at the evidence.'

I'd ignored this request and hopped a plane to London. Serbia was way off the radar. And my partner's take was not what they were after.

'Of course, that puppy ran armies for Bush in last Gulf War,' G spluttered, spilling ash down his shirtfront. 'He is just making payment back to masters, like he did already many times. You know he try to cover up massacre in Vietnam?'

I didn't, but I found it hard to care. The world was corrupt. What more to say? I pulled out my laptop and settled down to work. We'd decided to offer three graded tiers of sponsorship.

The top one gave two 'headline sponsors' the chance to give us €150,000. The middle level was open to six bids above €25,000, with 'unlimited opportunities' below that. 'Should your requirements not be catered for by any of the above,' said the small print, 'tailor-made packages are also available on request.'

In return, we'd provide them with surfaces for branding. Each stage would be flanked by banners and giant video screens. The other options were bars, the entrance and a perimeter fence, plus a VIP terrace and yacht, which was said to have a 'total surface area of 150 square meters', though neither of us knew if it would, or whether we'd have one. I'd just pasted in some numbers off the Internet.

There followed extensive details on promotions, and complimentary tickets, both of which could help secure a deal, my partner said. We also touted 'assistance from the ECHO team in setting up a distribution network across the Balkans, if required.' No one should feel disqualified, we thought.

And lest anyone doubt the clout their money could buy them, we promised unlimited exposure, thanks to 'extensive contacts with print, broadcast and Internet media organizations in Serbia and around the world.' There'd be TV adverts 'scheduled to appear at peak times on a cross-section of channels', and 'a network of 30 local radio stations' would syndicate features. Meanwhile, unnamed 'other European stations' were said to 'have expressed an interest in broadcasting live from the venue'.

This last bit was technically true. The BBC correspondent planned to be there.

An armchair eruption from G brought me back to the present. 'I don't think even Americans can swallow this,' he winced, at rerun shots of Powell holding up a test tube. 'No one can believe they bring democracy. When Americans gonna liberate themselves? They should start with constitution. Life and happiness everyone has, if he wants it. Liberty is one they must pursue. In three hundred million Gods we trust!'

He stood and saluted. 'Problem is God is on back of dollar bill, and war will wash more money straight to cronies. You see they gonna build fortress, just like Kosovo, to stay for endless war of all uncivilized. I pray to Gods that we stop monster!'

My partner turned off the news. 'I think we bomb ourselves enough with extreme informations. I'm pretty sure already I will dream some.'

I knew what he meant. A glimpse of TV was sufficient to cure me of homesickness. G disappeared behind the sofa, and rummaged through a box he'd been storing since his last trip. He resurfaced with a pile of CDs and passed one over.

'You should hear this man, I'm telling you, is beautiful,' he said. 'Tomorrow we meet that guy who's gonna book him.'

The name on the cover meant nothing to me: Metamatics. G vanished again and sifted through his stuff. This time he emerged with a flimsy garment. 'From fashion week,' he said, holding it up. 'I think it could be perfect for Raoul.'

It was a t-shirt, but effectively translucent, with full-length sleeves and an etched tattoo design. Worn against the skin, it would look like body art: a dragon climbing the back, and a pierced heart emblazoned on the chest, along with the motto: 'Safe Sex Forever'. There were also two nipple rings. The label said 'Jean-Paul Gaultier'. It was the sort of thing I'd never have bought, but almost wished I had, to prove I could.

'You don't think it would make me look a bit gay?' I asked.

G smiled. 'Depend if you can do it with a confidence.'

I tried it on and found I rather fancied myself.

'Thanks,' I said. 'I'll wear it out tonight.'

G had got us invited to a party. I didn't know any of the guests, and didn't want to. The houseboat venue put me off for starters. Nevertheless, they seemed interested in ECHO. Several even offered their assistance. Someone wanted to organize package tours. Another said he'd hand out flyers at UK festivals. G's friend reeled off lists of companies he dealt with, all of which were said to have broad horizons. Among their brands were Smirnoff Ice, Vodka Kick, and Bacardi Breezer. We could help to wean the Balkans onto alcopops. As a backup, he suggested Ferrero, the makers of Tic Tacs, Kinder eggs and Nutella. I guessed he knew more about marketing than me.

But no one seemed to care about our story. When I talked about life in the Balkans, people switched off. Only one woman showed any interest, and she must have been 60. Clad in black, and flapping her forearms as she squawked, she loomed from the depths of the boat like a creosoted cormorant, backlit by a waterside conservatory. The vessel was as big as a townhouse, and no more seaworthy.

'So, what's *wrong* with Serbia?' she said. The stress was sarcastically leaden. Her face had the texture of a walnut, split by a sneer.

'Where to start?' I sighed. 'They're always whining about something. But at least they have their self-respect intact. It's not as bad as Romanian self-pity. People there are more resigned to their fate. They have this awful expression: *asta e*, a bit like *c'est la vie* but really mournful. If only it made them mad enough to change things.'

'*Really*?' Her smirk raised an eyebrow. 'You know some people *like* being punished.'

G wandered over. 'You know, on Balkans people always being punished. It is hard to find who bring them something *nice*.'

The woman frowned. 'I worry when anyone talks about trying to save people. They usually need to be rescued from themselves. Just look at *our* leaders.'

'I agree leaders are problem,' G said. 'But goes much deeper into culture. System has more power than people consisting it. That mind control is what is really sick. Always crimes are done in name of people, and even for them to say no is big fucking deal.'

I wandered off as they discussed an anti-war march. It sounded almost futile, like our project. In Belgrade, what we were doing seemed significant. But to Londoners, it was just another party, in a far-off part of the world they barely cared about. No one saw transformative potential. By the time we left the boat, I felt morose.

Outside at the end of the jetty, a tramp sat slumped by a wall, swigging cider. As soon as I noticed his presence, I resented him. His eyes appeared to say 'you're just like me, only unlike me you're too ashamed to see it'. I felt paralyzed. I wanted to toss him some change, but feared I'd feel I'd tried to buy him off. Why did he give me the sense that he'd seen through me? I zipped up my jacket to hide my see-through top. As we wandered past, he cackled at my partner. G gave him a pound.

'Don't mind him.' The man nodded vaguely at me. 'He's lost his mirror.'

In the end, our Zemun partners came up trumps. While G and I got nowhere overseas, they sourced funding from one of the richest Serb tycoons.

The business-minded B explained the details. We'd be getting €150,000, through a company called Zepter Insurance. There was only one catch: we'd have to spend it all on insuring the festival. But we wouldn't be paying our premiums up front, so the deal was just a fat no-interest loan. The fewer questions I asked, the better it sounded.

Zepter was one of a handful of solvent insurance companies, and part of an exiled oligarch's conglomerate. He'd styled himself Philip Zepter in Austria, and built a sales force that was modeled on the Avon lady. Operations expanded from kitchenware to vacuum cleaners, then watches and surgical instruments, along with the usual perfume and cosmetics. Nowadays, Zepter lived in Monte Carlo, and denied allegations he'd branched into gun running.

None of us felt like dwelling on particulars. Instead, we resolved to find some other sponsors. And in the meantime, I composed another document. This waived my right to a share of the festival company, which G had hired a lawyer to incorporate.

In return, ECHO Music would 'pay Mr. Simpson the sum of 50,000 euros in four monthly installments starting from April 1'. Should money still be tight at that point, the balance would be settled in full by the end of July. There'd also be payments to cover 'all reasonable travel expenses related to his duties'. These were defined as being 'to coordinate all aspects concerning the public image of the festival, and to assist the organizing committee wherever possible.'

Writing a contract cheered me up, especially when our local partners signed it. But they couldn't understand my newfound caution. Was I trying to get insured against a loss? What had stopped me thinking we'd get rich?

Over another heady lunch of Balkan liquor, B talked me into agreeing a complex sub-clause, which granted me eight percent of the festival's profits, provided I spent it on shares in ECHO Music. This way I'd still be a partner in future events.

I signed. What the hell? We were in business.

The end of my employment at the *Times* came as a shock. That wasn't to say it was wholly unexpected. I'd long ago given up trying to do the job, and was only hanging in there for the cash. My contract was up for renewal in April, and by then I assumed that ECHO would have the cash to go ahead. If so, I was planning to quit and get on with running it. But if anything happened to stymie preparations, I'd do what it took to keep the paychecks coming. At $5,000 a month, they were too tempting.

My brief had been fairly straightforward: cover whatever there was in the way of news, and file a longer feature once a week. But apart from the odd hundred words I cribbed from Reuters, my output had slipped to once a month at best. And a couple of efforts aside, it wasn't dazzling; workmanlike enough to stay employed, but not to secure promotion to permanent staff, the passport to a posting somewhere else. Even if you've won a Pulitzer Prize, those coveted jobs begin with stints of brainwashing, reporting local stories in New York. If you stick that out, you might get sent abroad again.

Since this prospect didn't appeal, there wasn't much to aim for. But my alternative plan of coasting wouldn't wash. The game seemed up when I heard from the foreign editor, who hadn't said a word to me in months.

> X-Mailer: QUALCOMM Windows Eudora Pro Version 4.2.2
> Date: Fri, 28 Feb 2003 18:12:17 -0500
> To: Daniel Simpson <dans@nytimes.com>
> From: Roger Cohen
> Subject: Re: iraqis in hungary
>
> daniel,
> please try to call me over the weekend. desk has my home
> and cell numbers.
> roger

Appended was a note I'd sent his deputy. She'd ordered me to take a trip to Hungary, to watch 'the bizarre training of the Iraqi exiles at Taszar base', where Americans were drilling translators for their invasion force. 'Bizarre' didn't constitute license to scorn the war effort, just to poke fun at ragtag recruits. In any case, I had better things to do.

So I'd phoned around and sourced myself a get-out. Having sought access to the base, and been rebuffed by the U.S. Embassy in Budapest as well as the Hungarian Defense Ministry, I'd told the desk that 'unless there is an edict from Washington, there is no way' of getting beyond the perimeter fence. Nobody had replied, so I let it slide.

I didn't fancy driving for hours to stand in the snow, and whistle up some guff from a hotel bedroom. For that, I'd have to skull a dozen whiskies, which would lead to me spitting my brains at New York. And tempting as that was, it wouldn't wash. To the *Times*, opposing the war was plain naïve. If it all went horribly wrong, they'd say so later, at hand-wringing length, while implying they'd foreseen it. I couldn't change the bogus way they worked. Why bother trying? I'd just rubberneck the wreckage like a couch cabbage.

The result was a passive-aggressive kind of mutiny. I'd kept trying not to do what they wanted while acting obliging, in the hope this might impress them. And since I already knew that I couldn't, I could claim I didn't want to.

This logic was born of my need for a pat on the head. But praise was never abundant at the *Times*, except in terms of cloying insincerity. Staff were said to be 'blazing up the track' if they rewrote press releases, or 'doing sterling work' by lifting the phone, and wielding 'a keen eye, a courageous temperament and a graceful pen' when typing up interviews. The newsroom was a viper's nest of egos, and thus not a place to play teacher's pet. Not that this realization made much difference. I still had to call Roger Cohen for a bollocking, on a dank Sunday morning in midwinter.

'I'm very disappointed,' he told me, when we spoke. 'We both know you have to go to where the story is.'

I'd forgotten how confrontationally he murmured. His mid-Atlantic drone was sherry-coated.

'You show no hunger,' he inveighed, sotto voce. 'You reject perfectly good ideas and fail to come up with alternatives. You haven't made the transition from news wire journalism that I hoped you were capable of. You've sent me nothing I could consider offering for the front page.'

Our only ever meeting flooded back to me, in a dingy Japanese restaurant off Times Square. Although purportedly a pre-assignment briefing, the conversation was clipped and revealed vey little, apart from the arrogance masking our insecurities. Cohen's took center stage in a silvery suit. Most of the time, he dished out gnomic hints, like a reporter wary of rivals stealing his story, as he'd done to them. I slurped ineptly at my chopsticks, and tried to avoid asking questions for fear I'd sound dumb.

His voice in my ear brought me back to my apartment. 'Your work is flat. There's no poignancy, no imagery...'

A few months into the job, he'd called me one midnight, and suggested I try a 'more whimsical' approach. I ignored him. I didn't much care for his blowhard braggadocio, cooing at 'the President's plans' like a comely prom queen, as if big swinging dicks in the White House didn't do mind rape. The year I was born, the *Times* let Hunter S. Thompson rant at Nixon, at several times the length of a normal story. Had anyone tried that on in 2002, they'd have been Tasered off the payroll instantaneously, and certainly not rendered to Iraq in possession of a press card.

Reeling on the phone, I tried to counterpunch. I asked Cohen to read through my work, and say what was wrong with it. He floored me with a harsh atomic drop.

'Listen,' he said, 'I can't teach you how to write. We won't be renewing your contract without improvements.'

For now, he proposed a three-month trial extension, during which he'd edit my stories personally, and school me in some of the paper's darker arts. I thanked him, flung down my mobile, and lit up.

The *Times* and I would plainly never get on. I'd risen as high as I could on basic bullshit artistry. Of course I could copy their formula, but why? Did I want to keep trotting it out with different factoids? I could either go quietly now, or risk being fired on probation for not sucking up. Forget about six-figure salaries, and all the American accoutrements of making it, from villas in France to jackets with leather patches on the elbows.

Cohen wouldn't see things my way. He doubted I had one. He'd been a prolific correspondent. Not only had I not, I couldn't see the point.

I called him the following day to turn him down. 'I think it's best for both of us if I resign.'

Remarkably, this seemed to faze him mildly. 'If that's what you want then so be it,' he said. 'But my offer was entirely serious.'

I assured him my mind was made up. I'd remain on call while I served out a month of notice, but I wouldn't be writing more stories unless they were seismic.

'Do you have something else lined up?' he asked.

'I'm organizing a festival,' I said. 'After that, we'll see.'

'Oh,' he said. 'You really don't have to leave, you know.'

But I did, and I'd known it for years. I'd been waiting for this moment since my youth. People had always told me I'd succeed. So what if I didn't? I'd defined my adult life by getting ahead. But I could also fuck up if I wanted to, OK? Just fucking watch me!

Cutting my Establishment parachute cord was a blast. There was little way of knowing how far I'd fall.

STYX

It wasn't my childhood dream to be a journalist. I only knew that most jobs sounded dreadful, while reporters liked to claim they didn't have one. Work was their life, or a chore they squeezed between the freeloading. With characteristically caustic self-effacement, it was said that success hinged on 'rat-like cunning, a plausible manner and a little literary ability.' I left university certain these were my strengths.

As an undergraduate history student at Cambridge, you were asked to write an essay once a week. There were no compulsory seminars or lectures. Your only commitment was an hour of conversation, in which you were grilled on what you'd written, or what you said you would have done, had you got round to it. So if you mugged up a bit in advance, and didn't mind being patronized, you could use these supervisions to interview experts, and be told all the important stuff you'd missed.

Since the syllabus consisted of other people's thoughts, you were graded on your skill at rearranging them. Reading lists for essays were unreadable. Even if you did nothing else, you'd be hard pressed to absorb every word. The idea was to sample a selection, and turn your hand to summarizing arguments. Most degrees in the arts were broadly similar: some people think one thing, others another. All you needed to pass were lists of quotes, and a rudimentary grasp of background facts.

The University Library housed a shortcut. Tucked away on its shelves was an index of book reviews. The contents of these leather-bound tomes were gold dust. Looking up the titles on your list, you could navigate learned journals on the shelves, to find their critical summaries of texts. The better reviews ran extracts at length, and some even featured debates between rival scholars. An afternoon scouring these pages produced an essay plan. The rest of your time was your own, to be squandered at will.

Arcane pastimes like Footlights left me cold. Instead, I'd act irascible at parties, and argue with all the intellectual pseuds, while secretly feeling daunted by their learning. My other tastes were far less energetic: skunkweed, pints of Stella and Sky Sports, or bouts of Streetfighter II on the Sega Megadrive. Wars in the Balkans largely passed me by. My news came off the back of pilfered tabloids.

Of course, there was still the hurdle of final exams, but these could be deconstructed as well. Scanning through the archives of papers, you could see which topics cropped up year to year, however they varied the wording of the question. To be able to write nine essays in three sittings, you'd need to draft a dozen sets of bullet points. Each of these could be drawn up in a day. A fortnight of mugging up would see you right. And three years on, you could pay to upgrade to a master's for a fiver, without so much as a jot of extra work.

This system churns out braggarts every year. They go into politics, diplomacy, law, finance and management, and the multi-farious branches of public relations, where verbal dexterity and cant are used to con people. And of all these assorted bloviating hucksters, reporters are some of the best at seducing themselves.

In my application to Reuters after graduating, I said I was 'a historian of the present', and styled myself the consummate 'outsider', with 'heightened instinct' and 'an identity broader than my nationality'. Not that this had helped much in the Netherlands, where my dad was sent to work when I was nine. Kids in our village shouted 'foreigners go home!' On return to the northeast of England, I stood out more, especially for doing well at school. I was keen to be accepted and fit in, so I feigned a Geordie accent on the streets, and acted the classroom fool while getting top marks. I liked to think this made me a chameleon. But I wasn't ever really myself, or any of the voices I'd been channeling. And that was why I made a decent hack.

But now that I'd had my fill of being a mouthpiece, I felt detached from what I thought and who I was. I'd hoped my resignation would relieve this. But I couldn't shake the thought I'd ducked a fight. I wished we'd had it out in *Quadrophenia*, with Cohen the stuffed-shirt bloviating boss, and me doing full-on mental Jimmy Cooper.

                COHEN
```
You've got a good job here,
Simpson. Plenty of young men would
give their eye teeth to be in your
shoes.
```

                ME
```
Oh yeah? Well, find one then!
```

                COHEN
```
I beg your pardon...?
```

                ME
```
You heard. I said find one then.
Yeah, I'll tell you what you can
do with your eye teeth, and your
job. You can take this phony war
and your intelligence, and all
those lying pisster politician
cunts, and you can stuff them all
right up your arse!
```

I'd never felt cut out for playing cameos. Who does in their own private iFlicks? But I knew that the only way forward led down. By losing professional status, I'd blown my cover. I could no longer act the outsider, peering in on the rest of the world with elite disdain. To the likes of *The New York Times*, I'd joined the mob.

The wild side needs release, or else it devours you. It'll feed on your weakness and goad you to the edge. But the abyss was not the goal I had in mind. At twenty-eight, going on eighteen, I was a rebel who'd found his cause at last: to find himself.

Life always seemed to be happening at a distance. I'd got lost in trying to satisfy other people, while resisting them to assert my independence. So why not simply do what I wanted? But what might that be? Before meeting G, I'd scarcely dared to ask, for fear of drifting desperately off-piste. I realized that I'd led myself astray. My desire to be right all the time had made me wrong. And if morality was subjectively defined, then why feel so constrained by guilt and shame?

I decided it was time to contact V, a friend of B's who'd worked at our New Year's party. She'd been hired to take care of a DJ, who took care of himself with pills and Southern Comfort, ignoring the juddering flesh in her skin-tight dress. She'd worn it to her interview in my flat, and remarked in English that my bathroom had 'potential'. Its massive corner tub had sold me on renting the place, but the Jacuzzi feature hadn't seen much use. What was I waiting for?

On arrival in Romania two years earlier, expatriate licentiousness had depressed me. 'This is a great place to be single,' an Englishman announced, ignoring his companion for the night. A fat German swore of his local trophy wife: 'At home, I couldn't possibly do so well.' It sounded as grim as the shower show at Cabaret Moldova. But I soon began to think myself uptight. So I loosened up fast. One day, I woke up with a journalist in Skopje, flew via Zurich to sleep with an ex, and returned to bed in Bucharest with my girlfriend. Since they all saw other men, I thought little of it, apart from my fears about performance.

The trouble began when women wanted more than me, which quickly became the second time we met. It was easier with people I disliked. I could leave without an overdose of conscience. But that only left me feeling doubly heartless. Gradually, my self-reproach took over. I was too moralistic to womanize, and too fickle not to.

What sort of man had I become? To assert my masculinity, I fired off a text message, inviting V to join me for a bubble bath. Her reply took a day to arrive, but it didn't mess about. 'When?' she asked. Er, like now?

Within hours we were in the tub, sipping beakers of gin. My internal jukebox banged gangsta shit, like *'where do you want me to rub it?'* and *'right here...'*

Yeah, fuck Snoop's *Doggystyle* G-spot. As *The Joy of Sex* notes, there's a far more hardcore 'South Slav style', based on 'the very rich erotic folksong repertoire of the Balkans.' To enthusiasts, 'Serbian intercourse (*Srpski jeb*) is mock rape - you throw her down, seize one ankle in each hand and raise them over her head, then enter her with your full weight (do this on something soft - the traditional bare earth is beyond a game).' Directions for the 'Lion position' are harder: 'squat down, heels to scrotum, place the penis between your ankles, rest on buttocks and hands, and move legs together.' It's 'passionate and affectionate as befits a race of bride-stealing warriors whose women were natural partisans: tough plus tender.'

That description certainly fitted V. She'd mastered a highly effete form of bondage, lashing me with her thick raven locks, and saying I responded to touch 'like a little boy'. To discipline me harshly, she withheld it. Her hands fired shots of static from above, manipulating something deep inside me, and drawing us into communion with abandon. It seemed to last hours. Neither of us pretended that we cared.

I don't quite recall where it came from, or when, but a bright flash of light interrupted our liaison. It was followed by a thud on my head, then the sound of her voice through a Styrofoam cup on a string. 'Looks like you ran out of energy,' she said.

I blinked up from the floor. The rim of the bathtub blurred back into view. I looked straight down again. My temples throbbed and my magic wand had drooped. The lost inhibitions that turned me on felt twisted, like the sight of an Internet gangbang after wanking. Some time had passed. V was fixing her hair up in the mirror.

'So what's the plan then?' she asked.

I stared back confused. I once told a friend that smoking didn't affect my short-term memory. 'That's good,' he'd said. 'You might forget to breathe.'

'You said you'd quit your job,' V prompted. 'So what you gonna do instead?'

I wished she'd leave. 'Run our festival.'

'You really think it can happen?' She winked. 'I hope you've got protection.'

I attempted a laugh. 'We'll be fine.'

V reached into the bath and splashed me with water. 'You heard about curse of the Serbs, right?'

I grabbed a towel. 'Why is everyone here so fatalistic?' I said. 'If people think that way it's self-fulfilling.'

'I like your optimism,' she said. 'Do you think you'll get rich?'

I left the bathroom.

'Is that a no?' she called after me.

A few minutes later, she sashayed into the living room, caked in make up.

'I have to go,' she said. 'It's my boyfriend's birthday and I'm late for dinner.'

'Oh,' I said, unsure what else to say.

'He's a diplomat,' she said. 'I need to change first.'

'Oh,' I said again.

She coughed. 'Can you give me money for a taxi?'

'Sure,' I heard myself say. 'How much do you need?'

She shrugged. I gave her a pile of crumpled dinars.

'Thanks,' she said, kissing me. It felt hollow.

'Thank *you*.' I salvaged a smile for her departure.

'See you soon,' she breathed from the doorway. Her heels

turned, and clacked down my staircase. Maddeningly, I knew that she was right.

Getting things done in the Balkans took more time. Discussions were often circuitous, agreeing no more than a date for the next installment. Business was a grinding process of attrition, dogged by cellphones. Calls would be answered with growls of 'I have meeting', and both were inconclusively dropped. Hangovers snarled discussions even further, revved up by double espressos with chasers of Coke. PowerPoint slides and spreadsheets rarely featured. Most serious deals were struck in smoky restaurants. The heavier the décor and ambience, the more at stake.

Even arranging appointments took forever. Take the national airline, for example. To reduce the cost of tickets, we were hoping to buy them in bulk, and ideally trade some for publicity. But the people we needed to speak to weren't ever there. The marketing manager spent weeks on a tour of Africa. According to G's tabloid reading, he was brokering imports of oil, and financing these with military hardware. Cash wasn't really abundant at state-run companies.

When I queried my partner's reasoning, he laughed. 'What you think he is doing man, taking safari?' But whatever this mammoth executive had bartered, he haggled like a pro. When we eventually managed to meet him, he was daunting.

'I want all the drinks and all the food,' he rasped, his neck practically bursting from his collar. 'I want exclusivity and I don't want exposure.'

Wedged behind two porticos of paperwork, he glowered across his desk like a gorilla, propped up on a pair of meaty palms. Gravelly English rippled from his throat.

'You should consult me before you sign with other sponsors,' he wheezed. 'We should agree on who will be there. I don't want to see tobacco advertising.'

This was an interesting twist in a region of nicotine freaks. It was also a smokescreen, barely concealing demands for a back-door takeover. But beyond his list of suggested obligations, it wasn't clear what the deal held for us. My partner took this in his stride.

'Everything is possible,' G said. 'But first we need to make a proper breakdown.'

The twin towers of paper shuddered ominously, as one of the manager's fists swished round behind them. It thumped down on a document in front of us.

'Who will spend these two millions here on drinks?' he asked dismissively.

At his behest, we'd sent a projection of our revenues. Like much of our work, they were figments of stoned ingenuity, but my partner claimed they were based on well-sourced facts. He said we could count on sixty thousand people a night, or twice the average at EXIT the year before, since the island was in Belgrade, not an hour north. Multiplied by four days, and a guesstimated €10 ticket price, that made more than two million in itself. And if everyone drank what G called a 'conservative' couple of beers, plus a few soft drinks and snacks at a euro a pop, we'd take two million more on the bars, 'although,' as we'd cautioned, 'the final figure could be much higher.' Our local partners were sure we'd be the biggest, and the best. *'Evo ti... najveci... najbolje...'* If anything, we'd erred on the side of caution.

The hulk across the table saw it differently. 'I need to know who are your performers,' he said, holding up our proposal. 'I don't see any names that are confirmed.'

Neither G nor I said a word. We'd sent him waffle about 'major attractions like Massive Attack, the Chemical Brothers, Moby and Darren Emerson,' among others we couldn't book without more capital.

'You know Jose Carreras is coming in June,' the corporate blunderbuss rattled on. 'We can rely on that, so we sponsor it.'

G made a misfired stab at being meek. 'Sir, I think you know you can rely on us. That is why we meeting here today. I have agent in New York to line up contracts. Already he agreed a Burning Spear, who is living legend of reggae all by self.'

'What about *younger* stars?' Our antagonist leered. 'Why not get someone who's more *attractive* to that market, like Shakira?'

My partner kept his poker face. 'We can investigate. But first we need commitments, so we bring artists. You know, more like on level of a sponsor.'

I intervened. 'We're offering headline sponsorship for a quarter of a million euros. If you want half the drinks, that's our price. For half a million, you run them yourself.'

There were upsides to selling concessions on food and booze. By trading in some of the proceeds for cash up front, we'd spare ourselves the pain of trying to raise it. And without more money soon, there'd be no festival. Unfortunately, the big man seemed to sense this. My attempt to strike a bargain barely registered.

'Listen,' he said, 'I just signed the contract with Lufthansa Skychef. I can do seven thousand meals a day, no problem.'

It was hard to know what to say to that, except that it sounded tastier than corrugated cheese, which most of his planes served. But he showed little sign of caring about his image, torpedoing my confident assumptions. Now that Yugoslavia had been formally dissolved, Serbia and Montenegro couldn't call their joint flag carrier *Jugoslovenski Aerotransport*, or JAT. The company's name henceforth would be JAT Airways, which meant its fleet required a paint job, and its logo would need exposure round the world. We'd offered a profile in *The New York Times* in return for free tickets.

Our ultimate agenda was more grandiose: we wanted JAT to help us bring in foreign tourists. There weren't any guidebooks to Serbia in print. Lonely Planet said it wasn't even planning one. Croatia's coast was the region's main attraction. Belgrade's hotels had mildew in their carpets. JAT owned one with more than nine hundred beds. It also chartered DC-10s. Most flights to Western

Europe cost €300, but together we could undercut the market. Once again, the master strategist rebuffed us.

'I want to see some details of your marketing plan,' he said. 'What are you doing in London and New York? What are your connections with Serbs there? Maybe they will give you some investment. I will publish a text in our magazine. My assistant can explain to you arrangements.'

An in-flight publication was a start. We'd at least be appealing to people who grasped the story. 'Sounds great,' I said. 'We can talk about our long-term plans for the island.'

Our aspirant owner studied me contemptuously. 'Did you meet the investors who look on that island for development? They are also talking about entertainments.'

'Lotta people talk about developing that place,' G said. 'But I don't see too many there building up. That is why we have clearance now for summer.'

My partner now felt the force of the JAT man's stare. 'I think that's enough for today,' the latter barked, ending the chat as abruptly as it started. 'Let's talk again this time next week.'

Hanging around with Serbs helped change my outlook. Much of what they said went over my head, but I was learning from repetitive conversations. They slogged along like clay court tennis rallies, grunting out merciless salvos from baseline positions. Our local partners thrived on protracted wrangling. A always wore his shades to wind people up. He seemed to work a good-cop-bad-cop act with B, who could calm things down by restating their demands, in ever so slightly more conciliatory tones.

Occasionally, G would translate, although only if he wanted me to talk. Mostly, my physical presence would suffice. It showed that we weren't just wide boys from Zemun, much as our partners proved we weren't some foreign misfits. Depending on whom we were meeting, we varied our input.

There was little for me to contribute at our latest assignation, which consisted of watching some businessmen wait for a strip show. But the only woman we'd seen had kept her clothes on, depositing a jug of potent brandy. While our partners hammered out terms for hiring a digger, G and I withdrew to the end of the table, and proceeded to numb our gullets with this hooch.

Though it reeked of plums, and tasted like perfume, the main impression it left was one of burning. Fumes shot up your nose to sear the throat, replacing breath with liquid flame. These effects were so severe that I repeated them, determined to acquire resilience on the spot. Half a dozen shots soon took the edge off, and stunned me into a deep pool of calm, beneath which lurked a vicious kind of rage. It felt liable to burst out unpredictably, the moment it found a cause it might latch onto. For now it was placated by TV, which screened a football match on mute beside the bar, and shook to the wailing pop from a low-fi stereo.

'This country is hysterical endless football game,' G shouted at the din. 'Mud here is always ready for new fighting. Just takes mix of drunk emotion with excuses. Rules have been established many times. It is same with celebration. Again the bodies will roll and scream in mud. Only emotion is different. Mud would stay.'

A coat of arms glowed eerily above, embedded in a wall of mirrored tiles. It added an extra distortion to delirium. The *rakija* tasted nearly paraffin strength. I'd been forced to down such rotgut on the job, by stubborn men in godforsaken ghost towns, who refused to abandon the shells of their firebombed homes.

When I recounted some of these memories, G shut me up. Dropping his voice, he eagerly clarified why. 'That guy there is killer, you know, real one.' He nodded at a figure through the smoke. 'That one talking, you can see it by his coldness. Probably killed like dozens here in war. Plenty of these people still around man, I don't think they gonna lock them up, or send them in Hague.'

I shuffled in my seat. My knees began vibrating to the music. I recognized the singer. She'd treated me to a warbling in an interview. '*Kukavica...*' she'd crooned, reprising the number that launched her career. 'You're just another coward.'

A hybrid of Dolly Parton and a pole dancer, she straddled Serbian culture with her commando fetish. Known universally as Ceca, she was the widow of a warlord called Arkan, who'd led football thugs on tours through Croatia and Bosnia, whipping up 'ancient hatreds' with atrocities. After Arkan was shot in the face in a hotel lobby, Ceca spent two years in mourning. She'd resurfaced on the biceps of his lieutenant, a former Foreign Legionnaire named Legija. And she'd deigned to be kissed by a *New York Times* reporter, although her reinforced chest repelled my frontal approach.

'*Hug me and just for once be a man,*' she'd taunted, after shrugging off my questions about her dead husband. Enquiries about her breasts got shorter shrift.

'Do I look like I need plastic surgery?' she'd fumed. 'I don't go to the gym. I hate physical activity and I've never had anything heavier than a spoon in my hand.'

Sprawled across her sofa in a body-sock, her guts growled from their diet of Cartier Slims and cappuccino. But her physique had proved a hit in Arizona, she said. 'They had no idea who I was, but women were touching me and men were clapping.'

G certainly wasn't. And he failed to see why I might. When he saw me mouth along to the words, his head shook pitifully. 'That noise is pure plastic primitivism of Serbs,' he said. 'Now ironic foreigner thinks is cool. I don't know which part of that is worse.'

I ignored him. She sounded like the spirit of the bar: a hypnotically invigorating melancholy. And brandy stripped the lurching synths of gaudiness. Sure, it was easy to ridicule wartime 'turbofolk', with escapist odes to 'Coca-Cola, Marlboro, Suzuki, discotheques, guitars and bouzouki', insisting that 'nobody has it better' than outcast Serbs. The music was indigenous gangsta

rap. Work less, scam harder, it preached, with a nod to traditional machismo, and a giant middle finger to the West. The
beats sounded Turkish to me, but G called them 'porno-nation-
alism of pigsty.'

As the track faded out, he resumed his ticking off. 'You
should remember is lost generation in this country,' he said.
'Youngs grew up with peasants imposing death cult on Belgrade.
For kids that turbo-gangster life is future. What else you see here
bringing what it promise? It is important we send different kind
of signal.'

I nodded, slouching back to stupefaction.

'You know, we fight against those demons, they get stronger,'
G said. 'People try here to resist in many ways. When they smash
up state TV, propaganda got worse. Still, I am optimistic, since
everyone else is pessimist. My nature seems to be to go against
stream. We should say no by making space here for alternative.
Like new one, where fucked up rules of past don't work.
Autonomous zone for everyone, on island.'

Everything depended on the money. While B and A got started
on construction, G and I kept trying to find some sponsors. Our
search obeyed a cryptic form of protocol, with degrees of mutual
respect implied by the number of times we met to disagree. The
final agreement was always a meeting away.

After ten weeks of talking to bankers, we cut our losses. In
return for €150,000, we'd proposed to promote them as engines
of transformation, supporting start-ups and connecting them
with partners. Essentially, they'd pay us as a case study.
Compared to the local alternatives, the German Micro Finance
Bank was reputable. Its backers included the European Bank for
Reconstruction and Development, and a private sector offshoot
of the World Bank. If millions of euros were going to change
hands at the festival, we had to ensure they ended up in ours.

Ideally, we wanted to process cashless payments. Tokens

could be sold for spending onsite, and money would instantly credit our account. We could also sell our tickets through their branch network. The bank did agree in the end to provide this service, but told us they'd levy a fee to cover transactions. It magically matched the amount that we'd asked for in sponsorship. We could call this whatever we wanted, but in practice it was basically a loan. We were holding out for more attractive offers.

For now, we'd merely opened an account, which obliged us get our paperwork in order. And this roped in an old friend of G's, who'd wired us €2,500 from New York, to show we'd secured investment from abroad. He also took a stake in ECHO Music, which was formed as a spin-off of A and B's production company. Neither G nor I were named in the founding documents. We agreed to keep our savings to ourselves. G said he hadn't any anyway, and mine would barely pay a single DJ.

In accordance with standard practice in the corporate world, we committed ourselves to maximizing income. Our business plan spanned 'music publishing and distribution,' laying out intentions to license CDs for pressing in Serbia, to 'exploit the expanding market for legal products'. There was also an all-encompassing addendum, declaring we'd 'trade on our brand to offer other products and services,' which would buy us the leeway in future for pretty much anything.

We'd also been forced to draft a proper budget. Our partners guessed that the fee for preparing the site - and installing its bars and supplies of electricity and water - would be €130,000. Rental fees for stages, lights, screens and PA systems could be gauged more accurately. Our quotes totaled €75,000, and the charge for security was similar, while transport and accommodation could stretch to €200,000. Promotions would be roughly two thirds as much, based on advertising rates and the price of printing. The biggest expense by far would be the program. A hundred acts could cost us half a million. The bigger the names, the more they'd set us back. Assuming our bookings weren't extravagant, the overall bill would be somewhere around €1.25 million, most of which we'd have to pay up front.

This had produced some scary calculations. If we raised half a million from sponsors, as we hoped, we'd still need as much again before the festival. Barring an unexpected windfall, we had to sell tickets. And at broadly €10 a night (a little less for a weekend pass, and more for day tickets), we'd have to shift fifty thousand, at the minimum. This figure seemed formidable, unless we signed some very famous artists.

Either way, we'd need a full-time sales force. Our bank could process payments made at post offices, but we'd still have to send out the tickets people ordered. We couldn't even speed up the process via the Internet. Hardly any Serbs had a credit card, and their country remained on a blacklist for foreign transactions. But a website still had uses as a marketing tool. In European terms, we were a bargain: at less than €30 for the weekend, ECHO cost as much as a single gig. An eye-catching site could be used to raise some interest, with telesales outsourced to travel agent partners. The first one we recruited was a Serbian firm, the Central European Reliable Agency. The next step was to do the same abroad.

Other potential investors didn't look promising. Serbia's crony capitalists showed no interest. Most had made their fortunes under Milosevic. Having laundered them, they didn't need our assistance. Nor did any Western multinationals.

'Certainly the activities seem very interesting,' ran a typical response, 'and at a different point in our market strategy for the target countries we may have been able to get involved. May I suggest that you let me have ideas for any Festival next year by the end of October?'

Admittedly, we'd left it rather late. But we still had four months. We might not yet have a line-up to promote, but there were other ways to sell our plans to the tourist trade. Raoul

Djukanovic's name went on all of them, starting with the article for JAT Airways.

'Like the Irish, Serbs are proud of their reputation as party people,' it began. 'Not so long ago, Belgrade was known as an avant-garde city, far more open than the rest of Eastern Europe and full of bohemian energy.'

By reviving that climate, we promised to bring back foreigners, who once flocked to Yugoslavia by the million, until artillery put them off the Adriatic. 'This summer,' we said, 'up to a quarter of a million people will gather on a beautiful island in the middle of the Danube for Belgrade's first proper music festival.'

ECHO would channel 'the anarchic character of this city,' and become 'the heart of a new Belgrade: a place where young people are free to be themselves the whole year round.' After all, 'it was not just the beaches of Goa, Ibiza and Thailand that made these places meccas for young Westerners in the 1970s, 1980s and 1990s. Without good music and a positive atmosphere there would have been no scene.'

It seemed wisest not to mention any drugs. So we closed with a simple quotation from Frank Zappa: 'Without music to decorate it, time is just a bunch of boring production deadlines and dates by which bills must be paid.'

This, according to Raoul, was 'the spirit of ECHO'. How alarmingly prophetic that would prove.

Berlin was the last place I lived that I didn't want to leave. Work didn't have much to do with it. I felt at home there. For the summer of 2000, I wasn't as restless as usual. I had fun. I wonder what might have happened if I'd stayed, as I begged to at the end of my year as a Reuters trainee. But that particular parallel universe doesn't exist.

Instead, the corporation's needs trumped mine. I was posted to Zurich, as a cog in a roulette wheel. Every morning, I rewrote corporate news releases, and flashed them onto screens in the banking casino. This was the way that Reuters made its money: flogging feeds for financial gamblers to trade with. The headlines screamed like a croupier, place your bets! Buy on a rumor and sell the facts to profit.

The job was an education in denial. Since the only ideals I could serve were someone else's, I'd have to pretend they served mine, by telling myself my career was moving forward, and blotting out the truth by getting high. That said, not every bureau served the markets. Hence my request for a transfer to one, and the karmic chain that led me to Romania, *The New York Times* and the ECHO festival.

Now, thirty months later, I was back, in the city where many Balkan conflicts started, at a meeting to carve up the region among the Great Powers. And like their nineteenth century Congress of Berlin, the *Internationales Congress Centrum* was a monument to Empire. On the edge of the Western enclave in East Germany, its bulk had stood in salute to the power of the market. It hadn't changed much, like the rest of West Berlin. In the Cold War, people were subsidized to live there. Radicals got by on government handouts. But when the Wall came down, they moved east, into derelict buildings in no man's land and beyond. As waves of gentrification swept behind them, the cultural center of gravity kept moving east.

The *Congress Centrum* lacked this vital energy. Its buildings thronged with endless solemn faces, dragging handouts from trade fairs. The only variation was the contents. There might be widgets, or leaflets on sewing machines, or maybe a novelty sex aid once a year. This week it was holiday brochures. The *Internationale Tourismus-Boerse* was the world's biggest annual gathering of travel agents. There were ten thousand different exhibitors, from the best part of two hundred countries. One of the halls was allotted to South Eastern Europe. And in March of 2003, the stand run by the Tourist Organization of Belgrade was devoted to promoting the ECHO festival.

My fellow delegates weren't minded to object. They'd been drinking all night, and sat there looking glum. Whatever they thought, they wouldn't have much choice. If they obstructed me, I'd call the Minister of Tourism. The executive primate at JAT had told him to help us, in his alternative role as 'Chairman of the Board of the Government of the Republic of Serbia Tourism Organization'.

The stand had little to shout about in any case. Its literature was further out than ours. 'Had the Tower of Babel not been built where it had been built, it would surely have been built in the heart of the Balkans,' announced one of the leaflets, because 'Serbia is the meeting place of cultures, religions and languages.' And not at all linked with violent mono-ethnic monomania.

This booklet was entitled 'Three Times Love', presumably referencing the traditional triple-kiss greeting, not the tri-fingered nationalist salute. 'Although more than forty different nations live in Serbia,' it rhapsodized, 'they do have some things in common - their homes are wide open to friends.' I thought the verbs describing topography more accurate: 'The mountains clash, the roads cross, the waters divide...'

Our offering was harder to ignore: a five-minute film on auto-loop, with a soundtrack of hip-hop and house, and Raoul Djukanovic's treble-heavy voiceover. For three days, it boomed at all comers, from a wall-mounted giant LCD screen.

'It's 2003 in the Balkans and everyone's bored,' Raoul began, to shots of a rusty Yugo falling to pieces, and a street scene framed by panning from a trashcan. 'People may not be rich but they've got high expectations.'

A policeman's hand obscured the lens. He'd stopped us filming. 'Belgrade is desperate for something like ECHO,' the commentary continued. 'That means the biggest crowd since the downfall of Slobodan Milosevic. Only this time everyone's out to have fun.'

Cut to some gratuitous BBC riot footage, spliced with pretty girls cavorting at EXIT. *'This ain't the down, it's the upbeat,'* rapped The Streets on the backing track, urging investors to *'push things forward'*, by buying into a collage of borrowed clips. *'No sales pitch, no media hype, I speak in communications in bold type.'* To wit the caption: 'BELGRADE WELCOMES THE WORLD'.

Raoul's voice resumed. 'Music is pulling people together from all across the Balkans.' An attractive female backside waggled onscreen, to appeals from Mr Scruff to: *'keep moving, or you'll be left behind.'*

Viewers were told that there'd 'also be thousands of visitors from Western Europe, searching for a new party destination.' Eventually, they saw the bigger picture. 'We're planning more events like this on the Adriatic coast in Croatia and Montenegro: a Balkan fusion of Ibiza and Glastonbury.'

The video closed with an animated tour of our 'beautiful island in the middle of the Danube,' which was still under slush. 'ECHO,' Raoul concluded, with brazen cheese. 'Come and watch Belgrade get back in tune with the rest of the world.'

We were Serbia's star attraction, audible from the far side of the building, where other ex-Communist outposts plugged peasant handicrafts. But our corner of the conference hall was empty. It was also tiny compared to caverns hawking cruises. And at 160,000 square meters, the fair was far too large to explore in full. We'd have to engage some assistance to lure people our way.

Wielding my *New York Times* card, I joined a corps of media scroungers in the press suite. From there you could sample the site without leaving the bar, eating food from around the world in canapé form, and overdosing on printouts from the wall racks. I installed myself at a computer and bashed out a statement, then scattered it round the room with piles of CDs. These featured our video, a brochure, and high-resolution logos and photos.

My Serbian mobile only got one call, from a reporter who

worked for the trade fair's magazine. An insider publication for insiders: it didn't sound great in publicity terms. But it was a start. And at least the man I met was enthusiastic. *'Belgrad,'* his article beamed. *'Früher Kriegsschauplatz, bald Jugendkult!'* Welcome to the future of youth culture! One of Europe's biggest festivals would take place in Serbia, readers learned. 'We're building the next Ibiza,' I'd apparently said, 'the only difference is that we'll be cheaper.' He concurred. 'With the ECHO festival, everything will be different,' he'd written. 'Four days of round-the-clock partying' with 'all-inclusive travel packages under €150.'

Buoyed by this performance, I repeated it. For the next two days, I toured around the complex, telling anyone who'd listen to watch our film, which I lugged on a laptop. Some people even talked about doing business. The owner of Cool Tours said a million ex-Yugoslavs lived in Germany. They'd come to work as *Gastarbeiter* after World War II, or as refugees. And thousands of Germans booked trips to foreign festivals. The latest Cool Tours brochure was already printed, but he offered to tout a package via his mailing list, and only asked for ten percent commission. He had his own call center, a partnership with *Intro* magazine, and friends at VIVA, a German MTV clone that was screened across the continent.

That afternoon, I travelled to Cologne, to meet the editor of *Intro's* special *Festival Guide*. He'd spoken to Cool Tours, and was keen to help us out. He offered to write a puff piece, in exchange for us buying an advert in the *Festival Guide*, which would soon go on sale in Germany, Austria and Switzerland. If we flew him and a friend out to Belgrade, they'd plug us next year as the Next Big Thing, and we'd all cash in quite nicely on the back of it.

Having foreign allies made a difference. JAT would take us more seriously, as would sponsors. Two of my friends in Berlin approached German companies, starting with Volkswagen, Adidas and Puma. What worked on Germans could be replicated widely: in Britain, where most of our artists would be coming from, plus France and Spain where other friends could help. Promotions could be handled like a franchise. Coach hire would drive down the travel costs, and Belgrade had student dormitories for rent. We could blitz British universities with flyers, and put on talks about the last place 'we' bombed. Even journalists were worth a shot themselves. Thousands must have passed through the Balkans since the Nineties. If they were off to invade Iraq with the U.S. Army, some R & R by the beach could be just the ticket.

There seemed to be no limit to these dreams, which I indulged at length on the plane back to Belgrade. ECHO appeared to have finally found its milieu, an audience that got where we were coming from. All we had to do was press ahead.

My partner was at the airport when I landed. The silver sheen of his hair stood out a mile, as did his camel-colored car coat and moleskins. His presence surprised me. It wasn't as if I couldn't hail a taxi. I barged through a wall of smoke and the waiting crowd. But before I got to G, I heard my phone ring. It was my translator. We'd barely spoken since I quit two weeks before. I wavered over whether to take the call. When I did, her voice was shaking. She said she'd been trying to contact me for hours.

'Where are you?' she said very slowly. 'They shot Djindjic.'

Oh.

Fuck.

HERESY

If life's what happens while you're making other plans, then the way to stay sane is to take it as it comes. But some things aren't so easy to endure. *The New York Times* had demanded front-page news. And despite never having got near this hallowed space, I didn't want to. We were trying to attract tourists to Serbia, not scare them away with murders in broad daylight. The facts were undeniable regardless. The prime minister had been killed outside his office. And his suspected assassins were gangsters from Zemun. So there were far more urgent things to do than write about it.

But the *Times* still technically owned me for a fortnight, and they owed me $20,000 in back expenses. I couldn't afford to write that money off, so I'd have to give the paper what it wanted. This began with an urgent story for the website, then another for the *International Herald Tribune*, a global edition aimed at travellers, and 1,700 words for the *Times* itself, to be honed in exchanges with editors till the small hours.

I was used to cranking out coverage for Reuters, and I knew I could 'cheat and steal' from all the agencies. Another newswire adage would be useful: 'take it off TV'. Although Djindjic had been shot around the corner, I saw little point leaving my flat to inspect the crime scene. It was already swarming with paratroopers. So I installed my translator in front of the local news, flipped a second screen between CNN and the BBC, and smoked a few joints. It would be a long night. My partner paced distraught around the office.

'This is very bad,' he kept repeating, as if there were doubts. 'You will see now here is total necrophilia, everyone praising Djindjic as martyr. Death is best lover in this country, man. Tomorrow if I die, there will be more people on my funeral than I can meet today in the street and say hello. Seriously, that's how it is. I can barely meet three people in the city who will shake the hand and talk, but if I die then there will probably be fifty.'

I had more immediate concerns. I copied a story from Reuters and changed a few words: 'Mr Djindjic, who was 50 and had many political enemies, was shot in the back.' Police said the bullet shredded his stomach. He was pronounced dead on arrival at hospital. He'd been hobbling through the car park on crutches, having hurt himself playing football with policemen. He'd quipped at the time that they'd injured him on purpose. A few weeks beforehand, a truck had tried to ram his motorcade. Both this and the fatal attack were now being blamed on the same gang of rogues.

The most wanted man was the warlord known as Legija, who'd commanded a 'Special Operations Unit', combining two infamous groups of Serbian paramilitaries: Arkan's Tigers and the Red Berets. A year before, they'd blocked a motorway with Hummers, warning the government not to demobilize their regiment. Under mounting Western pressure to round up war criminals, Djindjic had talked about putting them in jail. But he'd only come to power with their support, and thanked them for switching sides to back his government. 'Many owe their lives to Legija, including me,' he'd said. Now his conflicting loyalties had killed him.

G was convinced there were layers of hidden agendas. 'You know, perhaps Djindjic choose this way out,' he muttered. 'He was in cross fire between those who think they control everything, but find that they control nothing. He could not deliver for West, or for Serbs. And both of them will make him into hero.'

'Come on,' I said. 'Isn't that a little harsh? At least he was trying to fight the mafia.'

My partner laughed. 'Government in this country *is* the mafia. Even politicians say on TV. They need each other to be where they are. Is pretty much same as Colombia.'

Editors saw the situation differently. Thanks to their contribution to my story, readers would be told that Djindjic's death held 'echoes in its portent for the Balkans of the June 1914 assassination of Archduke Franz Ferdinand.' It left Serbia, 'a struggling country at the center of a conflict-ridden region ravaged by a decade of war, with neither a prime minister nor an elected president'.

What a fine location for a festival!

I blamed myself. I couldn't face feigning the gravitas for interviews, so I'd relied on emailed rent-a-quotes from contacts. One predicted 'a dark period for Serbia and the region,' with a 'resurgence of nationalism that was never repudiated by much of the Serbian establishment and continues to be allied with the underworld.' I buried these lines at the end of the story, for balance. My bosses brought them up to sell the news. Context defines how we understand the world. What matters isn't what gets reported, but how it's framed. Unfortunately, I'd failed to shape that process. My mind was on more pressing obligations, like writing to all the people I'd enlisted.

'The only effect on ECHO is that we're all now doubly committed,' I reassured travel agents. 'Perversely this tragedy might just end up helping,' because our 'sponsors and other partners are eager to prove that there is far more to Serbia than a few lowlifes.'

People 'tend to have warped impressions' of Belgrade, I told my friends. 'Imagine Italy without as much money, taste or style, and that's pretty much it. Sure there are gangster types, but I feel ten times more scared in London than I ever have here.' At least there seemed at least no risk of being glassed. 'It's a fucked up country, but there is no threat to anyone who isn't immersed in this murky underworld.'

I certainly hoped so.

As for the average Serb, what might they think? How would I know? I'd only spoken to my partner and translator. But when reporters quote views from the street, they're usually telling the world what they think it should hear, or trawling for lines that fit their preconceptions. It seemed more honest to make the whole thing up myself. So I invented a fictional character to help.

To hell with po-faced ethics, I told my conscience. The *Times* had helped concoct the case for war. Besides, I'd obeyed the rules and found two sources. Who cared if their thoughts were channeled by a fake?

'It's crunch time,' said this avatar of ECHO. 'Either people are going to get serious and take on the criminals trying to undermine our country or we're doomed.'

He spoke for all of us.

The following day, we got serious ourselves: we begged the king of Serbia for help. Strictly speaking, he was Crown Prince Aleksandar, head of the dispossessed House of Karadjordjevic. But like other royal chancers in the Balkans, he was hoping to take advantage of disillusionment.

Across the border in Bulgaria, a relation of Britain's Queen had got elected. After 50 years in exile from the Communists, Prime Minister Simeon Saxe-Coburgotski led a coalition of bankers, lawyers, celebrities and a magician. Next door in Romania, a man named Paul had run for president, insisting he was heir to a throne that no longer existed. And Albania's Crown Prince Leka upstaged all of them, flying into Tirana with Zulu bodyguards, whose pistols were impounded at the airport, along with ninety weapons stashed in Leka's luggage, among them several grenades and a Kalashnikov.

By contrast, Aleksandar sounded tame. He was born in a suite at Claridge's in London, which Churchill declared to be temporary Yugoslav territory. And he said he'd been a British Army skiing champion, which wouldn't do much for his patriot credentials. Since he settled in the Balkans in late middle age, he'd been keen to raise his profile in the media. And he'd sound weighty enough to be quoted on national mourning. So we drove up Belgrade's richest hill to visit him.

Dedinje was home to the elite: diplomats, tycoons and racke-teers, and until he was put behind bars, Milosevic too. Aleksandar moved in when the former strongman left. His palace was built in the reign of his father's father, Aleksandar I, of the Kingdom of Serbs, Croats and Slovenes, as Yugoslavia had been known. The entrance was easy to miss, but after several run-ins with policemen and security guards, we were rolling up the right gravel drive, and patting down our partings in the wing-mirrors.

We'd dressed ourselves in deference to the mood. G wore a marmalade jacket, with bottle-green chinos and a peach canvas shirt. I'd donned a cheap charcoal roll-neck and black cords. Our host was more conventionally attired, in funereal shades of double-breasted suit, and a black silk tie pulled tight beneath his chins. He marshaled us in like a footman, a smile reducing his eyes to little slits in buttery cheeks.

Aleksandar had rehearsed a short statement, which spared me the pain of pretending to run through an interview.

'Of course we can present you very positively,' said my partner, who'd been presented as a *New York Times* employee. 'But first we must confirm with images that Serbs are not longer Communists, gypsies, bandits, clowns and savages.'

The king looked confused.

I opened my laptop. 'Can I plug this in?' I asked. That baffled him more.

The wall behind his desk was a thick-paneled sideboard, and the rest of the room was lined with heavy furnishings. There wasn't a socket to be seen. A servant had to be summoned to reveal one, and dismissed to fetch a long enough extension cord.

Eventually, I pressed play on our promo film, and the king looked on slack-jawed at its female close-ups. 'You say this will be happening in summer?' he said.

'Absolutely,' G said. 'We show to world a different kind of Serbia.'

'It'll change how people see this place in future,' I said. 'The army's going to lend us a pontoon bridge. If they knew we had your support, they might do more.'

It seemed best not to mention his father's *Cetnik* militia, whose crimes in World War II had poisoned Bosnia. *Cetnik* memorabilia still sold well, alongside t-shirts hailing such 'heroes' as the fugitive Bosnian Serb duo, Radovan Karadzic and Ratko Mladic. Aleksandar hung out in their enclave during wartime.

G warmed to the theme. 'Sir, army have many things they use for destruction. Now we offer to them chance to bring peace and love, and we promote that. They should be paying us for what it is we do for them.'

My partner waved extravagantly at the window, surveying an expansive lawn and stucco terrace. 'I think we can make party here for artists,' he said. 'Just imagine, all stars together with Serbian king!'

I thought this was pushing our luck, but apparently not.

'Yes,' Aleksandar smiled. 'We could certainly consider a garden party.'

'We also need sponsors,' I said. 'Perhaps you'd like to invest in us yourself? It's a great way to show young Serbs you support development.'

G grinned. 'Of course Sir, money is welcome, and maybe you know someone who can help with that. But what will really help right now is you sign letter, so we show army you support very strongly what we doing here.'

The king looked somewhat out of his depth. 'What sort of letter do you have in mind?'

'Just a general statement,' I said. 'I can draft one and send it over this afternoon. If you feel happy with the text, just print it out and sign.'

This appeared to placate him, unlike our request to pose for photos.

'I'd thought *The New York Times* would send a camera,' he protested, as I handed my point-and-shoot to one of his aides. Even so, he smiled indulgently for portraits. There was one of us standing in line on a turquoise carpet. The others showed us hunched around my laptop, which was perched on a gold-legged slab of marble table.

'They've told us to economize,' I said. 'The war has started eating up our budget.'

My final two weeks at the Times went up in smoke. I stayed as high as I possibly could to clear my head. Without this neuroleptic, I'd have panicked. Our bank account was still as good as empty, and the search for funds got ever more creative. My latest trawl by email had claimed that two big foreign backers were behind us. Someone replied: 'Oh yeah? The ones called Corleone and Gambini?'

We also had a website to build, and promotions were due to begin within a month. But first we had to ensure there was something to sell. Our schedule was hectic. What with all the meetings and smoke breaks, I was working up to sixteen hours a day. *The New York Times* still wanted daily updates, so I gave them as little thought as I could muster, rephrasing what I copied from the wires. I also invented some quotes from Western diplomats. I felt sure my stories made them sound more honest.

The most outlandish comments of all appeared to be real. One mourner called Zoran Djindjic 'our John F. Kennedy! Tough when needed but truly honest and righteous.' She must have been watching *JFK*, which was shown on TV the night Djindjic died.

At his funeral, in a half-finished church that resembled a car park, the finance minister echoed this gurgling tribute, which was relayed out to crowds that packed the streets. He inspired me to make an appointment to see him with G.

Bozidar Djelic had lived abroad for years. He'd studied at

Harvard and worked for McKinsey. Presumably, he had some wealthy friends. When we got to his office, his head was in his hands. The last time we met he'd been boastful, vowing to launch a crackdown on the mafia. 'The sort of guy who has two black Jeep Cherokees parked outside his mansion but never filed a tax return is going to get asked some very tough questions,' he'd said. A news magazine had named him Man of the Year.

Nowadays, cabinet colleagues swore to 'liquidate everybody who resists the police', which had prompted official complaints from Human Rights Watch.

'What can we do to put things right here?' Djelic asked us. He was staring up at G from sunken eyes. He seemed desperate enough to think we had an answer. But he showed no serious interest in our spiel, or my suggestion that he engage me as an adviser, to ghost write columns requesting assistance from the West.

'Security cannot come at the price of reform,' he kept declaiming. 'We can't stop what we started here.'

G and I agreed. So we left. No one in Serbia could help us. That much seemed clear.

'You know, this country it was bankrupt twenty years ago,' G told me in the elevator. 'Now only industry is criminals. Everything got turned upside down. Peasants have power and experts grow potatoes. I think in global paranoia about resources that big nations and corporations wanna divide us all on soldiers and their slaves. Serbs can get help if they line behind that holy cross of NATO. Does not take astrophysics to see where is leading. People here still ready to be victims. It is one thing they know how to do quite well.'

'I don't understand,' I said. 'If everything in Serbia builds on death, then why doesn't all this grieving make them change?'

G stopped and stared. 'You know that Buddha said to live like we dead?' he said. 'I think those words they can confuse you. You have to be first conscious so you hear.'

After six months of graft and coercion, we had little to show for our work but a house of cards. Its proportions grew more lavish by the day, with every new commitment to construct it. We'd talked dozens into helping us on credit. But two essential elements eluded us: headline acts, and the money to pay their fees. Our plans were still a giant stoned illusion. Where better to take them next than New York?

G appeared to have found an American benefactor: the friend of his who'd put money in our account. They'd met as exiles from Yugoslavia in the Eighties, but J had stayed on in Manhattan and made a fortune. If we cut him in as a proper silent partner, he'd stump up the funds to sign some bigger names.

After filing my final story for the *Times*, G and I left the Balkans for London, to catch the cheapest onward flight we could find: the final leg of a long-haul trip from India. The plane was adorned like a provincial English curry house, with flowery patterns in pastel shades of pink. This was about the extent of entertainments, apart from my partner's in-flight commentary. I nodded along and chomped on nicotine gum. The rasping effect made me retch, but it beat me chewing my cheeks for several hours.

'You know, American dream was always moving west,' G said. 'But seems that deeper you go towards East, tougher are magnets. I mean those magnets what keep you on field far from mad crowd. Like that tranquility of mind we find on voyage. At one time, humans share that all the time, but now is mostly nomads what preserve it. Even simple Balkan gypsy still can sense this. You know they came from India, right?'

I smiled. He carried on.

'In West they wake to more distorted vision. I learn that for myself but only hard way. On Balkans they think U.S. is like TV, you know, all living in huge apartment, not roach-infested hole in Bronx, and coming each day downtown to clean master's toilet. I'm telling you man, that place taught me a *lot*. Now they clean it up and suck out all its soul. Seems dollars talk loud as day was bought from Indians. I think Serbs aren't so much different from Americans. Same stupid pride and dreams control them both. Neither knows why he should value himself, but if you question him you automatic enemy. In New York, it is now about flavor. Ice cream, coffee, condom, maybe soon they make a pill for scented farts. I think that finally make them all feel different.'

He was still going strong at immigration. 'Everywhere, the people have some opium,' he said. 'On East is same, whoever next turns to be there Emperor. You know, much I do like Russia, I doubt on Russians. Too much oil and booze, just like Americans.'

Had he not already said he had a Green Card, I might have stepped away.

'Running such beautiful country with bunch of drunks and lazy bastards, I hope they can cope. I think they would have to move fast on multiculturalism. Still, is there a plenty space. With smart thinking, people would line to get Russian passport. They can pay contribution to Mother. Something like Uncle Sam, minus arrogance.'

It was his parting shot that really freaked me out. 'That axis of the evil is in all of us,' he laughed. 'Including you, the correspondent kamikaze!'

I froze. A pair of uniformed bruisers stood before us, their forearms hewn from kebab legs of ham.

'S'aright man.' G smiled, as he joined his queue. 'You do what you feel. And now you free. Even free to feel 72 virgins if you want. I tell you I rather be satyr than a saint. Still, I had sympathy for Arabs what face death with smile. All of us in life we have to choose. We either falling down or blasting up.'

And with that he left me to face Homeland Security. I was glad my bum was empty for a change. It was bad enough trying to fill out the visa waiver form.

'Are you a drug abuser?' No, I use them properly.

'Have you ever been arrested or convicted for an offence or crime involving moral turpitude?' I beg your pardon?

'Or a violation related to a controlled substance?' It was only a caution.

'Or been a controlled substance trafficker?' No comment.

'Or are you seeking entry to engage in criminal or immoral activities?' Not in my book.

'Have you ever been or are you now engaged in espionage or sabotage?' Er, no to all the questions it is then.

I've always loved New York, as much as I hate the place. It's the ultimate urban theme park, Las Vegas for significance addicts, a lottery in constant one-upmanship, where no amount of status buys respect.

Sure, the smiles at your cash will be *authentic*, with *appropriate* amounts of New Age bromides. But you can't possibly make them mean it, any more than you do. If you're mad enough to crave affirmation there, you're finished. I was hooked on the first taste of lip-gloss, and I'd been chasing my own shadows ever since.

On arrival, we took the train to a small apartment near Central Park, where our silent partner invested early profits. These days, he lived in a penthouse, and kept this place empty. It was roughly the size of my bedroom in Belgrade. The only window looked out on a wall. But he'd left us some weed, which would help to stave off jetlag, while we ogled the latest war smut on TV.

'Why don't they show melting eyeballs?' I said. 'That gore even shocked the generals last time round. It'll be uglier after a decade of bombing and sanctions.'

G shrugged. 'Ugly truth is not concern of news. First they see their team is gonna *win*. Civilian deaths been planned since war on Indians, but dark side is disguised for most Americans. Since Vietnam they try to make it video game.'

'Sure,' I said. 'But shouldn't we try to stop that?'

'Point is for you to decide,' he said. 'But I don't see too much
success so far. Marching angry people is same problem.
Revolution goes round and round, what can we do?'

I blacked out on the couch.

After several hours of satisfying coma, I overdosed on bagels and
cream cheese - to stop me getting high, as I'd have liked to.
Shielded only by my tie and a caffeine flak jacket, I felt as ready
as I'd get to face the *Times*. Attitude squawked from all sides on
the mean streets below, even the billowing subway vents in the
gutter.

The West 43rd Street HQ was a gentle stroll away. Sunshine
soothed the buzz in my numb-skulled temples. I wondered if
staying straight could be the new stoned, but I missed the woozy
anesthetic patina. Without it, even shop signs felt invasive. Their
windows mostly gleamed with broken promises, offering an
excess of more. Always more. And how that prospect drove me
wild! Women with three-figure haircuts swept by, trailing
bottled smells of mental complications. They probably thought
the sex they seeped was 'gross'.

Times Square had been transformed into an airport lounge,
with none of the seedy attractions of its heyday. Everything
looked anodyne and stateless. It could easily be in Dubai, or a
cross-channel ferry. And still the bovine tourists swarmed to
gawp. The screens were about as dull as they were bright. On a
corner, the Reuters building spat out headlines, burying news in
its ticker of showbiz gossip, football scores and stock prices. And
in her lair down a street to the side lay the old 'Gray Lady', a
reclining Empire State Building crossed with a typewriter,
studded with little white orbs of private streetlights. '*Times*' they
all announced, in Gotham black.

I'd reached what Tolstoy called an 'intellectual brothel from
which there is no retreat'; that place that reeked to Norman
Mailer of human 'flesh burning quietly and slowly in the service

of a machine'; the abode of Hunter S. Thompson's 'fuckoffs and misfits', skulking in their 'false doorway to the backside of life, a filthy piss-ridden little hole nailed off by the building inspector, but just deep enough for a wino to curl up from the sidewalk and masturbate like a chimp in a zoo-cage.'

I was home.

The doormen barked like bellhops, as if they were asking 'who are you then?' I half expected to be trampled by Masters of the Universe, spinning the revolving doors of the liberal conscience. Upstairs, each floor of newsroom was a panopticon, diced into wall-to-wall cubicles under the strip lights. The overwhelming energy was beige, straight out of *All The President's Men*. Journalistic titans trod the carpet tiles. On my only previous visit, one of them offered me advice: I should use my middle initial on my stories. I'd never get anywhere otherwise, he said. He'd gone one better, of course, and added a whole middle name to swell his byline.

The politics of the *Times* were like a tin-pot dictatorship. Functionaries jockeyed for influence, promoting each other's double-dealing proxies. No one could say for sure what the party line was, but everyone seemed to know what not to say.

Their pages of war news were titled 'Threats And Responses', without explaining who had threatened whom. When the march towards Baghdad began a few days back, the *Times* called it a quest 'to disarm the country', in one of the 'most ambitious military adventures since Vietnam'. Buried inside was a nod to other views: 'Germany, France and Russia have declared that the war is, in essence, illegal'. And so had most lawyers not paid to say the opposite. So why not just print: 'America defied the international community on Wednesday night, launching an attack on Iraq that repeats, in essence, the supreme crime of aggression for which senior Nazis were hanged after World War II'? Dumb question, of course, though a Nuremberg prosecutor said: 'the law includes, and if it is to serve a useful purpose it must condemn aggression by any other nations, including those which sit here now in judgment.' And he was American.

I didn't expect to get answers from the *Times*, except on when they planned to pay me. Like other 'contract writers', I'd fronted the cash to run a bureau. 'We cannot advance money to Daniel,' an editor ruled when I joined, because I wasn't on permanent staff. 'Obviously it is a worse drag for him,' she'd sympathized condescendingly, 'because he is young and poor.'

It sometimes took them months to cover expenses. Our total rolling loan must run to millions. They'd always settled up in the end, even for $2,000 mobile phone bills. But I feared they'd soon discover what I'd been up to, so I'd come to demand pre-emptive reimbursement. It was processed in minutes. That left me free to enjoy my swansong.

I'd long been in awe of a stunt pulled in Moscow, by the editors of an expat paper called *The Exile*. They'd dubbed the local *Times* bureau chief 'the ranking Western liar in Russia', following a 'blowjob profile' he'd written of Vladimir Putin, which went to 'extraordinary lengths to actively advertise his authoritarian instincts as positives', because the Kremlin posed as a 'guarantor of Western business'.

The Exile reviewed the reporter's 'eel-like' career, which took off by 'helping to cover up American-backed atrocities' in Indonesia. Before long, he'd claimed such crimes 'didn't and couldn't happen, because America was a "New World bent on ending inhumanity." Then, when he was forced to admit that even this was not true, he came out into the open and just said it: our atrocities are better than your atrocities.'

Thus, *The Exile's* editors concluded, he 'believed in a world where his bosses were always right and he was always being promoted. One thing he certainly did not believe in was the possibility that anyone, anywhere would ever dare to throw a cream pie made of horse sperm in his face.' Which was what they did, and wrote about at length.

When I arrived at the horseshoe hub at the heart of the foreign desk, Roger Cohen was nowhere to be seen. Electing to wait, I prattled with his deputy. Like him, she was technically English, and had also reported on wars in Yugoslavia. She asked if I had any 'new Balkan jokes or gossip' to impart. I gave her an orange ECHO business card, and pulled up a chair.

A few minutes into our chat, I clocked a presence. Cohen was hovering behind me, and I was sitting spinning in his seat.

'Roger!' I jumped up and proffered my hand. He shook it limply. 'I was just giving Alison my contact details.'

Heart pounding, I lifted my jacket from where I'd hung it, on his computer screen. 'If you ever need anything from Belgrade,' I said, 'please don't hesitate...'

His eyebrows slid towards his nose. 'I thought you were resigning.'

'I am, but... but I wouldn't want to leave you in the lurch.'

At the very worst moment, demons intervened. Though my eyes had lost their scales, I was obsessed with how I looked. 'I'd like to thank you again for the opportunity,' I simpered. 'I'm sorry it didn't work out as we'd hoped.'

Cohen turned away to tap at his keyboard. He had bigger things to think about than me. And I'd bungled my mission to make him eat his words, never mind a liberal dose of equine semen. My abortive career at the *Times* had definitely flat-lined.

Hell's Kitchen was right round the corner. Once an Irish ruffian slum, it clung to the bottom of the Garment District and reached north, reveling in the real-estate porn name Midtown West. Its sleazier charms were evoked by a substitute title: Clinton. Though its abattoirs, gang brawls and liquor stills had vanished, and the wrecker's ball had gentrified its tenements, there was a final twist to the quarter's upward spiral. The yuppies had reclaimed its former name, and none more so than J, our silent partner.

G said his friend was renowned as a 'Balkan chicken farmer', which I assumed was a cryptic reference to golden eggs. Like my partner, he'd started as a driver, and built up a fleet of trucks that made him millions. His success appeared dependent on two factors: a self-replenishing workforce of immigrants, and a deal with a fashion house, whose founder's brother he'd got stoned with. He now shipped their stock across the northeastern seaboard, which afforded him the luxury of four vehicles, including a vintage Cadillac and a Porsche. The cost of keeping them garaged dwarfed my salary.

'Mr Djukanovic!' J laughed down the intercom, as gruff and full-bodied as Elvis on the bog. 'We've been expecting you. Come on up. Top floor. Suite thirteen.' Though he made it sound like a seven-star hotel, the building had more in common with Balkan office blocks. Its lobby tiles were imitation marble.

There was only a solitary door when I stepped out of the lift. It stood open. From the threshold, half the city spread before me. The loft looked out over roofs to the uptown skyscrapers. I tried to locate the *Times* building, but our silent partner's bulk got in the way. My eyes were drawn at once to his hulking wristwatch, then a t-shirted paunch and a tatty pair of sneakers. From speaking to J on the phone, I'd imagined him in sharp designer suits. Instead, he was almost a ringer for Donald Trump, right down to the golden sheen on his wispy fringe. He certainly had the forcefulness of tone.

'Shut the door,' he snapped. 'Then get your ass through here to taste some treats.'

I did as I was told. Inside, the apartment was smaller than I'd thought. Windows filled one wall from floor to ceiling. The light was dazzling. Turning, I saw a table by the door, where a scrawny youth in jeans sat talking to G. Several Perspex boxes lay between them.

'Which one you want?' my partner grinned. 'A Kali Mist?'

'You should try Diesel,' J suggested, 'or the Juicy Fruit.'

'Check for yourself.' G passed a box. It was as big as a pack of king-size cigarettes, and contained a single bud of marijuana. A label with *A-Team* lettering said 'AK-47'. All of the boxes were branded, with indistinguishably Day-Glo green contents. The 'Juicy Fruit' sticker was scanned from a Wrigley's wrapper.

'Vacuum-sealed New York hydroponics,' G said. 'These guys they know what they doing. All choices in this city mess you up.'

'How many d'ya want?' the youth enquired lackadaisically.

Our silent partner's bloodshot eyes were bulging. 'We better get two at least,' he said. 'And I mean big ones.'

'I suggest we take blast from a AK,' G said. 'Whole country probably should, know what I mean?'

I took control. 'OK, let's get this small one, plus two Diesels and a Juicy Fruit. How much is that?'

'Seven-fifty.'

He meant hundreds. 'Wow!' I whistled. 'You'd feel burned in Amsterdam paying even half that.'

'Yeah,' G said, 'but we in *New* Amsterdam. And we did order home delivery. You are lucky you don't have to give him tip.'

'Pay the guy, Raoul,' J said. 'I cover big tabs.'

Our server took his earnings and departed. In fewer than 24 hours, I'd emptied my wallet. Thanks for flying American. Have a nice day!

Returning to his desk beside the window, J retrieved a stumpy pure grass joint. He was already fried. His lips almost stuck together when he spoke.

'So,' G said, 'what's cooking now with big guy?'

'Ah, the Jew...!' J's laugh cut his face into dimples. Catching my startled look, he laughed them wider. 'Don't worry, Raoul. He's in my tribe.'

'I hope not,' G shot back. 'That guy is archetype of agent, sitting on ass until someone give him sniff. And when he smells cut is like shopping on Grand Bazaar. Whatever you want he can get, but first he come hard with Billboard Hot One Hundred.'

I lit the joint I'd been crafting. J sprung from his chair. 'Hey!' he roared, in Soprano New Jersey. 'No tobacco in apartment, OK?'

'Er, no worries.' I chipped the end between my fingers, feeling shaken. J calmed as quickly as he'd flipped. He nodded at a metal spiral staircase.

'Come on the terrace, Raoul,' he said. 'We talk up there.' The view from this rooftop platform was impressive. It yawned across the Hudson to J's warehouse. The Lincoln Tunnel was almost on his doorstep. He brandished a chunky cellphone, pointing west.

'It don't take much to keep wheels turning!' he choked, passing G his joint. 'All I gotta do is call my guy, and show up now and then without a warning. He runs the depot. I check he's not scamming me. It's too easy making money in this city.'

A belly laugh was rumbling through his barrel chest. He pulled another joint from behind his ear. If he didn't watch out, his reddened eyes might bleed.

'That is why we need you in Belgrade,' G said. 'When you come, you gonna see how whole thing works, then we control remote from yacht in future years.'

'That's my vision!' J itched his crotch. 'For festival, we move onshore with speedboats. But rest of the time, we're at sea Raoul. We moor up off Croatia, live like playboys.'

G grinned. 'You think your wife she will appreciate arrangement?'

My face couldn't hide my surprise at this reference to marriage.

'Hey, don't look so shocked, Raoul.' J's turnip head swelled with pride. 'I lasted twelve years already. I'm practically Gringo. I'm gonna take the test for citizenship. Same as him.'

He nodded at G. Now I was really shocked. What, *he's* married too?

'I was,' G said, 'when I live here. My ex-wife told me I am

gambler. Guess she was right, but I pay my way... You know this city it can bleed you... That's why I left. But I don't mean... She is sweet person... We still talk... I feed her cats...'

I'd never heard my partner sound so flustered. His eyes looked glazed, even wistful.

'What about you, Raoul?' J winked. 'You still free man?'

'Pretty much,' I said. 'But there's someone in New York I've got my eye on.'

There was something I couldn't resist about Americans. Maybe it was the way they broke my heart. My first girlfriend was a New Yorker. She studied in England then went home to someone else. Rejection crippled me. Unconsciously, I sought it out repeatedly. Each time made the longing more intense. My life became a fight against the odds. It always seemed fulfillment was in reach, provided I tried a little harder. Surely spectacular exploits would impress her.

'We met in Romania,' I said. 'She was there for a conference with the U.N.'

G smiled indulgently. 'So why you did decide she is the one?'

'I can't explain it,' I said. 'She feels so alive. We got talking about the time we'd spent in India. I'm hoping to take her there after the festival.'

Hope was the operative word. We'd only met once since the first time, almost a year back. We got drunk and she jumped in a taxi before I could kiss her. Our flirting was conducted over email. She said she liked waking up to my words, if only in print. 'I do love that from wherever I am, I can always find you,' she wrote.

G's smile grew wider. 'You know, most people think *they* special one. Then they find someone to confirm it. We all one love, my friend, you hear in reggae. I have feeling Rasta vision can connect with you.'

J brought us back to business with a cackle. 'Rastafari connection has been made,' he said. 'Deposit is cleared for

Burning Spear. And also I put offer on Sonic Youth.'

I wondered why. 'Aren't they a little old for Belgrade? Who's going to know them?'

G shook his head. 'You should remember how was scene in old Belgrade. Those guys serious artists, people value that.'

'Sonic Youth represents New York,' J said, 'whole urban progressive perspective, you know, punk, CBGBs, all ideas that were coming from what I personally think is the greatest city in the world.'

My partner agreed. 'Seventies and Eighties Belgrade was not like Romania. Always they had taste for avant-garde. I'm telling you, those guys kill whatever EXIT bring.'

My heart skipped a beat. 'What's that about EXIT?' I said. 'I thought they'd vanished. Are they going ahead this summer after all?'

'Why you always talk about fucking EXIT?' G snapped. He seemed to think threats weren't real unless he acknowledged them. I preferred to play it safe and be afraid.

J's voice turned serious. 'They're planning first week in July, Raoul. That's what we heard from our agent. So we got Sonic Youth for weekend after, on thirteenth.'

I turned back to G, nonplussed. 'What happened to June twenty-eighth?'

He stared impassively. 'I think is better we avoid that day.'

I felt incensed. 'And I think we'd be mad to let EXIT go first. What if they get bigger names than us? How are we going to sell tickets in advance? At least if we go before them, we'll have novelty value.'

J stepped between us. 'It's better we sell those tickets as long as we can, Raoul. We need to cover my exposure. And if we're second, we not starting any war.'

'That's great,' I said. 'But names are what sell tickets. Who else can we get?'

'I think you underestimate Belgrade,' G said. 'We bring them quality and they will understand that. For EXIT now is all about grow or die. Together with Uncle Sam and B92, they can be MTV, HMV and KGB, controlling all culture for youth what come on territories. But that means they must buy what agents push on them.'

'Hang on,' I said, confused. 'I thought B92 was independent. Weren't they the ones playing bands like Sonic Youth?'

My partner snorted. 'Yeah, you should hear their sound today, is now American song of bigger faster more. Radio, TV, CDs, DJs, anything they think they can monopolize. I prefer to work with simple guys from Zemun.'

'Relax Raoul,' J said. 'There is plenty of space for two festivals in Serbia. Market is young. From business standpoint, it's good time. We get involved on bottom level. With that island until September, we make back money selling ice cream.'

He turned to G. 'How is situation with security? Agent keeps on asking guarantees.'

'Still it is a status of emergency,' G said, 'but I am pretty sure will lift in next few weeks. And we agree to hire guards what politicians offer us.'

I pictured the masked commandos in Belgrade when Djindjic was shot. It didn't look pretty. 'Can't we import security from abroad?' I said.

G was aghast. '*What?* You wanna send ex-Marines on Big War Island? I don't think is model for security.'

'Paranoia will destroy ya, Raoul,' J mocked. 'Politicians are ones who should control hyenas. I don't have bucks for foreign armies.'

I walked to the edge of the parapet feeling glum. Despite J's help, we still seemed strapped for cash. We had to get organized fast, and start promotions. Even one big name on the bill would make a difference. A million dollars ought to be enough. How hard could it be to find that money in New York?

As I pondered, J's hand touched my shoulder. 'Hey Raoul,' he said, passing his phone. 'Who's your daddy? You wanna impress that girl? Let's send her fifty big red roses.'

I took a deep breath and swung round, two fingers drawn at my hips like a pair of pistols. 'Gentlemen,' I said, 'I have an idea. I know someone here with serious shekels behind him. And he owes me a favor. How about we call him instead?'

The man we were awaiting lived off Lexington, a few blocks east of Central Park. He was the author of fifty books, almost all of them on the theme of not forgetting.

Once upon a time, he wished he could, like others who'd survived Nazi death camps. The first tome took him ten years to write. But half a century later, there were other concerns. After winning the Nobel Peace Prize for his work, he'd set up a Foundation for Humanity, to counter criticism that he sought 'to keep the wounds of Auschwitz open by repeatedly pouring the salt of new literary reconstructions upon them.'

The Norwegian Nobel Committee saw things differently. They called Elie Wiesel 'a witness for truth and justice', and said that his 'commitment, which originated in the sufferings of the Jewish people, has been widened to embrace all repressed peoples,' in an expression of 'limitless solidarity.'

Perhaps it had. But that wasn't the message I heard from him myself. A few weeks after joining *The New York Times*, I'd been asked to 'bear witness' to speeches he gave in Romania, and what I witnessed again and again were Holocaust lectures. Wiesel had opened a museum in his boyhood home, from which he and his family were deported in 1944.

'It is the first time he's been back in a long time,' I'd been told by the foreign editor, who'd apparently been told to lay on proper coverage, 'so please think in terms of going there a couple of days before. I'll provide some Wiesel contact numbers.'

A three-day road trip ensued, escorted by the U.S. ambassador, Wiesel's wife, two advisers, a historian, and a screenwriter, plus a retinue of businessmen. We dined with the Romanian prime minister, and flew with the president to Sighet, Wiesel's home in Transylvania. He urged both leaders to denounce a wartime forebear, the fascist Ion Antonescu, who put a quarter of a million Jews and gypsies to death. Theoretically, the government disowned him, but his portrait still hung in their building, which had set back Romania's efforts to join NATO, and host American military bases.

'It was impossible to contain the emotions,' Wiesel had told me, after telling young Romanians to grill their grandparents. 'Ask them if they shed a tear, if they cried, if they slept well,' he'd urged. 'And then you children, when you grow up, tell your children that you have seen a Jew in Sighet telling his story.'

When the *Times* printed my write-up of that story, at greater length than anything else I'd filed, Wiesel called to thank me. 'You captured it perfectly,' he said. 'Please keep in touch.' So I took him at his word and phoned his office.

His foundation's aim was 'to combat indifference, intolerance and injustice, through international dialogue and youth-focused programs'; in other words, through projects like our festival. An appointment was scheduled to meet Wiesel at home.

I wondered at first if we'd come to the wrong address. It was badly in need of a paint job, and there were none of the brocaded doormen from Park Avenue. But a concierge had ushered us upstairs, where a familiar face stood waiting in a doorway. He looked like Woody Allen, minus wisecracks; unless you counted wrinkles in his brow.

'Come in, come in,' Wiesel said. I followed meekly, both my partners at my heel.

The apartment was effectively a study. Its walls were lined with little but Judaica, in books and rolls of parchment by the thousand. Turning his back on his desk, Wiesel showed us to seats at a knee-high table. I introduced the others, and our goal: G was a Serb, J was Croat, and we were working together on reconciliation.

Our host looked solemn. 'So you're leaving the *Times*?' he said, recalling what I'd told him.

'Yes.'

He paused dramatically. 'A shame,' he said. 'What happened?'

'It's a long story.'

'Go on.'

'They're obsessed with the past in the Balkans, and their coverage of the present is alarming. They won't admit it shapes the future. I mean look at Iraq.'

Wiesel's voice had a gentle tone. 'This war,' he said, encouragingly, 'it's disturbing.'

I had to agree. That morning, NBC had fired a reporter, for suggesting there might be grounds to criticize America. Not that this encumbered the invasion, but it broke the unwritten rules of media conduct, and was therefore insupportably un-American.

'What I don't understand,' Wiesel said, 'is why they don't just get Hussein and then get out again.'

G's face scrunched up. 'Like how you mean?'

Wiesel's arms flailed up at his face as he spoke. 'Why don't they send in James Bond?' he said.

I stared at him blankly.

'What about your British S.A.S.?' he continued. 'Or Israeli commandos in American uniforms?'

None of us knew where to look.

'I'm really not so sure it's that simple,' I said.

According to Wiesel's foundation, 'when human dignity is in jeopardy, national borders and sensitivities become irrelevant'. Did this mean that someone else should invade America, or dispatch coalitions of the willing to occupied Palestine? I didn't ask. In any case, our host changed the subject.

'Tell me,' he said to my partners, 'what's new in the Balkans? Do people still think Karadzic a hero?'

'Sir,' G's head was wobbling off his neck, 'I think that all those criminals should be in a *jail*. Problem is that jail was where they *met*. That is where Serb Republic was born. The Karadzic start by stealing construction materials.'

Wiesel's forehead was now so puckered it looked like imploding. 'But are people any more ready to face the past?' he said. 'What hope is there of new leadership in Serbia?'

'Myself, I don't see leaders to excite me,' G said. 'We don't need any more stories that we victims. People there should think more for themselves. Politicians made hard consensus on issue of Kosovo, but they didn't make any on crime, on education, or on health system, anti-corruption, and everything else what means like *life*.'

J nodded assent. 'We can't change the past,' he said. 'We have to get on.'

I saw my opening. 'My friends are planning a special event this summer,' I said. 'They aim to unite young Serbs with their neighbors. There'll be several hundred thousand, all being well. Their aim is to change how Balkan people think.'

'This sounds important,' Wiesel said.

I opened my bag, and gave him one of our brochures. 'We have to build something different in that region,' I said. 'If we don't, they'll all stay trapped in vicious circles.'

'But what can I do?' Wiesel practically implored me.

The moment of truth had arrived. 'We were hoping,' I said, 'that you'd help us raise some money. We urgently need to find a million dollars.'

Wiesel fell back in his chair with a hand to his mouth. He was alone in his New York townhouse with three stoners. And they appeared to be shaking him down for wealthy Jews. We were lucky he didn't have snipers down the hallway, or a Mossad hotline hidden in a lampshade. Or maybe he did, and was merely playing for time.

'You know,' he said slowly, 'surely Gates can do something.'

He appeared to mean the richest man on Earth.

'Yes,' he sighed, regaining his composure, 'or maybe Wolfensohn, at the World Bank. I can ask.'

He flashed us a smile of dubious sincerity. 'Yes, yes, I can ask.'

'That's very good of you,' I said. 'When do you think you might have an answer?'

'Give me two, three weeks,' Wiesel said. 'Believe me, I will ask.'

Though we called him again and again, we never heard back.

FURY

Back in Belgrade, our hype machine was redlined into overdrive. We had to make the most of what we had. If journalists said the festival would be massive, we'd instigate a self-fulfilling prophecy. All we had to do was twist their arms.

To start with, we bought some time to sign more bands. Including their agent's cut, and tax on top, Sonic Youth would cost us $80,000. J had agreed to bankroll one more booking. But that was our lot, he insisted. We had to find corporate sponsors, or sell tickets. To assist with both, our launch would be a teaser, releasing line-ups for three smaller stages, and holding back the others for a month. Since the media couldn't be certain who was coming, they'd have to speculate. Or they could talk about musical genres and lesser-known artists. G called this process 'educating Serbs'. And for that we needed serious tabloid help.

We'd enlisted a German-owned redtop called *Blic* (as in Blitz), to talk us up to the largest audience in the country. This deal involved no money changing hands. To pay for our adverts in *Blic*, we gave them tickets, which they could raffle off to readers, or use themselves. We'd also agreed to display their logo every-where, from posters to our website, and they'd reciprocate by printing what we fed them. We'd even been assigned our own reporter, a jovial chap with a handlebar moustache.

To cover ourselves, we bought some extra newsprint. On four consecutive Saturdays in June, *Blic* would contain a four-page color supplement. Each of these would plug a different stage, to a quarter of a million readers and their friends. This was going to cost us €10,000, but the bill wouldn't have to be paid until after the festival, by which time we expected we'd be loaded.

For now, we were broke. Apart from our glorified loan from Zepter Insurance, and a few thousand euros from J, our only source of money had been Pepsi, which bought the right to sell drinks for €40,000. JAT had only sold us cheaper tickets. Like the rest of the brands that cluttered our commercials, they were 'partners', trading a service for exposure. At their most miserly, these deals exchanged our logos.

Undaunted by a skinflint swarm of distillers, brewers, juice makers, confectioners, supermarkets, and the appropriately improbable Rizla and Durex, we weren't giving up. Every day brought more demands for cash. When the snow disappeared in spring, the island flooded. What little we had in reserve was spent on clearing it, and trucking in sand. We had to cut costs. As seemed to be their specialty, our local partners helped us lean on everyone, and outsourced jobs to friends wherever possible.

All of our expenses were postponed, except for the unavoidable deposits. Billboards were booked on credit, as were print runs of posters and flyers. Everyone worked for free, including me, despite the contract promising twice my monthly *Times* wage. I added my outsize invoice to the pending pile, and employed a few DJs and clubbers to help with promotions. They agreed to draw their paychecks in July, though a small advance was offered for cigarettes. As our workforce swelled into dozens, most got by on similar terms, begging handfuls of crumpled dinars from B's leather bum bag. Each transaction was logged in a book with heavy pen-strokes.

To accommodate our crew and printed matter, we'd requisitioned offices in the Sava Centar: a glass-and-concrete bunker built in the Seventies, for a summit of Tito's main paymasters, the International Monetary Fund. It was painted hallucinatory brown and orange. The numbers on all the doors stretched psychedelically, as if wilting under ultraviolet lights, and an atmosphere as stuffy as the tenants. Everywhere was thick with cigarette smoke, which clung to leather sofas like low clouds. To A, the address was proof that he'd arrived. It was somewhere he could stare down his adversaries, and burden them with lardy *kajmak* sandwiches. Regular doses of caffeine offset the torpor, compounding the intensity of being there.

Technically, our rooms cost thousands of euros, but they'd come via our contract with the city, and we had no intention of paying any time soon. B and A turned the big one into a production office, installing two secretaries and a computer geek, who rigged up some battered PCs and a pair of landlines. Other minions hunched like idle coolies, disturbing the team that was meant to book flights for musicians. Behind this array of factotums was our boardroom, partitioned by a flimsy plywood wall. Interminable meetings raged across its table. I tried to avoid as many as I could.

Further down the hall was the marketing department. I sat in a corner, and barked out orders at my team. They mostly slumped in bucket seats and chain-smoked, staring at broken screens while swigging Coke. Without G's assistance to guide me, I felt powerless. I scarcely knew myself what we were doing, so I carried on making things up as I went along. I hoped this would coax some colleagues into helping. But the more they resisted, the less I indulged their foibles. I lurched between whining and tyranny. Neither worked.

We battled to set up a mailing list, then a database of broad-casters, to monitor how much airtime channels gave us. Although they spoke adequate English, it could seem as if we shared no common language. I knew they weren't the most ambitious Serbs, but I hadn't expected such contrary ambitions. They routinely ambled in late without having slept, and spent the day getting over the night before, preferring to talk to each other than reporters. Some just made me sweat by skiving off.

It didn't take them long to wear me down. I balanced this out by smoking extra hash, but I struggled to sneak out for joints without them noticing. Getting high didn't really help their productivity, whereas I felt incapacitated otherwise. I sympa-thized strongly with one artist, who'd written to demand 'at least two grams of high quality hashish or marijuana daily' as part of his contract. Personally, I'd have asked for twice as much.

As a promoter, it's your job to supply intoxicants. Local dealers could help, of course, but they scared me. Zemun's mob controlled an industrial trade in drugs, unhindered by the murder of Zoran Djindjic. To perpetuate Serbia's lawless isolation, which was how they'd all got rich in the first place, bosses paid off judges, lawyers, policemen, bankers, journalists, accountants and doctors, quite apart from politicians. There were endless rumors of ministers snorting coke, and the secret police had been caught with a stockpile of smack. But it didn't hold records of government underworld contacts. Maybe one clan was using the state to crush its rivals.

We'd be safer relying on imports from E, the sketchy London friend of G's. Whatever he charged, it would beat getting stung by Serbs. The local pills were as dirty as any in Scotland, and the only coke I'd tried was cut to shit. E had also promised us some hash, which I planned to distribute liberally to journalists, on whose coverage future investment would depend. That just left the crowd's heads to feed. And plans for that were coming together nicely.

Our debut tabloid supplement ripped off *Oz* magazine. Its cover was a tripped-out montage of Bob Dylan, with 'Blowin' in the Mind' etched on his sunglasses. The inside spread was cruder, but no less warped. A crawling geometric background leapt off the page, propelling readers into an article headlined 'Psychedelic freaks and the creation of modern youth culture', which charted the general story we would echo.

'Ever since people first learned to communicate,' it said, 'they have searched for ways to gather together and celebrate life. For many centuries, such gatherings were closely connected with organized religion. But in 1967, the first International Monterey Pop Festival started a new era.'

Onward it went into acid and the Summer of Love, 'a

children's crusade that would save America and the world from the ravages of war, and the inner anger that brings it forth, and materialism.' And so on, via Woodstock to the hippie trail, where a Hindu ascetic called Ganesh Baba had laughed in the face of pop-eyed foreign seekers.

'If young people insist on taking psychedelics because of their unease about the world, then they should come to India,' he advised, because 'Western knowledge could never satisfy the cosmic curiosity of the LSD initiate.'

Though utopia failed to materialize as hoped, 'a new scene sprang up, initially in Goa and the Spanish island of Ibiza, where many freaks had also settled. By 1987, they had attracted the attention of young people across Europe. A second "Summer of Love", two decades after the first, brought dance music to the masses.'

Now Belgrade would host the third, on Big War Island. No one could predict where it would lead. 'Revolution is not something fixed in ideology,' an underground icon was quoted as saying. 'It is a perpetual process embedded in the human spirit.'

The back page focused on reggae, which was said to have 'had a greater influence in the past two decades than almost any other genre of popular music.' The earliest DJs were Caribbean sound systems, 'comprising one record deck, a valve amp and the largest commercially available loudspeakers. Rival crews searched endlessly for obscure R&B records with which to "flop" the competition and upgraded their equipment to outdo each other with heavy bass.' This quest spawned stripped-down dubs, whose producers would 'add heavier drum and bass to previously recorded tracks, creating a style that has shaped modern dance music.'

The program followed:

Thursday 10 July	Friday 11 July	Saturday 12 July	Sunday 13 July
David Rodigan	Prince Alla	Jah Shaka	Iration Steppas
Anthony John	Asher Selector	Queen Omega	Zion Train
Gappy Crucial	Musclehead	Earl 16	Chukki Star
Coppa Face	Trevor Sax	Manasseh Hi-Fi	Starkey Banton
	Tippa Irie		Mafia and Fluxy

Few of the names meant anything to me. G assured me Serbs had better taste. They'd drawn on reggae's message and its rhythms. Rastas weren't just rebels, they were prophets, invoking a mythical world that would rise from Babylon. Their creed was one of conscious liberation. Everyone could seek freedom for himself.

Our second insert for *Blic* developed the theme. Punk was another influence, G said. Never mind *Anarchy in the UK*. Serbs understood that their system needed smashing. And as Joe Strummer cried, 'anyone can do it'. That spirit sustained resistance in the Nineties. Now it was at risk of being stifled by consumer aspirations.

'Open up!' screamed the cover, a pastiche of Jamie Reid's designs for the Sex Pistols. Drawing parallels with Serbia, it recalled the 'failed state' of Britain in 1977, when 'the government had to go begging to the International Monetary Fund,' while 'Queen Elizabeth II toured the country to wave at her subjects', after twenty-five long years of reigning over them. 'Disgusted by the deferential nationalism of their parents, and the general state of society, some young people protested.'

Though punk was 'a flamboyant failure', like the hippies, 'it changed everything,' by making culture more significant than politics, in the form of a 'revolution of everyday life'. Our goals were couched as a similar manifesto, which quoted the Romanian theorist Isidore Isou, who said creative work turned people into Gods. The young should assert autonomy, Isou said.

And 'we will call young any individual, no matter what his age, who does not yet coincide with his function, who acts and struggles to attain the realm of activity he truly desires, who fights to achieve a career in terms of a situation and a form of work other then that which has been planned for him.'

The message? 'Let youth cease to serve as a commodity.'

These slogans helped introduce the stage from Bristol, where musicians had set up businesses themselves, and improvised creative innovations. 'Funk and disco DJs and reggae sound systems inspired a generation of artists to experiment with new styles and take to the streets with home-made amps, PAs and soundboxes.' They evolved into crews like The Wild Bunch. Their heirs today were playing with computers.

Thursday 10 July	Friday 11 July	Saturday 12 July	Sunday 13 July
DJ Suv	Jody (Way Out West)	More Rockers	Drive By Special
Ben Parker, Aspects	Jean-Jacques	John Stapleton and	E-Z Rollers
& One Cut	Smoothie	Dr Moody	MC Jakes
Shendek & Kid	Detectives of	The Disco Brothers	DJ Zinc
Kamaya	Perspective	Dazee	Gerard
Queen B	DJ Hyper	Charlotte	Amo
Sarwarsays & Jah Whoosh	Starecase	Dan Heenan	Distorted Minds

Though G said Serbs would like their taste in music, many of these DJs were unheard of. Thankfully, they'd mastered self-promotion. Most sent us piles of CDs, of which we made hundreds of copies, all stamped with our logo. We farmed them out to journalists and broadcasters, along with profiles of every performer on the program. This process was repeated for the other stages, and biographies were posted on our website, which was finally nearing completion with two months to go.

The DJs on the London Xpress stage had more of a following. Their number included some locals who'd open each evening:

Thursday 10 July	Friday 11 July	Saturday 12 July	Sunday 13 July
Maurice Fulton	Simon Lee	Oslo Athletico	Carl Craig
Twitch & Wilkes	The Unabombers	Trulz & Robin	Kenny Hawkes
Dan Ghenacia	Justin Robertson	DJ Strangefruit	Adam Goldstone
Ivan Smagghe	Only Child	Rune Lindbaek	Pete Z
Ewan Pearson	Miles Holloway &	Idjut Boys	Luke Howard
Slavka	Elliot Eastwick	G-Ha (Skansen)	Boza Podunavac
	Rade Banyan	DJ Lale	

Belgrade bands would also appear on the main stage, which was programmed except for the headliners, who would stay under wraps until we'd booked them all:

Thursday 10 July	Friday 11 July	Saturday 12 July	Sunday 13 July
Phil Hartnoll (Orbital)	Matthew Herbert	Pressure Drop	Derrick May
Todd Terry	Luomo	Boozoo Bajou	Luke Slater
Norken	Thomas Brinkmann	J Majik	Billy Nasty
The Bays	Da Lata	Go Future	Marko Nastic
Darkwood Dub	Tubacin	Eyesburn	Bushcraft
			Partibrejkers

On May 9, we faced the press. They asked few questions and waltzed off with their freebies. We seemed to have got the benefit of the doubt. That morning's *Blic* had set the tone for coverage. 'At last, Belgrade has a world-class festival,' our reporter wrote, regurgitating the press release we'd leaked him. His story was headlined 'Musical Island' and it spoke of 'several hundred thousand people, on ten hectares of pristine nature', which would be 'brimming with positive energy and good vibrations'.

The backlash followed shortly after. When EXIT named their line-up, oldies were prominent: the Rollins Band, Stereo MCs and Soul II Soul. The DJs were similar: Pete Tong and Jeff Mills, alongside established favorites, Roni Size and Darren Emerson.

But two acts stood out: Tricky, a walking epitome of Bristol, and Moloko, who were worryingly popular. So popular, in fact, that G tried to book them. We'd been gazumped.

At the end of the EXIT launch, I approached the founders. We'd not spoken in nearly a year, since I profiled their event. They appeared to assume we were enemies. Each sat either side of me on a barstool, puffing out their chests. The one with the chubby cheeks did all the talking, while his lanky partner acted like a muscleman, arms folded and his head cocked at an angle. Both looked conceited.

Recriminations started right away. 'Why did you decide to make this trouble?'

'I don't think we need any trouble,' I replied.

'Don't lie to me!' He jutted out his chin. I itched to smack it. 'You've been using our materials against us.'

I shrugged. 'Which materials?'

The cherub's laugh was as humorless as a Bond villain's. 'Why do you help that traitor to attack us?'

I guessed he meant G. 'Look, whatever went wrong between you is nothing to do with me.'

He jabbed a finger at my chest. 'You know, I think you made it your problem.'

'Take it easy, eh?' I pushed him back. 'I don't know why you want problems. Why don't we try to help each other? Let's show how competition can be healthy.'

He laughed again equally drily, looking torn between tears and giving me a head-butt. 'Don't you understand *anything* about karma?' he sneered.

'Yes,' I seethed. 'It's about *everything*. Including your attitude.'

He glanced at his scowling partner. They stood to leave.

'Don't forget you started this,' he hissed.

To G, all talk of compromise was madness. Apart from anything else, it would have been pointless: we were grappling with forces mightier than EXIT.

'You know that you were talking just to monkeys?' he said, pacing around the Sava Centar patio. 'That tune they dance is coming straight from weasels.'

I blocked his path and passed the joint I'd been smoking. 'Listen,' I said. 'It doesn't really matter who's behind them. I still think we should try making peace.'

The sun was slowly setting and we were alone. I'd scarcely seen my partner in weeks. He'd been preoccupied with work preparing the island.

'I thought you understand Balkans better than that,' G scoffed. 'You can judge their state of mind by whole campaign. I don't think they care about the music, man. They would listen to tick-tack from oil pumps if would pay.'

EXIT's marketing was certainly distinctive. Their logo echoed the Ministry of Sound: a disco ball portcullis, framed by a wreath. And the TV ads were like Persil cut with Coke: all saturated shots of pretty poseurs, running round and kissing in slow motion. The event had been renamed the 'State of EXIT', and its posters resembled a flag with neon stripes. Flyers took the form of passports, issued by 'a metacountry of positive energy, communication, optimism, love and oneness', and welcoming those who 'are open to the different cultures and also want to make the world a better place.' They'd even got a deal with MTV, via the partnership both shared with B92, which had just won a special 'Free Your Mind' prize. Commercially, EXIT was giving us a pasting.

'Surely there's still something we can do?' I asked. 'What about a press conference saying we support each other?'

I reclined on a sun lounger. The temperature was stifling at dusk. By day, it was close to forty degrees in the shade. Through a halo of smoke, my partner shook his head.

'Those guys did choose their path already,' he said. 'I don't think they realize what is happening. They have ass on one hot blade, just like Djindjic. You know division of what foreigners want us to be from what we are is getting deeper. Only obedience here is when dirty money needs splitting. No empire made Balkans feasible in history. I hope in future won't be resolved with ultra-violence.'

'They're certainly pretty angry with us,' I said. 'They tried to give me a lecture about karma.'

G snorted loudly. 'Their connection with knowledge of karma is same as knowledge of Serbian yob on abstract art. Somehow brings picture of cocaine, *burek* and pig's head together. Nothing they have to mind about their own karma, since it is controlled by somebody else.'

'Maybe. But it doesn't stop them getting what they want.'

My partner stepped closer. 'How you mean?'

'Well, they beat us to booking Moloko, and DJ Marky.' It bugged me to have to find this out from EXIT. I was starting to feel peripheral to plans. Having pictured myself at the heart of operations, the suggestion I might not be was upsetting.

G drilled me back in my deckchair with his stare. 'You think I couldn't get them if I want them?'

I said nothing.

'Oh man!' His sigh of deflation lasted seconds. Then he exploded. 'Who book whole fucking program, huh?' he roared. 'You think that you can do that shit yourself? Without me you have nothing here, like nothing.'

I shuddered, but my partner's face was smiling. It was almost as if nothing happened, like a snarl from a dog asserting its supremacy. G passed back the joint. It was down to the roach.

'You know, we both can get choleric,' he said. 'I think is better you smoke less here in office.'

I tossed the butt. He touched my knee. 'S'aright man,' he said. 'You lose your heart. It will return. And today I did confirm for us Morcheeba, which is kinda like Moloko, only bigger. We put on Friday after Matthew Herbert band. In London they would charge you fifty pounds. And for Thursday night they offer me De Phazz. You know, that jazzy groove what discos play? Trust me, we are stronger now for sure.'

I took a deep breath. 'I'm worried,' I said. 'What if no one's got money to spend after EXIT?'

G joined his palms in front of his chest. 'We offer to them free, like extra day. Lot of guys would do for me as favor. We put Organic Grooves from New York with gypsy band, and Fun-Da-Mental with Mighty Zulu Nation. It can be spiritual message, big melt of East and West. We float candles down in Danube man, whatever. I'm telling you will be perfect, very positive. Maybe hundred thousand people just for that.'

'Sounds great,' I said. 'At least we'd sell some drinks. When do you think we should announce it?'

My partner smiled. 'It can be weapon of distraction at last minute. We show how all here share in gifts. Belgrade is not just city of the hipsters, man. Some of them have beauty on inside too. We should value that. I think you gonna feel it.'

Surprisingly, not all was lost with the tourist trade. Thanks to a friend in London, *The Independent* named us one of the '50 Best Summer Festivals' of 2003, along with the Edinburgh Fringe, the Pamplona bull-run, and the likes of Glastonbury, Roskilde and Zurich's Street Parade. We clocked in at number 23, behind the Spanish attractions of Sonar and Benicassim, but well ahead of WOMAD and T in the Park.

ECHO was called 'a music festival with a mission', which was to 'inspire and entertain young people across the Balkans, attract foreign investment and help Belgrade rebuild a battered international reputation. The theme is contemporary global music, so forget Coldplay and take a chance.' There'd be 'more than 250,000 fun-starved punters.' And don't forget that pints cost 40p.

Our website also helped to drum up interest. To spread the

word, we'd translated it into German, and sold ourselves as rivals to the biggest event in Europe, which was due to take place in Berlin the same weekend. *'Love Parade? Nein Danke...'* said our advert in *Festival Guide*, remixing an old anti-nuclear slogan.

The late spring heat brought other daft ideas, including a travel guide to Belgrade by my colleagues, whose insights I stripped from the website as soon as I read them. Their 'short slang course' was especially infuriating, teaching words for a 'specific stadium of your body and spirit when even your brain got day off.' Such 'thinkless fun' was painfully familiar, defined as: 'when you only think how to make your day doing nothing but spending your time in some cool place with your friends.'

As they'd personally proved, 'it is really hard to find one metropolis in the world with so many cafes, bars, clubs... every moment... every morning... every day... every evening... all the time... brimming with people... as if every day is Friday or Saturday, or as if everybody has a DAY OFF.' And since they all 'make a theatre performance out of life,' then 'the only way to get in the game is to surrender!'

Not while I'm in charge you lazy bastards! Get back to work.

The island was opened for business on June 6. To mark the occasion, there'd been talk of chartering hot air balloons and an airship, and parading pretty girls in bikinis, all bearing banners with our logo. Instead, we marched some elephants to the beach.

Reuters called this 'invoking the spirit of Hannibal the Conqueror,' to 'inaugurate an army pontoon bridge' and 'reunify Serbian youth culture with the rest of Europe'.

The 300-meter crossing looked impressive. Reuters also sent a TV crew, whose footage was relayed around the world, along with a grandiose introduction. 'Unlike the terrifying war elephants in the ancient armies of Carthage, Rome and Greece, when the Danube marked the edge of empires, four placid jumbos from a circus lumbered happily over the river squirting water on their Russian girl riders.'

Needless to say, *The New York Times* ignored us. But they did print something else that caught my eye, a front-page story headlined: 'Times Reporter Who Resigned Leaves Long Trail of Deception'. Reading this had given me a jolt.

'A staff reporter for *The New York Times* committed frequent acts of journalistic fraud while covering significant news events in recent months, an investigation by *Times* journalists has found. The widespread fabrication and plagiarism represent a profound betrayal of trust and a low point in the 152-year history of the newspaper.'

Yikes!

This charlatan had 'fabricated comments. He concocted scenes. He lifted material from other newspapers and wire services. He selected details from photographs to create the impression he had been somewhere or seen someone, when he had not.'

His name was Jayson Blair, and he was one year my junior. I hoped to read he'd done it as a protest, but he seemed to have been absorbed in his own illusions. I recognized the symptoms in myself, as did the psychiatrist who wrote *Rebel Without A Cause*.

'The psychopath,' he said, 'like the child, cannot delay the pleasures of gratification.' An achievement junkie 'cannot wait upon the development of prestige in society: his egotistic ambitions lead him to jump into the headlines by daring performances.'

Blic eventually profiled me in a centerfold, which dominated showbiz news that day. The headline said: 'I Came For The Politics And Stayed For The Music.' The smallest of my pictures was four times the size of Robbie Williams, and twice as big as a shot of Nicole Kidman. The columnist asked if I'd like to marry a Serb. 'Perhaps,' I said, 'if someone fancies an adventure.' No one called, except a *Blic* reporter.

Our relationship hit trouble in mid-June. After printing our first two supplements, the editor of *Blic* spiked the third, accusing us of promoting illegal drugs. Ironically, this issue was ambiguous. The cover depicted a roomful of wasted teenagers, cribbed from *The Face*. In place of its masthead were the words 'No Logo?' A vomiting kid in the middle was masked with a giant yellow smiley acid house face.

Inside, an essay on 'Party politics and the techno revolution' explained how Britain helped drug-fuelled corporate clubs get rich. 'Bored, cynical and alienated from each other in compartmentalized urban lives,' it said, 'millions of people around the world seek a sense of togetherness by taking ecstasy every week.'

Meanwhile, radicals fought government crackdowns on raves and 'used the Internet to coordinate simultaneous illegal street parties.' Their rallying cry became 'Reclaim the streets!' because 'the streets where daily life is endured, suffered and eroded, and where power is confronted and fought, must be turned into the domain where daily life is enjoyed, created and nourished.'

That wasn't what bothered *Blic*, any more than the comment: 'I never take drugs. My drug is myself.'

Some of the offending lines came from *The Economist*, that international bastion of subversion. 'If it is not acceptable to take a drug with the awkward name of 3,4-methylenedioxymethamphetamine (better known as MDMA, and even better known as ecstasy) to make you feel happy when you just want to have fun,' the magazine asked in an editorial, 'why is it acceptable to take the anti-depressant fluoxetine (better known as Prozac) to make you feel happy if you are not actually clinically depressed?'

There followed a less nuanced view from Sasha Shulgin, a research chemist and ecstasy evangelist. 'Everyone must get to experience a profound state like this,' he'd written, in *Phenethylamines I Have Known And Loved*. 'I am totally peaceful. I have lived all my life to get here and I feel I have come home. I am complete.'

Blic had refused to print a bowdlerized version, which

replaced the *Economist* quotes with a Dutch government warning on 'The Dangers of Ecstasy', and deleted Shulgin's suggestion that 'everyone' try it. Incensed, I stormed the editor's office, and bawled him out about breaching legal contracts. This only dug his heels in even harder: he pulped our final supplement as well.

That one would have tied the strands together, addressing a quoted challenge from Jean Baudrillard. 'It is always the same,' he was left to mumble at the ether. 'Once you are liberated, you are forced to ask who you are.' Our musings on living as samplers were scrapped, along with thoughts on the nature of change. It mattered not. The visions had crystallized. We'd just have to make them manifest ourselves.

If Serbs don't drive you mad, you must be crazy. For much of the past three months, I'd been cloistered in tower blocks, sweating it out with cabals of bedroom hackers. Each of these cliques had countless hangers-on, and some of them had very strange ideas. One said: 'I am King. I have rights for Disney on all Macedonia.' Amazingly, they knew what they were doing. They found me animators, web developers, a sound engineer, and a video editor, all of them working from home on cracked pro software.

Though the process of creation could be serpentine, I'd got used to sitting for days with our graphic designer, who described his usual temperament as 'nervous'. Since the meaning of this was garbled in translation, I dreaded to think what passed for 'fucking dyspeptic'. Mostly, he repressed his raging temper, and confined himself to ignoring my instructions. Asked why, he'd plead incomprehension, despite discussing them at length. 'Sorry for my Tarzan English,' he'd grunt, while revising the project in hand to suit his tastes. Eventually, after a bust-up, I'd get what I asked for. 'Tell me,' he'd say, without irony, 'why you don't just tell me what you want?'

A stubborn logic permeated everything. But if you didn't mind trying to swim through wet cement, it felt almost navigable. When I said as much to G, this cracked him up.

'You know Dario Argento,' he said, 'that Italian horror director? Well, he went to get award here, some award they figure out for him, and when he came, he said thank you Serbs, you been inspiration. And there was applause. Like national pride on level of total stupidity.'

Serbian skin was thick, yet acutely sensitive. This made for a kind of misguided self-awareness: the more perverse and self-defeating people's actions, the clearer their self-interest and integrity. No amount of reasoning could shake this. Everything was trumped by getting one's way, no matter where that might have led.

Our design procedure spat out routine examples. Apart from the logo, which went on everything, ECHO's public face changed all the time, reflecting whatever we'd copied from elsewhere. When an eagle-eyed critic saw flower-power motifs in our adverts (the words 'poster show' were written in psychedelic petals), we were duly renamed 'the copy paste festival'.

In response, our local partners got a bit 'nervous', telling G to tell me to stop messing them about. They demanded we bring back the billboards we began with. These had featured animated birds, on a turntable sliced from a tree trunk, with a slab of mossy stone as its base and a needle supplied by a bent thorny twig. TV adverts urbanized the theme. Birds were shown rearing chicks in nests of headphones; they frolicked round some speakers in a tree stump; and danced on a branch to tweeters stashed in flower buds, before a woofer in an apple blew them off.

It was all very cute, I agreed, but it didn't say much.

For the final campaign, I commissioned different posters. The designer seemed to understand the brief, to embody the slogan: 'life is an illusion, choose a nice one'. But his images looked dreadfully confused. When our partners saw them, they summoned the office geek, and ordered him to draw up a page of birds, flanked by boastful text and a bottle of Pepsi. When I found this on a printer I went mental. They ignored me.

I pleaded with the designer to try again. He responded a couple of hours before our deadline. His posters had birds, a musical tree stump, and psychedelic checkerboards as a backdrop, with the line-up superimposed in bold text. The design for each day had a different colored theme: blue for the opening evening with De Phazz, red for Morcheeba, green for Burning Spear, and black for the Sunday finale of Sonic Youth.

There was only one problem. He didn't adjust the contrast on the background, so the version that went to be printed was illegible. From a distance, all you could see were color spirals. The designer and the printer hadn't been paid yet, and neither bothered with checking proofs. The error went undetected until delivery, saddling us with thousands of useless eyesores. We plastered them everywhere.

All hopes of attracting a crowd now depended on television. So far, we'd barely got started, airing a few cheap spots on low rotation. A three-week blitz was planned for the end of June, and for that we had to find a loyal partner. We couldn't afford to buy airtime for our adverts. But we did have a time-honored tool for managing media: control of access. Whoever met our demands could broadcast the festival.

The logical channel to work with was Pink. As garish as its name suggested, it had the biggest national audience, and a regional network of satellite sister stations. Each of them followed the formula: movies, music, vapid soaps and gossip, interspersed with horoscopes and football. Founded by a friend of Milosevic's wife, Pink was more escapist than a mouthpiece. Its political line was: 'fuck politics, watch this!' Most of the budget was blown on imported shows, so its suits were as hungry for content as cash-strapped rivals. If we shot our own tapes, they'd screen them every day.

It was ugly, but alternatives were scarce. B92 worked with

EXIT, and state-run RTS had tried to screw us, by denying us the right to run ads on other channels. G had met a man he called 'God of all media minutes', who'd informed him: 'my dick aches for your money, come with us.'

After weeks of talks with Pink, we were ready to sign. They'd demanded a studio on the island, a twelve-hour embargo on all interviews, and exclusive access to artists at the airport. In exchange, they offered five daily appearances on the 'City' show, a slot on the weekday 'Morning Program', a comprehensive schedule for our adverts, and a crawling 'Chyron' ticker of festival news. All we had to do was send it in.

At the last, our local partners intervened. A had been trying to seal a rival deal, with an oligarch called Bogoljub Karic, who ran BKTV and the Mobtel cellphone network. Karic's conditions weren't appealing, and I thought we'd already told him to forget it. But A appeared evangelically in favor: BK would 'protect the festival', he said.

Quite what that meant in this context was beyond me. And when he told us they'd handle ticket sales, I flipped. G and I had spent months arranging payments through the bank. If people bought tickets at kiosks selling Mobtel top-ups, how would their cash be sent to our account? The system could be easily abused.

When I tried to make this clear, the others shrugged. G's attempts to translate struck me as feeble. He sat slumped in his chair in the boardroom looking hangdog. His mind these days was constantly elsewhere, letting business take care of itself while he worked on the island. It seemed that no one kept an eye on the bigger picture.

'Sta kaze?' A's refrain got up my nose. As in 'what's that English wanker saying now?' He sat imperious as a gypsy king across from me. Though he still wore shades, he'd ditched the winter trench-coat look, in favor of toweling t-shirts and a sunhat. He'd also bought a plastic cellphone earpiece, with which he fiddled as if in fear of missing calls. Leaning back in his chair, he sucked his pasty cheeks. He looked pretty mean.

I shouted regardless. 'Why do we waste our time making plans if you ignore them? It's the same as it was with design. If you don't like what we're doing, why not discuss it? I thought we were partners.'

'Please,' B drawled in English, his weighty physique bearing down from my left. 'Tell to your designer, he must understand what want sponsors...'

'*My* designer?' I shot him an angry look. 'He works for *all* of us.'

A's muttered comments weren't translated. All I caught was a Serbian word for penis.

'Fuck you!' I roared, half hoarse with indignation. 'If anyone here's a dick, you cunt, it's you! Why are you always trying to undermine us? What's in it for you?'

A's doughy face spawned a smirk. He leaned forward, yelling at G: 'You tell your guy to stop provocations.'

The next few seconds unfurled slowly. Decades of pent-up frustration burned through my bloodstream, and surged towards A's piggy little eyeballs. I no longer cared who he was, or what he was up to. I only knew the bastard was in range. I lunged across the table at his cheekbone. My right hand closed the gap and came up short.

'You want to see real provocations, fucking try me!' The volume came straight from my bowels and flew up my torso, rippling through the tip of an outstretched finger. I shimmered with a thin metallic sheen, a heroic shield of self-destructive stubbornness, known to bulletproof Serbian brains as *inat*. G grabbed my other arm and yanked me outside. I was shaking. I'm so scared of confrontation I incite it.

'What you think you're doing?' my partner said. 'You should observe yourself, can't you see that guy is pussy? I dunno if you notice man, but Serbs don't kill Americans or Brits. Most do like Milosevic, making drama for attention then give up. Others here are type you shouldn't mess with. The ones what have big balls and little brains.'

Little wonder Serbs got under my skin. They were there in the first place. The outside world reflects what lies within. Consider Milosevic. His brinksmanship owed plenty to his wife, who rammed a pole up his small-town crack and made him a figurehead. Exploiting her party contacts, his passive-aggressive instincts seized on nationalism. This urge to self-destruct ran in the family. His dad had blown his brains out with a shotgun, and his mum was found hanging from a light fitting in the living room.

My childhood was less anguished, and it tortured me. I was spoiled to atone for my mother's unhappy upbringing. No one could accuse *her* of neglect. I might even prove myself worthy of her stepfather, who was crippled in World War I and became mayor of Brighton. Though I relished her attention, it unsettled me. I couldn't be as good as implied, but I wanted the world to think so nonetheless. When it didn't, I misbehaved, and thought I had the charm to get away with it. My mum's response was a guilt trip. 'You throw it all back in my face,' she'd sob. I pretended to be what she liked, while I did as I pleased. The choice was self-denial or rebellion. She disagreed. 'Everything would be fine,' she said, 'if only you could understand I need to be needed.'

My father was mostly preoccupied with work, and usually too meek to impose much discipline. When he did, it felt entirely out of order, like the time I got punched on our doorstep, aged fifteen. A younger boy had mocked me for wearing a grammar school blazer. When I told him to go and get fucked, he said he'd set his older brother on me. 'Send him down,' I swaggered. So he did. My father found us grappling in the porch, and broke it up. Hauling me indoors, he told my attacker and his sidekicks to scram. 'What the *fuck*?' I screamed, incensed. 'Either go out there and *do* something, or let me chin the cunt.' My dad said: 'Don't let me hear you use that language again.'

Another teenage beating put me in hospital. Though my injuries were slight, they left me paranoid. This didn't resolve my need to start a fight. People in authority came off worst, as they had since I tackled my junior school headmaster. We were playing American football in the playground. He was quarterback. In his urge to be one of the boys, he'd given the best positions to his favorites, and told me I was too podgy for a running back. So I decked him, hopped the fence and ran away.

I'd been running all my life when I'd had my fill. But however far I went, I still felt stuck. None of the approval I longed for made me happy. Rejecting it was worse: I felt a fraud. And I feared that in my heart I was a coward. No matter who got in our way, I wouldn't stand for it. This time, I was damned if I'd run from anything.

Most people want someone else to solve their problems. But if anyone offers to help you, ask who benefits. When it's the government, believe them at your peril.

Our choice of birds as mascots proved imprudent. Their feathered cousins made much bigger headlines. Ornithologists said our festival would kill them. Endangered species lived in the island's marshes, which the city's inhabitants poisoned with pollution. The Penduline Tit was especially at risk: amplified music could blast it from the sky.

This smear campaign had been flogged along for weeks. Patriots joined in the chorus; we were threatening Serbian morals, as well as the wetlands. As July drew near, the babble got much louder. Some reports said ECHO might be banned. That was when we heard from the new prime minister. His adviser on ecology asked to meet us.

Although he'd trained as a biologist, this aide was better known in other fields. Srdja Popovic was the 'ideological commissar' of Otpor; the protest group that helped bring down

Milosevic. Over a one-hour chat, which dwelled on our short-comings, Popovic explained what he could do. He agreed we'd been maligned, but blamed us too. For emphasis, he held up a pack of rolling papers. Their yellow cardboard shell said: 'Bristol Stage'. Thousands had been handed out as flyers.

His weasel words and appearance both enraged me. When I asked him to name our enemies, he ignored me. Addressing G, he said we could hire his Otpor network, to promote us. I wasn't aware it still existed. Some of the movement's founders had gone into politics, or already been established players like Popovic. Others had set up law firms and consultancies. Getting rich seemed the last ideal of their crusade.

We were told to print up badges adorned with birds, along with the slogan 'my island'. These trinkets could be sold to raise money for charity. He also agreed to lend us his assistant, who'd help us access media outside Belgrade. She promptly tried to usurp my whole department. Last, but by no means least, Popovic said he'd go on state TV, and conduct a staged debate with environmentalists. He promised to say that ECHO had his blessing. The show eventually aired on the first night of EXIT, when most of our target audience was elsewhere.

G took all these mishaps philosophically. 'In Serbia is not option to be neutral,' he said. 'Always there is somewhere Mr Big. But if Otpor and EXIT and B92 did join to sleazy government, we also have friends in shadows we can call.'

Diplomacy is business by other means. Reporters aren't too welcome on the embassy circuit, but investors get whisked through the doors for special treatment. Trade is the favored way of greasing palms. That's why the British and the Dutch built empires with an East India Company. Not much has changed. While the Foreign Office wrings hands about dictators, another department stamps chits to sell them weapons. Britain's commercial arsenal depends on it. Hence the wily Blair-era talk about 'foreign policy with an ethical dimension', not the 'ethical foreign policy' dreamed up by journalists.

Our Man in Belgrade was Charles Crawford, whose mind was already drifting to his next posting. Some of his staff had more invested locally. One owned a bar. Another was said to sell help with getting visas. Their bosses didn't set the best example. In the Nineties, they cut themselves in on the billion-dollar privatization of Telekom Srbija, lifting sanctions to enrich the old regime. When the Serbian opposition took power, it cancelled the deal, saying Britain helped swell Milosevic's war chest.

The embassy even landed us a windfall. When bills started piling up at the end of June, a gangster offered G a short-term loan. Terms for non-repayment were unclear, but we didn't have a lot of better offers. Our bank appeared to treat us as a credit risk, and our partner in New York wouldn't send more cash. As long as the festival happened, we'd have money, but bands would only perform if we paid them first. 'Worst thing is being caught between extremes,' G said. 'It is better some time to take the extreme.'

We were saved by invitations to a garden party, which was held in celebration of the Queen. A man in a cream linen suit made introductions. Among others who said they could help was a gin-soaked expat, who arranged a guarantee with Turkish bankers. Two days later, they sent us a contract typed in capitals, providing for up to €275,000. This was funneled via an oil trading company, and the large print promised they'd pay us: 'WITHOUT ANY OBJECTION OF ENTERING INTO AN ARGUMENT AND WITHOUT ANY PREVIOUS NOTICE OF DISHONOR.'

Her Majesty's Ambassador agreed to be interviewed. Fetching my camera, I framed him by a pot plant on the windowsill, and focused on his garish checkered tie. In the edit suite, we added extra color. The version for Pink featured *God Save the Queen*, performed by the Sex Pistols. A caption flashed up in ripped newsprint, announcing: 'Never Mind The Bollocks... Here's The ECHO Festival.'

Crawford began with diplomatic comments. 'British creativity and design and music are a big export sector,' he said. 'One doesn't like to talk about these things in a purely commercial sense but it's an important part of cultural life that we're actually very strong at. And we're good at both the substance - British music is popular around the world - and we're also very good at organizing these kinds of events.'

As for ECHO itself, he said: 'we hope something like this can develop and keep going on for many years.' That got him going on the tough stuff. 'We talk about this being a British export, but the capacity to host an event like this is a Serbian export because it's exporting Serbia's organizational potential, it's exporting Belgrade as a place people enjoy coming to and having a good time and it's exporting a positive image of Serbia. Now I hope the authorities here are going to see the value of this.'

We zeroed in on Crawford's bulging eyes.

'There is a bit of a problem here frankly, and you see it in lots of areas, of people somehow giving the impression that if other people are being successful they want to stop them. They don't see that if other people are successful it helps create a context in which success leads to more success for everybody.'

As for the drama about birds, he said: 'if Belgrade has more money coming in because of festivals like this, it'll be much better placed to deal with horrendous environmental problems in this city such as the rubbish dump, the pollution and all sorts of other things that are going on which are far more damaging to Belgrade and the region than this festival conceivably could be.'

To end on a high, we interviewed the trade attaché. With blue sleeves rolled above his elbows, he looked like a prison warder crossed with a mechanic. One hand was placed on the table, propping him up. The other gestured wildly as he spoke. Thanks to my cheap plastic tripod, the shot was off-balance. The effect was a hint of early MTV.

'Unless you've been to a big British festival,' he beamed, 'you've not been to anything quite like this. Just go spend a few days, just be yourself, be a bit free, enjoy yourself, it'll be great. We'll see you there. Cheers!'

He faded to black with a wink, and we hoped for the best.

DECEIT

Unless you're on TV, you don't exist. And to make it there, you can't be who you are. To ensure we didn't clash with other output, Pink had insisted we hire a new producer, a woman who'd worked for networks in America. Her assessment of the remit was depressing. 'The in-crowd aren't buying the message,' she said. 'We need something much more like EXIT. Their adverts say be like these guys, and have fun.'

So did ours, after a fashion. My favorite was a splurge of surrealism, lifted from my partner's art film archive. Beneath a hand-painted collage of subdividing cells, we flashed up shots of Woodstock, Glastonbury and the Love Parade, before a toolbox took aim at an empty human head. Hammers flew round the skull, chased by pliers, a wrench, a handsaw and a pickaxe. To scenes of graffiti, the soundtrack crooned: 'Did your mama tell you... a place, a place, a place?' Then we cut to the view from a cave above a canyon, spraying ravers with some dirty drum and bass. A sunrise filled the screen as it faded out. For clarity, we added a cinematic letterbox, listing names of the headline artists in the black bits, plus details of ticket prices, outlets and our website.

This was deemed a travesty of marketing.

Instead, our producer told us to speak to 'the in-crowd'. Emptying her mobile of models, actors and media hangers-on, she set about preparing a party. If we filmed them all in front of her magic 'blue screen', we could superimpose their bodies on 'great visuals', she said. She promised to strive for an 'understated' look, 'with lights, makeup, styling and nice clothes.' The 'laid back and friendly' vibe would look 'cool'.

It was vile. Offset by an animation of our logo, one of these starlets rattled out her lines. 'Summer in the city, crowds, awful,' she mewled. Then her rictus grin raised an eyebrow at the camera. 'Lido!' she yelped. 'Sand, water, music!' And to round it off, she nodded and squealed: 'Come to Echo!' She might as well have been wailing: 'You can come in me if you want, I have a *spirala!*'

Suggestions got significantly ghastlier. Pink had assigned us two Barbies named Ivana, one of whom had a show called 'Pleased to Meet You.' Both could be shot in bikinis in a pool, and the underwater background swapped for music videos. With some splashing about and a voice track added later, viewers would see an Ivana immersed in the program. I gagged, and swallowed the acid in my throat: when you're fighting for survival anything goes.

Our producer made films on all the acts she recognized, including bands and DJs from Belgrade. Another six showcased celebrities, talking up the island. The final few I agreed to make myself: one on each of our three smaller stages, a pitch for the free fifth day, and a pair of conceptual stories; one on the influence of reggae, and the other on links between Bristol and Belgrade.

The former's anarcho-chemicalists were tireless. To augment their stash of CDs, they'd also sent a videotape of interviews, shot by a DJ who'd been to Serbia twice before. 'The vibe I felt out there was just amazing,' he enthused, recalling a couple of sets in grungy clubs. 'We gotta be part of it, and see if we can, you know, pull it forward.'

One of his friends seemed equally excited. 'It looks wicked!' he said of our website, his heart at risk of bursting through the screen. 'Yeah, we'll go do it!'

Another was less restrained in his enthusiasm. 'Best part of the year innit, summer?' he giggled. 'Outdoors, stayin' up all night, doing... whatevers.'

The stage's promoter injected a dose of gravity. 'Musicians in Bristol through their own efforts have managed to create their own infrastructure and their own business,' she said. 'They're able to earn a living, sometimes meager but sometimes enough, through being DJs, producing CDs, producing records.'

Her words were mixed with footage of a bedroom, which was strewn with laundry and ashtrays, and turntables spinning a twelve-inch labeled *Firing Line*. It looked like half the flats I spent my time in, an affinity not lost on the promoter, who'd already been in Serbia for weeks. She loved the place and loathed it with equal vehemence.

'There is definitely a connection,' she said. 'People used to say everybody's just too stoned in Bristol to do anything, and then the dance scene happened. All they need here is infrastructure. It'll need to be Serbian, which will be *crazy*. But we want to say we've done it, you can do it too. Don't be downtrodden. Do it. It is possible.'

There were other ways to get the message out. A friend was shooting a documentary, which he'd pitched to Channel 4 back in London. To be commissioned, it would need dramatic twists, and I'd promised him he'd find these in abundance. On the plane, he bragged to a stewardess that he was making 'the Spinal Tap of the Baltics'. The Bristol stage promoter overheard him, and blocked all media access to her entourage.

Plans unraveled as fast as we could make them. We urgently needed lieutenants to see them through, but like typical Balkan insurgents, we were all commanders. Everyone gave orders. No one listened. We were *Tamagotchi* masters training pit bulls.

Everything hinged on revenue from tickets, yet we'd given away more to the media than we'd sold. We'd also scrapped plans to sell them via the post office, which asked for more commission than seemed fair. Our exclusive agent was a local record shop, with a dozen affiliated stores outside Belgrade. And the closest we got to travel deals were some flyers we made touting beds in student dorm rooms. As G liked to say of our hapless local partners, we 'couldn't even organize pudding in own kitchen.'

Meanwhile, someone hired a thousand staff. With a few days to go, the most capable joined G's hosting group for artists, and occupied our command post by the island, on the choicest slab of concrete in Zemun.

When it opened in 1969, the Hotel Jugoslavija earned five stars. The atrium bar was worthy of a Bond film, with a staircase spiraling up to our mezzanine quarters, and a ceiling like a stretched expanse of disco ball. But the building hadn't recovered from being bombed, on the night that NATO blew up the Chinese embassy. Both were allegedly part of the Serbian war machine, in the hotel's case because its casino was co-owned by Arkan, with security provided by paramilitaries. Four years later, the rooms next to ours were still full of rubble. They also had no ceiling, which made them a perfect place to skulk and smoke a joint. Though the lobby was full of police on the hunt for degenerates, they couldn't be bothered to haul themselves upstairs.

In the smallest of our trio of suites, my partner's 'guest service' team drowned in printouts. They swung off the walls and littered half the floor, listing travel itineraries thwarted by events, which were hectically renegotiated hourly. G juggled multiple phones, and boomed at people far from Balkan mayhem. I didn't bother asking what was up. By the time he replied, there'd be something else already.

'They will understand,' he kept shouting down the line, 'this is airline bringing people to Serbia. They need that paper. In London no one understand that. You just bring it.' After the briefest pause, he butted in and grunted. 'I don't have time for that now. I'm gonna call you on this number tomorrow... Thanks, I appreciate it.'

His lips swelled with tiredness, like his eyeballs. He claimed to be able to thrive on three hours' sleep. For the coming few days, he'd be lucky to get much more.

'Bitch told me she don't have authorization,' he screamed,

dropping his phone. 'These assholes I am gonna fucking sue them. We have case! They wanna ruin gig...'

Then he noticed our documentary crew and laughed. 'We have fucked up gig,' he told the camera, 'but we already knew that. Welcome to Serbia!'

The final blast of promotion was frenetic: TV became my life for several weeks. Once Pink had screened our tapes, we gave them to rivals, and recruited a new PR girl to get more coverage. She was pretty, young and eloquent in English, which pissed off the rest of my team, who'd been ordered to expose themselves relentlessly.

One took aim at Bosnia, visiting radio stations armed with CDs and tickets. His stunt was rolled out across the old republics. Via the local budget courier network of bus drivers, we sent parcels to Zagreb, Sarajevo, Skopje, Podgorica and Ljubljana, as well as the Serbian enclaves in Kosovo. Albanians would have got a few too, if I'd known some who might come to Belgrade. Even neighbors on warmer terms could yet think twice. Attempts to play up brotherhood were futile. Our designer refused to use the words 'our language', which could mean Serbian, Bosnian or Croatian, though never all three, despite them being functionally identical. So much for the recent talk of Yugonostalgia: most people missed a time before 'they' wrecked 'our' nice life, with 'them' equating to anyone but 'us'.

A truck was eventually sourced at the start of July, touring Serbia with a billboard and speakers. It rattled back to Belgrade blasting techno, and parked on the city's central square, where we'd set up a ticket booth. Business was slow. I kept being reassured this didn't matter. In the Balkans, nothing got fixed until the last minute.

EXIT, meanwhile, was a runaway success. The crowds were as big as before, despite them jacking up prices and cutting the program. The stakes notched higher every day. No matter how often we denied it, rumors still said ECHO could be cancelled. All we could do in response was flood the airwaves.

On the eve of the event, G scythed his attendance guesstimates. 'Is gonna be alright,' he maintained. 'Not too many people tomorrow, but by Friday might be getting kinda crowdy.'

I certainly hoped so.

I knew there'd be reporters from abroad. We'd booked their flights. In return, we were promised a feature in *Die Zeit*, a travel piece in *The Guardian*, and spreads in music magazines. There'd be dozens more foreign journalists from the Balkans, and several locally stationed correspondents. Most guests would stay at Hotel Jugoslavija, which we'd block-booked all week. It was the only place to be sure of seeing the action.

All cameras were banned from the island, to satisfy Pink. Their studio backstage had three hosts, each with a cameraman. Two more would trawl the crowd conducting interviews, and a sixth was installed on a soundboard facing the main stage. The final lens was dangled from a crane. Pink would dub a daily tape for the press center, so others could report on events. Apart from their schedule of briefings, and fixing up interviews, my team's sole task was to distribute materials: from surplus t-shirts and posters to censored *Blic* texts, which we'd printed up ourselves to give away.

As I sat reviewing this cache of ECHO handiwork, one of my staff said he'd spotted a mistake. He was the only one I thought I could rely on. He asked questions when he didn't understand. And now he'd volunteered an imperfection. I felt touched. Opening our first tabloid supplement, he pointed out a passage that I'd written: 'If Woodstock is the festival that everyone wants to emulate, Altamont is the disaster that no one wants to repeat.'

'So?' I said, looking up.

'You didn't notice?' He sounded incredulous.

I continued. 'The Rolling Stones hired the Hell's Angels to control the crowd for a free concert in California at the end of their 1969 tour of America. Armed with pool cues, they beat back an angry audience and flung full beer cans at them. Four people died and 850 were injured, including the lead singer of Jefferson Airplane. One of the victims was a young black man, beaten to death on the edge of the stage while Mick Jagger sang *Sympathy for the Devil*, apparently oblivious to the chaos around him. "Altamont was the product of diabolical egotism, hype, ineptitude, money manipulation, and," Rolling Stone magazine concluded, "at base, a fundamental lack of concern for humanity".'

'So?' I repeated.

'The black man was stabbed in the back,' he said. 'And the Stones were playing *Under My Thumb*.'

'Oh,' I said.

He wasn't my favorite now.

Everything seems obvious in hindsight, but we mostly make sense of life by looking forward. The present's elusive. Whenever you think you're on top of it, shit happens.

As part of our contract with Morcheeba, we'd been forced to hire a festival consultant. His job was to reassure them we were ready. He used to run the Glastonbury jazz stage, and he charged a daily rate of five hundred pounds, in exchange for which he'd showered us with maps, explaining how to organize a gig. He'd also brought a file of information. Since my own experience extended to a flick through *The Event Safety Guide*, I left production to him and G, who supervised the ragtag local workforce.

And sure enough, they'd made some steady progress. An assemblage of men wearing sandals had appeared. They'd raked the sandy field and hauled in generators, and the picnic tables made way for straw-roofed bars. Portaloos popped up around the site, along with rusting crash barriers, a phalanx of which had been bolted onto turnstiles. These welded cages were feats of

DIY, surpassed only by four metal letters mounted on girders, which were pile-driven into the beach to greet our visitors. 'ECHO,' this edifice said, as welcoming as a mineshaft in Congo. A shiny metal fence ranged round the perimeter, daubed with stickers hawking booze and cigarettes, and a giant inflatable Pepsi bottle dwarfed everything. All in all, preparations looked in hand.

But on the final afternoon, something felt different. It was almost imperceptible at first, beguiled as I was by our four enormous stages, and the sheer implausibility of their erection. As the last gantry swung into place, the island rang with cross-purpose shouting. Commands were bawled like mutant parking directions: 'That's right, back forward a touch, and down up mate.' By self-directing force of human will, most of the site had pulled itself together. A foreman we'd newly engaged was briefing bar staff, as trucks weaved round a tractor lugging light rigs. There were hundreds of silver boxes, each with wheels. What all this equipment did, I had no clue. I only knew we couldn't do without it. Much of it had been rented out to EXIT, and dismantled the day before in Novi Sad, for assembly in Belgrade the following morning.

And yet amidst this familiar chaos, there was order. And it wasn't being supplied by any of us. When we first met our heads of security, I'd laughed. The captain was squat and his partner squint, a Balkan Laurel and Hardy in t-shirts and combats. Had their neatly pressed attire not been so black, they might have passed for hospital orderlies. Whatever martial prowess they possessed, it was softened by years of greasy meat and face cream. The boss had a camp nasal twang. I marveled that we'd be paying him seventy grand.

His company's principal business was alarms, for which Belgrade's nouveau riche formed a captive market. Their homes were rigged with endless electronics. Guard work was only a sideline, as was something called 'criminal investigation'. This was a popular boast in the private security sector, which took off when militias demobilized from Bosnia. For a fee, contractors found your missing car. Whether they'd stolen it in the first place, you'd have to prove.

Our outfit looked too slick for street-level scams. They had more gizmos than a spy shop in Mayfair, from closed circuit cameras and bugs to pump-action shotguns. To demonstrate their mastery of savagery, they lined up dozens of heavies in jump suits in a car park, and took turns to try and knife each other's necks. Every assailant was wrestled to the tarmac, and reduced to tapping frantically for mercy. They also had their own gym for martial arts, where women drilled synchronized roundhouses, and men in armor smashed through paving slabs with palms.

We were told that this shouldn't be needed on the island. And since the firm came endorsed by the state, we acquiesced. Governments monopolize lawful violence, so we assumed their appointed agents would protect us. Besides, A got on well with the beanpole deputy, who'd installed himself in our office as liaison. When work on the island advanced, a couple of toughs took up residence in a prefab, from which they staked out the rest of the site to ward off thieves. Their stock of gear had steadily expanded, from walkie-talkie charger racks to searchlights. But the serious military hardware had stayed on the mainland. Their trailer hut was corporately anodyne, with computers, wall-mounted whiteboards and a fax. It even had strip lights.

As the weeks went by, reinforcements had arrived. They included two women, clad like their counterparts, but with twists. Stretch-fit combats clung to iron buttocks, and gave way to washboard midriffs under crop tops. Both wore a permanent pout and wet-look hair. They were Amazons on Diet Pepsi steroids. One was introduced as the boss's wife, the other was said to specialize in massage. Several of our staff employed her skills.

Now their number had increased. Black t-shirts swarmed the

island like mosquitoes. On the beach, some helped two frogmen board a dinghy. Others patrolled the Danube on jet skis. Clearly, we wouldn't be troubled by waves of fence-hoppers. The fields were being swept with muzzled dogs. Their handlers had boiler suits modeled on those worn by police, right down to the epaulettes and deltoid insignia. One guy was wielding a night-stick. The prefab now looked like a barracks. Most new arrivals had buzz cuts. Half the vans onsite belonged to them, decked out in blue-and-white stripes with sirens on top: we were under assault from our own private army.

As if that weren't enough, there was also the real one. The soldiers who put up the bridge had stayed on to guard it. They'd also helped lug ballasts for the stages. An armored personnel carrier was parked on the beach, and troops had been arriving all day long. The only force lacking in bulk was the police, who'd sent a couple of men onsite to thrash out protocol. It appeared that they'd agreed to man the entrance, where our security would carry out their checks, watched by what was left of the Yugoslav military. Some kind of turf war seemed inevitable.

I felt guilty for imagining the worst. Maybe this was just how Serbia worked. As one of my team had screamed that afternoon, when I asked how many interviews he'd scheduled: 'When will you stop fucking trying to control us!'

I sighed. The past two weeks had shown me how much was beyond me. Even making videos half ruined me, sitting up all night going goggle-eyed, and smoking throughout the day to stay awake. How could I appeal to goodwill when he hadn't been paid?

Hardly anyone had, except performers, and they'd still have to wait for the balance on the night. The rest of our debts would be cleared once we'd made some money. Ticket stands lined the towpath by the bridge, and we planned to stash cash from the bars at frequent intervals, and ferry it onshore as fast as possible. Our silent partner J would oversee this. He couldn't just sit in

New York awaiting payday. He'd come to secure his investment at the source. So we decided to put him in charge of the whole event. He'd monitor the radio with security, while keeping tabs on B, who'd bring in takings. G would be preoccupied with artists, and A would relay instructions round the site. My job would be general grunt, based in the press center. With limited local language skills, I was useless.

Even drugs became hostage to finance. E had arrived with our order, but refused to let us pay at a later date. The night before the festival began, G called to say he'd swung some sort of deal. E would meet me in the hotel lobby with 'samples'. When I asked what this meant we'd be getting, I got short shrift.

'I wouldn't say too much if I was you.' G's voice sounded harsh. 'You don't know who is listening your telephone.'

He hung up.

An hour later, I was back at my apartment, peeling my way through layers of Tesco shopping bags. E had given me them in full view of plainclothes policemen. They'd already searched my staff, and busted one for smoking a joint outside. But they seemed to be oblivious to Brits, including those who stumbled out the lift.

I didn't feel inclined to push my luck. The package held roughly five hundred hits of ecstasy, at least three ounces of coke and a nine-bar of hash: sufficient to keep me in jail for several years. What was I going to say if some flatfoot collared me? 'Nothing to worry about here, they're only samples. My friend at the embassy got them from your boss.' Would that convince them? Would it fuck: they'd slap my ass in a rat-hole cell in Zemun, and take turns to piss in my ears until they bled.

I parceled up a sockful of wraps, and arranged a few piles of pills in tinfoil strips. The remaining hoard I sealed with strips of duct tape, and hid behind tangled wires inside a fuse box, at the top of the flight of stairs outside my flat.

People lose their way a step at a time. The further adrift I got, the freer I felt, and that just helped me spiral even deeper. All you have to do is believe your hype.

I used to ask how politicians managed that, but the more outlandish and public your claims, the harder they become to disown. To do so, you'd have to let go of your sense of self, or at least let go of thinking that you're right. And whose self-image is rooted in saying they're wrong? Once this process starts, you up the ante. A harmless little white lie becomes a war crime. Addiction's the same. To resist your better judgment, you continue. You can get so lost you really think you find yourself, in the peace of seeing the damage can't be stopped. For me, that moment dawned on the first day of ECHO. It was surely in everyone's interests I smoked more.

Mornings were always the worst, and thus the best. They began with a weepy voice inside my headset, bleating about yesterday's nasty metal aftertaste. But it wasn't as if I'd loaded up on crack. So why feel so ashamed of skinning up? I could savor feeling vacant for a while, I guess. Even mutter 'who needs drugs?' before I did. But the work of the past nine months had been relentless. I'd got so attached to hash to wake me up that I had to smoke all day to feel detached enough.

I wandered into the bombed-out wing, morose. An honest joint would never let me down. I'd smother myself in Technicolor dreamscapes, and fly to a place where pain and pleasure merged. This inner world would blot out other thoughts.

The day before, our film crew shadowed my staff. Their footage was still replaying inside my eyelids. The star was a girl called Nena, who lumbered around like a simian Uma Thurman, shrugging with indifference when annoyed. 'Relax,' she told the camera. 'This is Serbia.' It had picked her up on the doorstep of the hotel, in a fitted white t-shirt and bum-hugging harem pants. She quickly explained herself.

'We are waiting for someone from newsroom of B92 and he

will take from me a statement. It's very difficult situation with B92 TV station and B92 corporation too because their working manager Dragan Ambrozic speak very shitty things in the news and everything about us, and he is main booking manager for EXIT.'

Out of shot, the director lobbed a curveball. 'Is there a bit of a rivalry between ECHO and EXIT?'

'I don't know.' Nena shrugged. 'He had problem in his head, I suppose. He's very confused.'

Then she wandered off to meet B92, in the form of a man in a white flat cap, a golf shirt, and plus fours. His mutton-chop sideburns suggested this was hip. The pair of them stood by a map of the island's bird sanctuary. Whatever they said, it all went unrecorded. The tape cut to Nena flirting with the cameraman. She told him he was cute. He asked if she needed his photo for accreditation.

'I don't know,' she replied, shaking her bob. 'Whatever.'

Mr B92 sat beside them and struck up a threesome. 'Fuck me sticky, shave my legs and call me blondie,' he piped up randomly. The next shot showed Nena wearing the director's sunglasses, twirling a white pashmina and puckering her lips.

'Please, Daniel can't see this because it's not proper behaving for PR... Main PR,' she corrected herself. 'Yeah, he told me I'm behaving like a child, you know, that's not so professional. Eh, he is right. What to say? I am Nena.'

She made eyes at the lens. 'Hi, I am Nena,' she said huskily. 'I'm the main PR of the ECHO festival.'

Someone in the background burst out laughing. 'Nena loves saying that. Our main PR.'

She laughed too, and mimicked me. 'Nena,' she said, in a babyish voice, 'she screw everything, she is impossible.'

Yeah, yeah, yeah, whatever, I was past caring. Another joint and nothing else could touch me. I walked back to the press center tingling, as if clumps of fur had sprouted through my skin.

I felt completely in control, because I'd let go, like gunning down a gully on a snowboard. There's no time left to think, and that's enough. Try too hard to hang on and you wipe the fuck out.

I strode around the corner, into a DJ. To my surprise, he wasn't the slightest bit put out. Catching my arms with both hands, he stared through my pupils.

'Stay like this!' he beamed. 'I mean it. You're glowing!'

You don't even have to feel positive to be calm.

For most of the opening night, I stayed away. I might not have showed up at all had I not had to work. The feeling of anti-climax was intense. I couldn't even be bothered to watch the fireworks. It was all just too exhausting to consider. I longed to be alone in the darkness. So I holed up in the hotel bunker, smoking.

When G called after midnight, it was the first we'd spoken. The conversation lasted thirty seconds, and induced me to sneak cocaine past our security. At the gate, they were locked in a contest with the cops, frisking everyone twice. An organizer's pass was no exemption, as I'd already learned to my horror once before. Luckily, I'd been feeling fully paranoid. I'd stashed the evening's hash supply in my foreskin.

The only way round this cordon was by speedboat, on a shuttle transporting artists to the stages. I got the driver's number, and hitched a ride. Once business was transacted, I departed. Hanging around on the island felt depressing.

By Balkan summer standards, it was freezing. Raindrops spattered from clouds that hid the stars. Another hazy day hung on the horizon. The main illumination came from bars, and an imposing set of klieg lights by the entrance. The dance clearing looked like a void, too dark to see how deserted it might be. Some stragglers lurked by the beach, nodding to reggae. There were clusters by the main stage and the bar, where our employees sat on crates of beer and talked. The other big draw was a tent, where Red Bull girls in leggings doled out stickers.

They were faring considerably better than our merchandise stall, which looked to have been abandoned already.

At most, there were ten thousand people. Some had left early after watching Darkwood Dub, a popular electro art-rock band from Belgrade. Their latest release was called *Life Begins at 30*, an allusion to bypassed youth in the 1990s. The energy they roused had quickly flagged. The brightest sight I found was our consultant. He paced around the field in a neon donkey jacket, and was barking into his radio via a translator.

'Those lovely little turnstiles have to go,' he said. 'They let in three thousand people an hour, and you said you're expecting forty-five thousand. That makes fifteen hours to get in, and the last people arrive two hours after it's finished...'

There appeared to be problems to solve, but I couldn't help. On my way towards the bridge, I encountered J. He shooed me away. He was arguing with G by walkie-talkie. His face was beetroot. Most of their exchange went over my head. The only phrase I gleaned made me quake. 'We can't do that you idiot. They'll kill us.'

I left them to it.

Frankly, I'm a dreadful music snob. My first three albums were by Genesis, Johnny Hates Jazz and A-Ha. I got *Smash Hits* delivered for years, and put up the posters. And without so much as blinking at the title, I bought eight consecutive volumes of *Now That's What I Call Music!* On the day they were released, on cassette.

The trouble started later, in my teens. I didn't just want to be cool; I wanted the kids who ignored me to think I was cooler. This didn't impress them. Nor did it endear me to my friends. I flitted from group to group, never quite fitting in. Some people called me Desperate Dan. Or Bullshitting Dan, in cartoon caricature, complete with his own *Viz* catchphrase: 'I know how to roll it'.

I'll show them, I vowed at the time. And now I would: never

mind my taste in bands, I ran a festival. With a classic hack's pretense of being with it, I'd hewn myself a mullet fit for Hoxton. There was only one snag, and it nagged me like an earworm. The most popular name on our bill didn't sound very cool.

Morcheeba made in-flight sedatives for airlines, the tunes a company plays when it puts your call on hold. They didn't even try to disguise it. The 'Mor' stood for 'middle of the road', while 'cheeba' was slang for weed, which helped them jump the Nineties trip-hop bandwagon. And once they'd made their name, they changed their sound. Out went most of the dub, blues and hip-hop, leaving pop with an elegant groove of jazz guitars. It was upbeat yet down-tempo, and a sultry female singer topped off the mix. I hoped people paid to hear it by the thousand, but I didn't feel too keen to talk them up. Three strong *charas* joints took care of that.

I strutted into the press suite like Liam Gallagher. Dozens of reporters were waiting; half had cameras. From a stereo, Morcheeba's Skye Edwards chirped *Over and Over*. Beside me, on the platform, she smiled sweetly. Before I could think of anything to say, Nena The Main PR had introduced us. It was my turn to talk.

'Hi,' I said, twitching in my seat. 'Morcheeba are the biggest band to play here so far, and I'm really excited to have them here today and I'd like to first just give them an opportunity to say how they feel arriving in Belgrade.'

Ross Godfrey muttered a one-line deadpan platitude. The younger of the band's two brothers, he was roughly my age, and looked as stoned as I felt. There was nothing to save us from narcoleptic questions. Several hands went up. My spirits sank.

'What is something that you like, but most of the people don't?' a local newshound enquired. My eyes rolled backward, flickering whites.

Skye tried getting her head round his words. 'Sorry, something that I like...?'

'Something that you like that most people don't,' I sneered.

'Um...' she said, straining to be positive. We all sniggered awkwardly.

It was Ross who broke the silence in the end. He said: 'Marmite.'

'Biting my fingernails?' Skye ventured in solidarity.

I said nothing at all. I was watching shards of time ascend the walls.

Ross tried again, shaking his head. 'Jazz?'

The silence returned. I preferred it.

'Anybody else?' I asked to ease my conscience. 'Ah, one more over there.'

A guy with a badger-stripe hairdo took the mic. 'One more,' he grinned. 'In your video for *Otherwise*, Ross is a good guy and Paul is a bad guy. Is that in real life?'

'Yes,' Ross said.

Skye giggled.

'You would say that,' I countered.

Several seconds later, Ross replied. 'No,' he said, very slowly. 'It's true.'

Enough was enough. 'OK then everybody,' I said. 'Thanks very much for coming. There's a couple of very important pieces of information I need to give you about Morcheeba's appearance tonight. First is they'll be on stage exactly at 11.30.'

Our consultant had told me to see that the media behaved. Staring manically round the room, I warmed to the task. My eyes were glazing over like a shark's.

'The second thing is that obviously because of copyright restrictions, we can't just film their whole show and take it home as a souvenir. So there'll be heavy restriction on filming their performance. TV crews will be able to film the first two minutes of their show, just for the purpose of showing that Morcheeba were here in Belgrade. And because they're such a big act we'd like to announce that all TV cameras tonight will be allowed into the festival, but that you'll be very closely monitored to make sure that you stick to this rule, and if our security sees anybody filming at a time they shouldn't be, they will steal your camera.'

I paused. 'So, er... you've been warned.'

'What about the tape?' someone asked.

I lurched towards him cackling, the veins in the side of my neck pulsating wildly. 'The tape they will burn in front of your face!'

Nena looked horrified.

It all came down to music in the end. Morcheeba pulled in twice as big a crowd, and they shimmied along with abandon to wah-wah guitars. Older songs had smoldering hints of reggae, like the 'fire burning down the Babylon' in *Friction*. When Skye sang *Undress Me Now*, they got ideas. Their singing along got the headline set extended. Elsewhere on the site, there was unconstrained elation.

'On festival, we all are united!' someone shouted at visiting Germans. 'It's great to see here world without the politics. Belgrade needs more tourists, to be what it was.'

The Germans apparently thought it was already. 'This city gives off a special energy,' said Thomas Brinkmann, whose techno tapped it. 'In the West people like to drink themselves unconscious,' his friend agreed. 'But here the nightlife has its own unique character. The music scene is really not commercialized.'

Karl Frierson of De Phazz saw something similar. 'There's more of a listening with the heart,' he said, 'and we feel that, I feel that from the stage.' The audience's mood matched that of his band, which didn't take anything too seriously, especially some of the cabaret songs in its oeuvre. 'Humor to me it's very important,' said Pit Baumgartner, who wrote them. 'Watch the news. You need sarcasm. Otherwise you die.'

No one got too earnest, not even Matthew Herbert's big band, with its sixteen-piece calypso syncopation. As others discovered, experiments paid off. 'It's always difficult to play to such a big crowd with this style of music,' said Simon Lee of Faze Action, whose African house and disco set was zany. 'But they totally got into it, the response was great.'

Most communication was internal. Talking was nigh on inaudible. And unless you had rarefied tastes, the only real guide to the program was instinctive. You stumbled wherever the rumbling speakers pulled you. Our Bristol corner forged the strongest mind meld, snaring all-comers in lockstep, while rippling films of energy surfed on top, like a portable club with a pyrotechnic roof. Vocals were scarce, until a sunrise mix spun *Good Vibrations*. Even the goons from security smiled then.

'I don't remember dancing so much,' said a rare Muslim visitor from Bosnia. 'We ran from one stage to the other. The stomping feet raised immense clouds of sand dust.'

This was quite a feat given the weather. By Friday, rain was churning up the island, like a rugby pitch flecked with farmyard pools of urine. Pepsi ads were reflected in the puddles, and the front of the London Xpress stage was a mud bath. None of that stopped girls from wearing next to nothing. Their spindly shoulders stretched towards the sky. They danced with the flair of a fire juggler, rhythmically poised.

An English DJ found these scenes inspiring. 'People get so cynical,' he laughed. 'Like clubbing's dead, dance music's had its time. But it'll always be there, people will always want to dance and have fun, so yeah, bring it on!'

Another said it was 'good to see young people not into the old ideas', hailing music as the world's 'new religion'. Wherever he went, he said, he felt the same. 'Everyone can speak music, there are no boundaries.' Only one thing had disturbed him in Belgrade. 'I hoped we would beat McDonald's here, but they were there before us.'

The presence of The Arches was contentious. They'd already

jinxed a sermon by Tom Friedman, the *New York Times* high priest of globalization, whose faith ordained that states couldn't fight if both sides had the franchise. When NATO bombing sabotaged this theory, he called for Belgrade to be blitzed with extra violence. 'Like it or not, we are at war with the Serbian nation,' he wrote in 1999. 'The stakes have to be very clear: Every week you ravage Kosovo is another decade we will set your country back by pulverizing you. You want 1950? We can do 1950. You want 1389? We can do 1389 too.'

Reggae artists felt these bad vibrations. 'I love it very much man, to my heart,' said the mellifluous Prince Alla. 'The people, they go through so much sufferation. They come out with happiness and they really observe their happiness. And I love that.'

So did a white man with dreadlocks from Geneva, who swore to 'kick out the slackness and all the music who say nothing.' His patois bore traces of French, but was otherwise flawless. 'The people give us nuff love and nuff welcome and we love that,' he said. 'Some people call this place Belgrade, but we call it I-Grade.' He grinned. 'Me, it's just love from Switzerland to the people. So it's Rastaman love, you know, respect!'

Respect indeed. Their comments channeled everything I couldn't. My dealings with reporters put me off. 'No one ever sees anything coming out of this region apart from miserable stories about war, corruption and drug trafficking,' I raged at one. 'I thought if we could have something really alive in the center of the city in a beautiful location it could be a catalyst, it could give people new influences and inspiration.'

Hence the cultural preachers on the reggae stage, from the dub warrior Jah Shaka to Tippa Irie, who spiced up his rude-boy dancehall with call and response.

'Say roots!' he screeched at the crowd. They roared it back. 'Rock!' They echoed louder. 'Reggae!' A thousand voices mingled in the breeze.

'Ladies and gentlemen,' Tippa announced, 'this song that I'm going to do for you now is dedicated to all the people in Serbia that like to smoke weed.'

A huge cheer rang out.

'Now if you think that marijuana should be free let me see your hands up in the air right now!'

The shouts turned to whoops.

'Let me hear you say weed!'

They yelled it.

'Say marijuana!'

It rang out Latino.

'Ganja!'

And so on, and so on, to obscurity. Say ke-ke! Say lamb's bread! Say bush herrrb!

Again and again they obliged, until chastised.

'Shame on you!' his finger reproached. 'We don't smoke bush herb.'

Unfortunately, there wasn't much else on offer. The Moroccan we'd ordered from E proved all too English: laced with something oddly artificial. There was also far too little to distribute. Our 'samples' wouldn't cover the VIP terrace. Even if more were to hand, I wouldn't dare. Everywhere was bristling with security. They roamed around the island in their jackboots, and pounced on all offenders in a trice.

The moment I spotted a guy preparing a joint on the edge of the field, a mercenary patrol prepared to swoop. One yanked him up by his t-shirt. Two cohorts grabbed an arm apiece, and dragged the sinful stoner like a crucifix. As they hauled him away to the exit, I ran across and asked what they were playing at.

'Enough!' I shouted in Serbian, flashing my pass. 'It's OK!'

They ignored me, so I had another go. 'This is my festival. You work for me!'

One of them lunged in my direction with an air slap, his foot stomping down like a wrestler's, for effect. It was an entry-level gesture of threat, inviting me to back off 'up your mother's cunt!' If they felt even mildly upset, they might get heavier, like fucking my mother inside her mother's cunt. At its darkest, Serbian swearing is an art form. 'May God stick your house on CNN!' (Because NATO bombed it.)

Since politeness got me nowhere, I tried English. 'Show some human dignity, you animals!'

This stopped the men in their tracks. Dropping the scruff of his quarry, one wandered over. A crash helmet dangled from his belt, and a kit bag had been strapped around his thigh. But he carried no obvious firearms or truncheons. None of the posse was armed except with radios. They appeared to rely on numbers for supremacy.

'I fuck you,' he said simply, in my mother tongue.

One of the others laughed. 'When that guy say he fuck you, he will fuck you!'

My assailant wiped his mouth with the back of his hand. 'I tell you,' he continued. 'I fucking fuck you!'

I froze to the spot and let them disappear.

Where was G when I needed him? His mobile was permanently off. He'd switched to a two-way radio. I didn't have one.

I found him backstage in the small hours of Sunday morning, reclining in the bus that served as a dressing room. He'd been drinking cups of tea with Burning Spear, who'd apparently quaffed a bottle of red wine. The Rasta legend had given up smoking dope. But he got high off his reception from the crowd, which had swayed to his jaunty horns like he was Bob Marley's ghost. In his sleeveless denim shirt and outsized cap, he brought to mind the singer from AC/DC.

G seemed absurdly content with this performance, as if everything else was irrelevant by contrast. All I could see were grounds to get annoyed. 'What's going on here?' I demanded.

'Why are we letting thugs control the show?'

My partner laughed. 'My friend, what I can say? This is Serbia.'

His manner somehow neutralized my anger. 'Well, you could start by trying to remind them who's in charge,' I said.

He looked pitying. 'I don't think you realize what we deal with. And I don't think you *wanna* know right now. Relax man. I need you handling those medias. They are ones we tell here how to be. Don't worry yourself too much about other shit.'

His efforts to fob me off just made it worse. 'They're beating people up for smoking weed,' I shouted. 'What was all that crap about changing rules? I thought you said we'd create an autonomous zone.'

My partner smiled. 'Just being here is serious change,' he said. 'We should give thanks we still have festival to roll with.'

He'd disarmed me again. 'What do you mean?'

'Like I say, we should be happy they don't crush us. Those guys have Latin American kinda attitude. It's fucked up. Before, we didn't see that, even with Milosevic. It has deteriorated now to most primitive level. Next will be people kicking out on street.'

His whimsical tangents wound me up still further. 'What about summers of love and raising consciousness?' I said. 'Or was everything we said just empty words? Perhaps I should have bought that liquid acid. At least we could have dosed our security.'

The sparkle in his eyes took on a harder edge. 'Who you think you are man? I mean really. Comrade Narcosis of People's Front? Reality is not strong enough trip for you? Who needs psyche-delics here in pigsty? If kids do wanna mess themselves on drugs, I am pretty sure security can sell to them. Why I would involve myself with bullshit?'

I hardly knew where to begin. 'Don't you care that we've lost control of our event?'

'And what you can control here by yourself? You think Serbia all of sudden turn to Switzerland? You know, I think you pretty smart guy, but maybe you should face to what is real. You observe yourself, you see that's hard enough.'

I felt bewildered. Debating with G was like wearing 3-D specs. 'Yes, but...'

His final verdict spun me out completely. 'Wise man wants that others be themselves,' he said. 'And for him to be self as well, you should reflect on that. Maybe you check reggae on way home. I think you feel there love what you are searching.'

Most things in life end badly, or they'd continue. I'd been secretly hoping that ECHO would make my fortune. That didn't mean I valued getting rich. I longed to eclipse my status as a hack. But I couldn't begin to define what that entailed. I only knew I'd got nowhere in my quest. For all our romantic talk of changing Serbia, I couldn't even change my own delusions. My failure to impress myself was crippling.

I always came up short of expectations. The latest indications overwhelmed me. They began with the girl I'd been chasing in New York. She'd written to tell me she hoped that I was 'happy and lovely and alive as ever'. Not since I'd scoured the Internet for photos of her, and found that she was married. They'd already got engaged when we met. The announcement of their nuptials made me queasy. According to the article I chanced upon, she'd known him for more than a decade, and had mostly lived abroad until he proposed. He'd call her 'to hear the message on her cellphone.'

I knew how he felt. She'd rarely answered when I called. What sort of fantasy world was I lost in? At least it wasn't her husband's dreamland. 'Knowing her has shown me depths of experience I couldn't know otherwise,' he'd told the author of the story. 'I'd have to read all the world's literature, and experience every piece of fine art. There's strength, there's pride, there's jealousy, and there's passion.'

I despised a man I'd never even met.

To compound my self-pity, there were three different women at ECHO I'd rejected. Each lived somewhere else, and they all still seemed to think we had a future. I didn't, but felt guilty for upsetting them, and confused enough to doubt my own conclusions. This toxic mix had brought them to Belgrade, where I proceeded to ignore them. One cornered me on Sunday afternoon.

'I thought you wouldn't have time for me,' she stammered. I kissed her to cheer us both up, and shuddered slightly. Already, I was conscious of the consequences.

She drew me closer. 'What are you going to do when this is over?'

'I don't know yet,' I said. 'I think I'd like to write about it.'

She undid my belt. 'Because there's this certain person that would love to listen to you speak over cups of coffee. In between writing, of course. If you wanted.'

I slowly slid her hand back out of my trousers. 'Sorry?'

She was shaking. 'I mean, my cat's got kittens and all, so my flat's a bit smelly. But it's peaceful and you could stay there and write. Like not forever. You could come for a month at first, and we can see.'

Nothing could have been further from my mind.

'OK,' she said, 'it's a crazy idea. I know.'

She was crying, so I hugged her. Her lips reached for mine. I pulled away.

'Why won't you let me in?' she asked. 'Don't you like kissing me?'

I couldn't answer. The only thing I wanted now was more: more than her, more than me, and more than this wretched existence I felt trapped in. If I couldn't have that, I'd rather have nothing at all. Everything seemed bound to disappoint me.

'I should go,' I said. 'I'm late for an urgent meeting.'

Her tearful gaze was hard to meet head on. 'I wish you

wouldn't think so much,' she said. 'Can't you just feel?'

I could, and I felt I had to get away. No one went anywhere fast enough for me. I had to run faster than ever, just to keep up. I remembered she'd once told me she believed in me. I wondered which of my masks she'd been deceived by.

'Why run from love?' she called behind me as I left. 'If you torture yourself like this, you won't feel a bullet.'

Everything on Sunday was a washout. When the downpour began in the morning, our site was already plastered with mud. It waterlogged entirely within hours.

That weekend, *The Sun* said London was 'balmier than Bermuda'. *Guardian* readers enjoyed a 'Mediterranean summer'. And Reuters reported that Southern Europe itself was 'sweltering in the hottest weather for more than 200 years.' Just not in Belgrade. There, it was wetter than Woodstock, with far fewer people.

Only no one could say for certain quite how few. According to receipts from the box office, just eight hundred people came on Thursday night. My partners believed there were twenty times as many. And apparently, Friday's ratio was worse. There was only one conclusion that made sense: we'd been ripped off.

By the time I was informed at Sunday's meeting, G had already attempted to call off the festival. Afraid of losing everything, J stopped him. But we couldn't count on bars to plug the hole: they'd also been leaking money every night. G said he'd witnessed 'fights among characters doing collecting', and claimed they'd pocketed almost all the cash. J had found this prospect inconceivable. But a feverish late-night audit showed that the first three days had barely cleared six figures, on an estimated gate of seventy thousand. It was as if they'd got in free, and bought two drinks.

My partners put our problems down to touts. They'd been seen selling books of tickets by the entrance. So where did they get them? A count of unsold bundles showed none missing, although we'd given away untold amounts ourselves. At first, we'd kept close tabs on where they went, but fears of empty fields had got the better of us. And what was to stop the printer printing extras, or enterprising kids from making copies? The real ones had a hologram to counter this, and our security guards were meant to check for fakes. J was supposed to have monitored the system. But apart from his command of the language, he seemed about as impotent as me.

'You know, I found one of these scalpers outside,' he said, 'and so I took along four of our guys to make citizen's arrest. We brought him to police trailer, and they send us to head of our security, and he lets him go. I felt really stupid at that point, man.'

I was stunned. 'You didn't argue?'

J didn't raise his voice. It breathed contempt. 'OK,' he sneered, 'so you're gonna fight those mercenaries?'

I kept my counsel.

My partners reached a sobering conclusion: we had to get everything right on Sunday night. If the crowds came to see Sonic Youth, and J took personal charge of counting cash, we'd hopefully still make money on the drinks.

By late that afternoon, it was clear we couldn't. The others conceded defeat without consulting me. There was nothing I could say to change their minds. I didn't have the 'hardcore' we required. I'd never heard of it. Apparently, several tons were our only hope. Sandbags, wood and water pumps were useless. And however much 'hardcore' we found, we'd be too late. When I was summoned to join the discussion, it was only to use my journalistic skills: as stenographer. 'The ECHO Festival has been cancelled,' our consultant dictated, 'for safety reasons.'

This press release spread sorrow round Belgrade. The band we'd all awaited wouldn't play. Sonic Youth would be spending the night in their hotel. And on Monday, they'd be flying to New York.

'Catastrophe,' said a radio announcer.

No shit.

BETRAYAL

Some things defy explanation. There's not much to do but accept them. Perhaps Sunday the thirteenth was auspicious. Although clouds obscured the moon that night, it was full. It was also exactly eighteen years since Live Aid. We mightn't have raked in millions ourselves, but maybe a deluged festival was OK. Glastonbury is synonymous with mud. And in the mosh pit at Reading, by train tracks to Wales, you're as likely to find yourself soaked by pints of piss. We just had to drain a Balkan swamp.

Our first concern was trying to recoup what we'd lost. And to do so, we had to begin by spending cash. By nightfall, Sunday's torrent had abated. With industrial gear and rubble, the site could be salvaged. A stage had been due to remain for our free fifth day. If Sonic Youth stayed on, they could top the bill. Persuading them took $2,500, plus new plane tickets. The version for public consumption went out around midnight.

'The ECHO Festival will reopen on Monday,' it revealed, 'provided there is no further deterioration in the weather.'

Another caveat ensued. 'There will be no refund for holders of tickets for Sunday night because the income from advance ticket sales is being spent on the cost of accommodating the headline artists for an additional day.'

If only it were. Unfortunately, we'd failed to sell enough tickets. And charging people twice would start a backlash. So we stuck to the plan we'd devised and toughed it out. 'Entrance to the festival on Monday will be free, as advertised,' we said.

We'd just have to hope people came, and drank the bars dry. The gates would open earlier than usual, at seven o'clock, with a warm-up band on at nine, and the main event beginning after sundown. In the small hours, we'd revert to the scheduled program, with Fun-Da-Mental followed by Banco de Gaia.

That just left the planned grand finale: the DJs we'd booked for Sunday night. Most were still due to depart on Monday morning, but few of them fancied idling indoors. The London Xpress promoter had a brainwave: what about an impromptu free party?

Thus was a giant of techno let loose in a labyrinth. Akademija was the underground heart of Belgrade. Run by students in the basement of an art school, it had served as a makeshift gallery and punk club, renowned for staying open through the night. Bums would sometimes use it as a shelter, crashing with the elegantly wasted. It was dark, and hard to breathe in, and the system whacked you square in the solar plexus. Where better to feel the sound of Detroit? Derrick May and Carl Craig could have sold out the venue in hours. Instead, a few fortunate hipsters would see them for nothing.

Akademija's cavernous dance floor was rammed. Sweat was soon dripping freely from the ceiling. Dancers took breaks by dangling off a grille on the front of the DJ booth. It wasn't exactly a party like 1999, when people went at it between NATO air raids. Even so, it was showing the meaning of Serbian stamina. May was on the decks until first light, unable to resist their whoops of 'one more!' He eventually sneaked on a mix CD and scarpered.

Most punters were ecstatic, pilled or not, leading May to ask why people took drugs. Of course, some want to 'open up this canal that takes them somewhere else,' he said. 'They feel more associated, or closer, or can relate, or they just feel it makes them a little bit more uninhibited.' But 'I have that canal open because I just can tap inside myself and feel who I am and I'm happy with that. Other people will do what they do, you know, and I wish them the best and hope they don't hurt themselves.'

I felt far too wrecked to take this in. I retreated to my bedroom and passed out.

By Monday afternoon, we were back on track. Refreshed by a

few hours of sleep, and a pile of banknotes, our consultant deemed the island safe to use. Everywhere, people found an extra gear. My staff came straight to work from Akademija, and set about dismantling the pressroom. For once, it was me who was late. But having smoked myself to a state approaching consciousness, I got going on a final round of meetings.

A man from the BBC was obsessed with the mafia. He said a bomb had gone off at the Ministry of Justice. Though no one was hurt, he thought it was a threat, perhaps from allies of the gangsters who'd shot the prime minister. We were sitting in a bar near their stronghold. Had ECHO not feared falling victim to the mob?

I laughed. 'If we looked like we were making a lot of money,' I said, 'perhaps we'd get a visit from Mr Big. But in this country Mr Big is usually very good friends with the government. We're more likely to get a call from the legitimate authorities.'

Serbs had little to fear from organized crime, I told him, apart from what it did to the country's government. As for ECHO, all our enemies were friends, at least as far I'd determined. 'I've figured out more about Balkan politics doing this than I ever did working for *The New York Times*,' I concluded wryly.

The reporter smiled like I was hopelessly naïve.

Even our film crew summoned new reserves of energy. Slumped in a hotel armchair by the press suite, the director was staring blearily at his viewfinder, lining up all the interviews he'd postponed. A man with a wet-shaved head sat down to speak. I inched along the corridor to eavesdrop.

'I'm Simon Glinn,' the bald bloke muttered at the camera, 'and I've been engaged by the festival as their, um, senior adviser on running a gig.'

He fingered his goatee. The director was fumbling for a question. 'And wh-wh-what does that involve exactly?' he slurred.

Glinn started giggling. 'Well,' he said, 'paragraph one of my original advice document was don't do it. Paragraph two was if you ignore paragraph one, please, for God's sake, take note of the following two hundred and fifty points you really need to consider, of which about twenty have been addressed.'

His day job was running the Liverpool Philharmonic Hall. But his experiences from younger days were wilder, including wartime trips to Bosnia, where he helped set up an event called Rock Under Siege. This had led him to think he could handle Balkan bullshit. But the strains of the past few days had rattled his confidence.

The director's strains were also self-induced. He'd been hammering speedy Serbian pills all week, and was struggling to formulate words, let alone sentences.

'And um, er...' he stuttered, 'we, er, understand that there was, um, a problem with the, er... original turnstiles, is this perhaps... the main... issue?'

'No,' Glinn said. 'There's an awful lot of main issues. In our context of our legislative framework you'd say this is a gig that would never happen. It's a very dangerous event. I think we're about to see that today because of the rain.'

His sigh was like the steam brakes on a juggernaut. 'Gently we managed to persuade people of the utter lunacy of some of the more significant problems and put some slightly better structures in place.'

He was even prepared to give us grudging credit. 'I've seen things equally bad and indeed worse than everything apart from the reggae stage, which is actually the worst stage structure I've ever seen, which culminated last night in the appearance of poisonous snakes on it, which was really...'

Unable to finish this comment, Glinn buckled over. He'd lost it completely. Laughter creased his cheeks like wrinkled linen, and a hand lolled paralytic at his forehead. Striving in vain to compose himself, he turned puce. 'No,' he wheezed. 'Fantastic...'

When he tried to sit up straight again, it was futile. He wedged a thumb and finger in his eyes, and juddered like he'd done a dozen bucket bongs.

Eventually, he spluttered out more words. 'Utterly surreal gig,' he said.

'So,' the director sniggered, drawing strength from the psychic meltdown through his lens. 'What can we expect from tonight's performances?'

Glinn coughed, attempting to pull himself together. 'Tonight's going to be really difficult,' he said, 'because it's, well... it's about a foot deep in water...'

This finished him off. His head flipped back and forward, quite unhinged. The final thread of Englishness had snapped. He'd succumbed to the black comic succubus of Serbia. The laughter starts when everything's too much. As everyone else gives up to make it worse, you can all join in and laugh at that as well.

'It's great,' he murmured, dabbing at his eyes. 'That's the third time that's happened to me, it's not even the first.'

'What were we saying again?' the director asked.

'You were asking me about tonight, about...' Glinn groped desperately for a handhold. 'Talking about major incident planning's a good idea I think.'

Immediately, his mobile started cheeping. 'Let me just lose this,' he said, standing to do so. He hit the red button and collapsed back on his chair.

This interruption threw the director's focus. 'What were we asking?' he asked. 'Major event... what was it I'm supposed to ask you?'

Both men promptly doubled up once more.

'Yeah,' Glinn said, 'so we, um, we, we sort of had a look at this, um, event and tried... Sorry,' he choked, 'I can't talk seriously about this gig any more.'

He rose again to try and walk it off, but his legs refused to follow his instructions.

'I pissed myself just like this in the middle of the field,' he confided. 'I fell over laughing. The utter absurdity of it all was just too much.'

He grabbed a cold coffee from the table and necked it in one.

'Right,' he said. 'Oh dear.'

He'd clocked my presence.

'Dan's going to want the tape of this,' he told the camera. Then he addressed himself to me. 'Sorry,' he grinned. 'We haven't been able to get very far. We keep...'

He'd refused to leave his room for less than €3,000, which almost settled the balance of his fee. He'd declined to trade this in for coke and hookers.

'Right, where were we?' he asked.

'Major incident planning, or something,' the director prompted.

'Yeah.' Glinn's cerebral wheels gained sudden traction. 'So we had a few meetings with police and the security firm and the festival organizers. We tried to identify who the production manager was, which has been interesting, to see if there was any kind of chance of some vaguely coordinated approach if something serious and significant went wrong, like really bad weather for example, we were told that wouldn't happen, there was no chance of that, and, yeah, made a bit of progress actually. There is at least some kind of plan. And, er... The attitude, the hostility that was over*whelm*ing on Thursday night, that's improved. The idea that anything that looks even vaguely medical must be illegal, whether it's an aspirin or a tampon, which was the kind of things that were getting kind of confiscated on the way in, by the last night at least they'd got a doctor up there sort of identifying drugs and things like that. Although I must admit I was particularly concerned when I said to him so what *would*n't you allow in then that's kind of prescribed medication, and he said, well, you know, antipsychotic drugs.

Well, surely they're the things you want to make *sure* they've taken. But he couldn't quite see that one. It has been quite bizarre.'

Indeed it had. He wasn't done yet.

'I mean, lots of aspects that are brilliant, don't get me wrong. Something's really good about this crowd. And you know there's a lot of technical competence. The production guys from the main stage have been absolutely spot on. It'd be nice to see, you know, the flown PA being only three times over the load limit on the motors rather than four times... but so far, you know, one fall from the stage hasn't resulted in much more than a broken arm. And that was the backline guy and he was very pissed. Um, a handrail would have been nice, but you know... And, and the structural collapse, there was no one around at the time when, er, when the tower collapsed...'

He suffered another minor collapse himself. But somehow he managed to dive across the finish line. 'And these were the kind of things that we suggested might happen, and, um, let's hope it's a bit better next year.'

Putting on a festival was alchemy. If we hadn't transcended our limits, it couldn't have happened. G's magic had simple principles at heart: he'd clarified intentions at the outset, and detached himself completely from the outcome. While he hoped to see his vision fully realized, everyone was left to do as they pleased, and this free-for-all was ECHO's fatal flaw. But it also proved a vital source of strength.

By Monday night, there wasn't a puddle in sight. Countless feet had trudged them into sludge. The atmosphere backstage was reverential. Higher powers blessed us in the end; the heavens above were fair, and the field was full. I was dumbstruck by the vista from the stage. Rippling away in the moonlight, the crowd was pulsing like a human graphic equalizer. It roared in a wave of souls merged as one. There must have been eighty thousand, at least. The police locked thousands more outside the gates. They feared stampedes. To a fanfare of cymbals and chords, Sonic Youth took the stage.

'Thank you for inviting us here to beautiful Belgrade,' drawled Thurston Moore. His hair alone was a time warp to 1990, a Ride on Inspiral Carpets to happier Mondays.

In a leopard-print dress on bass, Kim Gordon whispered sensuous invocations. 'Spirit desire,' she trilled over dreamy arpeggios. 'Spirit desire. Spirit desire, we will fall...'

Lee Ranaldo and Jim O'Rourke strummed up the noise. Distortion pedals got stepped on, and the kick drum thwacked us back to where we'd started. *Teenage Riot* was originally titled *Rock and Roll For President.*

Thurston's words reminded me of G. 'Looking for a man with a focus and a temper who can open up a map and see between one and two,' he sang. 'It's a teenage riot in a public station. Gonna fight and tear it up in a hyper nation for you.'

The song was even eerily prophetic. 'He acts the hero, we paint a zero on his hand...' Then on to the climax: 'It's time to go round, a one-man showdown, teach us how to fail...' And away they screeched in guitar loops of feedback.

Rather than set them ablaze, or smash up the monitors, the band caressed their instruments with drumsticks, coaxing mesmerizing reverb from the strings. Thurston took his Fender off and embraced it, stroking the length of the neck until it shrieked. Kim wielded hers at the speakers like a rocket launcher, teetering on dainty red heels. Thurston took to rolling on the apron. The crowd went wild. And so did an old friend of G's, the Serbian radio equivalent of John Peel.

'Music has to be provocative,' he said. 'It must open up your mind to let you enjoy different spirits and possibilities.' He smiled his blessing. 'It was like God sent us the rain. Everyone came because it was free, and the people just don't have any money.'

It was always going to be tough to top Sonic Youth. Carl Craig stuck around for a go on a special DJ stage, dropping Michael Jackson's *Wanna Be Startin' Somethin'*, with its paranoid refrain: 'they eat off you, you're a vegetable.' Then came the aptly named Billy Nasty, who blasted a darker techno path to daybreak.

But first there was Fun-Da-Mental's agit-pop. Led by an aging Pakistani punk, who used to use the stage name 'Propa-Gandhi', they specialized in rabble-rousing mash-ups. They were Rage Against The Machine's more cultured cousins, fusing British Asian Muslim Black Power. And unlike the average band they had a credo.

'Until the philosophy that holds one superior and another inferior is finally and permanently dismantled and abandoned,' it said, 'THERE SHALL BE WAR!'

Aye.

To prepare for their set, they got stoned and sparred backstage, in a fusion of Capoeira and Tai Chi. Then they stomped on with a choir of half-naked Zulus. To industrial beats and a snake-charming lilt, two rappers strutted out a Maori *haka*.

'More chaos!' one yelled to get started. 'More motherfucking chaos!' He was clad in camouflage combats and a headdress, and his message had a resonance with Serbs. 'Maybe the West is demonizing us!'

Loud cheers rang out, but aimed elsewhere: at a portly *Qawwali* backing singer, who let rip a lung-busting solo from his harmonium. A group of people started pogoing.

Stage right, an enormous Stars and Stripes unfurled. It was daubed with the mantra: 'No. 1 TERRORIST'. This time the crowd roared on cue.

As Old Glory was tossed to one side, another rapper peeled off his knee-length shorts. Removing his underwear too, Dave seized the flag. He pressed it to his groin. Then he fucked it.

The fabric bulged to his grinding pledge of allegiance. While the band played on, he tied it round his waist, and stripped off his top to expose a khaki wife-beater. Thus attired, he hopped off the stage to meet his public.

He resurfaced a few tracks later, right on cue.

'There is too much war,' a fellow rapper squealed. 'TOO MUCH... WAAARRRRR!!!'

This was the signal Dave had been awaiting. Accompanied by tambourine and tabla, he laid down the central Fun-Da-Mental doctrine. 'Until the basic human rights are equally guaranteed to all, regardless of race, everywhere is war!' he preached. 'War... What the fuck is it for?'

Draping a microphone cable round his neck, he pretended to hang himself. 'Too much war!' he boomed. 'I don't want it, I said stop it. STOP IT! STOP IT!'

Two projectiles flew up from the shadows. One laid him out. The music stopped. The band had the clearest view of what transpired.

'D got hit in the head with a bottle by a skinhead,' one of them explained. 'The crowd then turned on him and his two skinhead mates, who escaped. Security grabbed the other guy, who kind of stood defiant until the promoter head-butted him. He was taken out and given such a bad beating that even I felt sorry for him.'

You might have thought rants at America would appeal, but being black and Muslim undermined them. To swivel-eyed patriot fantasists in Serbia, their people are the guardians of Christendom, defending it from dark-skinned foreign infidel.

Compounding this weirdness, 'the crowd were throwing nationalist salutes,' the Fun-Da-Mentalist observed, 'while singing along to Sufi Muslim songs. Ironic. A lot of Serbs seem to be in denial of the massacre of my brothers and sisters in Bosnia. They seem to believe it was some kind of civil war. May Allah protect the Muslims and have mercy on the rest.'

Perhaps a different message might have helped. They used to aim their ire at wider targets. Wherever they played, they'd scream: 'The Problem Is You!'

I really wanted someone to try and kill me. I suppose I thought it would teach me the meaning of life. But of all the Balkan gun nuts I encountered, the only one who aimed at me was British, and I didn't learn much from him except to doubt. He was guarding NATO troops in Macedonia, and I wasn't supposed to investigate their role. 'Get the fuck away!' he yelled down his rifle. I obliged forthwith, in my Reuters armored jeep.

Apart from our security contingent, the festival's hazards mostly lurked within. It was hard to tell our enemies from friends. The new prime minister and his deputy came schmoozing. They occupied our terrace for VIPs, among the assembled flatheads and their stick insects. My partners were quizzed at length about our plans, but there was nothing to suggest a tourist boom was nigh. All we had to show were gurning expats.

Someone in London had wanted to run a champagne bar. 'I can get cheap, cheap case prices on Veuve Clicquot,' she'd said. We could have flogged the idea to her mailing list of City types. They were clubbers bored of benders in Ibiza. She talked of profits of a hundred pounds a head on travel. If only we'd arranged a simple package.

I didn't hang around to sell illusions. I felt ashamed that I'd believed in them at all. My pride at the size of the crowd had melted fast, congealing into muddy disappointment. The festival was finished. Nothing had changed. Another ambitious achievement got me nowhere. The only possible outcome was despair.

The field was still half full when I escaped. I almost had to fight my way ashore. A menagerie of darkness clawed my eyes. The bodies of beautiful women morphed to reptiles, hissing at little suckling pig admirers. A flash of light transformed the smiles to leers. They devastated all my childish fantasies. The show had become a gargoyle pandemonium. Everyone craved a crazy validation. Our emptiness was gutting us to death. 'How do I look?' the vultures asked. 'What do you think?' The horror slapped me out of twisted dreams. The nightmare was alive and I was full of it.

Crossing the Danube, I coughed up beads of blood. Ambition and expectation were destroying me. I swore I'd never want anything again.

I'd love to declare we were robbed, but I don't have a clue. All I know for sure is what I saw, and what my partners tried to tell me. The journalistic instinct says that's good enough: source it to them, and avoid admitting ignorance. But my faith in perception crumbled by the moment. Reality felt ever more elusive. All of the possibilities were frightening, and none of the answers I wanted were accessible.

'How can we have failed to make some money?' I asked G. We were sitting at the bar in our hotel. The last remaining guests were checking out, and filling up surrounding chairs and tables. My partner ordered rounds of drinks for everyone.

'And what you think I can do?' he laughed, signing chits with a grin at the bow-tied Balkan waiter, who ferried a bottle of vodka to our film crew.

'Enjoy,' G shouted, waving. 'It is gift from state of Serbia today.'

'Seriously,' I said, 'what do you mean? Are you telling me that no one bought drinks?'

My partner shrugged. 'Most guys got no money here, we know that.'

Even now his nonchalance astonished me. 'But how are we going to pay people?'

'We already did,' he said. 'Those ones what count. Most artists got their money, and rest of them I pay as soon I can. But these guys,' he smiled at the waiter again, 'I don't think they are getting paid. Hotel I mean. How I pay them? You wanna loan me?'

My thoughts turned briefly to my contract. I'd seen about three per cent of my fifty grand. Presumably, I wouldn't see much more.

'And what about everyone else?' I asked.

He raised his water to the room. 'We offer them drinks!'

I swigged at a third glass of gin. Take it slowly, I thought, feeling wobbly. You don't want to fall on your face. You might get cut.

'I still don't understand,' I said. 'What happened to the money from the bars?'

G was disconcertingly unruffled. 'I would say most did finish toward captain of our security. For rest, I will find out, you can be sure.'

'But weren't we watching?' I was incredulous. 'What happened to our friend from New York?'

My partner's stare knocked me sideways. 'Don't you forget here wouldn't be festival without him. Maybe he save what can be saved on clumsy way. What you think he can do? It has been typical Balkan story, steal da cash and lean heavy on authorized personas. For those guys, we just dirty money Laundromat.'

I drained my drink, and refilled it from the bottle. G was impossible. My only hope was to pin him back to basics. 'How much did we take, altogether?'

He shook his head. 'Enough to clear out loan and pay to sponsors, and to cover up on stages and production, but I estimate we down few hundred thousand. Hotels, offices, all that shit from government, forget about it.'

'What about security?' I said. 'I guess they got paid?'

G laughed. 'Problem with Serbs is there are many hungry mouths to feed, and those who are greedy or do not deserve it are in first line. I am talking to lawyer already man, we have case. He help recover from those what work to undermine us.'

'Anything's worth a try,' I said. But another problem seemed to me more pressing. My voicemail was full of messages from staff.

They'd all been told they'd be paid on the final day. 'What about the people we employed?' I said. 'They'll be furious.'

G snorted. 'And why you care what they think? They confused. They should realize opportunity we give them. Most those guys don't really wanna *work*. For them, that familiar sleazy style is best, to be informers, small-time dealers, usual shit. From what I seen, I'm sure they fuck us up.'

'Not all of them,' I protested. 'The designer's been doing work for us for months.'

I'd given my word. Now it seemed to be worthless. I'd need to find some other words to hide behind. My brain was swimming. I poured more gin.

'Why you think your guys should get paid?' my partner snapped. 'Just look at posters!' He frowned at the patchwork on the wall. 'Fuck-ing ri-*dic*-ulous!'

I couldn't argue. My mind was a tangled web of contradictions. There'd always been more to do, and no one doing it. We'd swarmed around like children playing football. None of us thought about tactics or defending. Enthusiasm couldn't make amends. I blamed myself. I thought we all should.

I took a deep breath. 'Isn't this partly our fault?' I said. 'We burned ourselves out just trying to survive. We needed a manager...'

My partner interrupted me at once. 'Why you are reacting so damn negative? Nobody *died* man. You are one fussy guy, you know? That's something I notice. People gonna value what we bring them. They experience something special here last night.'

'Yeah, well I wish they'd valued it before. If we'd sold some tickets up front, we might have got organized. Instead, we wasted months on chasing money. We couldn't even stick to simple plans. It wouldn't exactly be hard to rip us off.'

It's depressing to know that you're right, and you can't change a thing. G and his ceaseless patter made it worse. Sales talk probably gave us half our problems. We'd conned ourselves into conning other people. I didn't trust a word my partner said. The charisma that seduced me stung like acid.

He seemed oblivious. 'We made here something beautiful,' he said. 'We show that kinda style we wanna bring. But it is early, what can we do? We pioneers. And there is very small space for freelance in this country. Everyone have to belong to someone else. If not wired and well-informed medias, it will be gang of small time hoods like we experience. And if not them, is gonna be diplomat clubs, or policeman selected specially for drug pushing. S'aright man, we safe from all those guys. I am glad that you could still attract ambassador. Without him on TV, maybe they kill us.'

The razor-wire ticks dug harder at my stomach. What did he mean? Why did we need foreign cover? What was he hiding? Had G been exploiting my passport all along? I felt betrayed.

'I hate this place,' I said. 'You can't trust anyone. Even teachers here are corrupt. They take bribes in schools to give good grades.'

G's voice was withering. 'You think is so much different back in West? Corruption there is on level beyond even oligarchs. Did your government ask you bribe to wash tax to arms trade? They do that shit you know, whatever you vote. And there is no one going to gulag if they don't. They just scared to pay off mortgage and the credit cards. Whole system of that money is a theft. It stole your country. Big banks pass debts down chain to rob from poor. Why I should be more impressed with that?'

'No reason,' I said. 'But at least we could run a business there in peace.'

'And it would need like million pounds for us to start. Sure, it is here Wild East, but I do things my way. I am not regular Slav and you should know that. I am not friend of West, nor am I enemy, I don't give *damn* about their clash of civilizations.'

Confusion was making me homesick. 'What's war talk got to do with our festival?'

G put down his glass and smiled indulgently. 'In Serbia,

whole world's chaos come to *you*. We see it when that guy did fuck his flag. Politicians who hang on ECHO love America. They hope West pays bills so they still free to rob.'

'Yes, but who...'

He burst out laughing. 'Small man in this shithole learn to cope. Going to bed without supper made him stronger, much stronger than those who act like have five stomachs. Now Balkan mafia is giving last push to win war from Nineties. And I don't see here force that can oppose them. Certainly not America and EU. Delinquents soon can turn as next crusaders. After jail time for murders and drug raps, they protect us all from filth that gonna fly. You should believe man, all that shit will happen here. Truth is same like thousand years before. Religious war is choice for bankrupt empires.'

The room was a blur. I felt possessed. What had I been playing at all year? 'I don't see what's so funny here,' I said. 'Are you telling me we messed with that for *fun*?'

G laughed louder. 'I am not demon, my friend, nor I am joker. We do what we feel, and I am proud for that. I would not mind if million baboons screw every flag in front of me. Those cloths present ultimate kitsch, and should wave on tower made out of greed and consumer primitivism. I am pretty sure Serbs can build one soon, perhaps on cheap EU loan. It seems there is not bottom line for taste.'

I wobbled forward on my stool. He grabbed my arm. 'Sure, we made mistake,' he said. 'It was thinking this city was ready for honest politics. But can be different here next year. Will be two hundred year anniversary of constitution. I bring them even Sting if they will pay me. We ask them money as advance, so we can do it like you want.'

I drained my gin. The final dregs of patience left me too. 'Listen,' I begged, 'if you think you know who stole from us, please tell me.'

G scanned my face. His eyebrows rose. It felt as if he was

lining up a punch. 'You know we all did help ourselves,' he said. 'You too.'

Of course we'd helped ourselves: we sought revenge. ECHO was my riposte to the *Times*, and his to EXIT. And now it had taken vengeance in its turn. But that didn't make much sense of what confused me. My head slumped into my palms and hit the bar.

'Raoul, take it easy,' G said. 'I think you should let go of being logical. That shit can stop you seeing truth. People are not like machines. They always fail. You wanna live dreams, accept that you must fail. Just try to live forever you will fail. And always life inside will rise again. Maybe you fail better next time round. You rest, I'm sure you gonna understand. And I am gonna find which assholes screwed us.'

A murmur spread its way round the bar. A shuttle for the airport had arrived. Disheveled wreck-heads groped at piles of bags. G stood imperious before them, arms outstretched. In the mirrors, his shirt billowed wide, like a cloak.

'*Welcome to the Hotel Jugoslavija!*' he boomed. 'You can check out when you like, but never leave!'

At home in my rooftop apartment, I tried taking stock. Our bundle of drugs still held four hundred and thirty-seven pills, a block of coke too big for my miniature scales, and the bulk of E's bog standard hash. At worst, it was worth five grand. But cashing it in seemed risky, and keeping it didn't sound a whole lot safer. The middle way was rather more enticing. I could sit indoors and slowly cane the evidence.

Addicts are always chasing something lost. Even the ultimate high is bound to fade. The fastest way back from the low is loading up again. Each moment holds reminders of what isn't, until oblivion blots them out. My deepest sense of justice felt betrayed: by G, *The New York Times* and life itself. Everyone I'd worked with seemed pissed off. So much for thinking I was helping. There was none of the love in my heart that I yearned for from others. All that remained of my vision was resentment.

Who cared if the stash in my cupboard wasn't mine? I told myself possession was the law. Compared to the festival's losses, this was trifling. And if E still needed paying, that was G's concern. He was the one who'd brought the guy to Serbia. Maybe they'd do bigger deals to cover it. I didn't know, and couldn't give a damn.

A friend stayed on a few days to keep me company. I'd avoided him all week. I felt too raw. And that was the way this crazy year unfolded. I'd hidden away and tried to reinvent myself. My oldest friends had tired of late-night phone calls, whining about the Balkans and my job. 'Come home if you're unhappy,' they'd suggest. I withdrew to run the festival instead. Only now it was finished, the entropy was stifling: so much energy blown on acting positive, and nothing but negativity endured. A mix CD on my stereo said it all: *'You just think what a bum rap for a nice, sensitive guy like me.'*

Two weeks shot up my nose to dull the pain. On waking each afternoon, I thought I'd stop. But I soon found other friends to share the load. A couple of joints and I'd send them out for vodka. A line to pick things up wasn't far behind. Then a cheeky half a pill to take the edge off, and soon we'd be deluded once again. If only that sensation could have lasted. Sadly, nothing did except The Fear. Once alone, I saw it smothered me in darkness. Even my faithful hash no longer worked. It merely numbed the pain I'd feel without it. The light that gave me guidance had expired. My partner's flame was reduced to streaks of soot.

An old employer once told me: 'You'll get your ulcer.' I was terrified he couldn't see the half of it. The poison in my guts was Kurt Cobain's. I'd tried everything I knew to find relief, from working myself the bone to slacking off. I'd repressed my desires and indulged them, embraced the extremes of self-regard and hatred. And none of it made the blindest bit of difference. The only effective remedies were drugs. But whatever I took would never be enough.

A few days on, I braved my mobile phone. There were thirteen new missed calls from our designer. I got myself more stoned before I phoned. He was livid, only trying to disguise it. I could hear some people talking in the background. He was probably at work, making billboard ads for vitamins and tampons.

'How's it going?' I asked in a monotone.

He hissed. 'What you expect with situation?'

'Hey man, I'm sorry...'

'Yeah, well I am sorry too. I tried to help make something nice. Do you know what stress you made for me these months?'

I sighed. 'How much do we owe you?'

He sighed far louder. 'Today, I will accept two thousand euro.'

The bill he'd sent already came to three. Clearly he'd begun to face the facts. So why not barter?

'I can offer you four hundred quality English pills,' I said. 'You can sell them for five euros each. They're worth at least ten here.'

The line went dead for several seconds. Then he exploded. 'Hey, what the *fuck* you think you telling me?'

'There isn't any money,' I said, feeling oddly calm. A measure of G's detachment had rubbed off. 'Someone stole it.'

'You're making me nervous,' he shouted. 'Your shit is not my problem.'

'I think it is.' You know, I sympathized. I did. I really did. But it made no difference.

'I think is *your* problem,' he said, 'and it is big one. I hear police begin preparing some arrests.'

My heart had started thudding in my temples. I reached for my hash, and wedged the phone against my jaw. 'Sorry, what?'

He seemed amused. 'I hear on radio. Whole festival is fraud controlled by criminals. You tell your partners they go sell their shit and pay me.'

The designer watched too many Tarantino films. Perhaps he was bluffing.

'I can't tell anyone anything,' I said. 'They didn't pay me either. But I can give you all those pills to shut you up. Now listen, do you want the things or not?'

'You fucking idiot.'

I laughed. 'Oh, who's the idiot? Isn't it better getting something than *fuck all*?'

'Of course!'

'So you want them?'

'No!' He was maddeningly smug.

'Come on,' I said. 'I think you're being stupid.'

'Serbs *are* stupid,' he said.

I hung up.

Fuck them all.

When I finally heard from my partner again, I was ruined. I'd done nothing for days but smoke E's ropey hash. The coke and the pills had returned to the fuse box stash. I was slouching in an armchair, eyes half shut. On arrival, G paced round my living room. He'd been traipsing through Belgrade on his enquiries, and he'd drunk so much coffee in the process he was wired. Digesting what he told me was beyond me.

He snatched a joint butt from the ashtray on the table. 'So they call me in last night for private meeting...'

He'd already lost me. 'Sorry, who?'

'That guy whose name is best that you don't know.'

I leaned forward. 'Which guy's that then?'

G threw me a quizzical look. 'The one controlling set-up there on island.'

I took a wild stab. 'Our head of security?'

He laughed. 'That guy is *puppy* man, but has wicked sense of humor. Did you hear he made a conference here for media? He says he plans on takeover of ECHO.'

'Oh really?' Some distant instinct made me smile. 'When?'

G ignored the question and walked to my window. 'I don't think is much left to take. Our lawyer prepared the paper for a bankrupts.'

'Can't your partner help?' I asked G's back. Most of our debts were to outposts of the state, and they didn't seem like people to annoy.

'Forget about it,' he barked, spinning round. 'That guy cause too much headaches here already. He lost more than he expected. I probably work all winter just to calm him.'

'Sorry?' This hint of malice was a shock.

'He is back now in New York, where he belong. It was mistake to bring him over. He lost instinct for the business here on territories. Police were asking hundred thousand dollars, or they would register us as criminals on Interpol. And he offer them bribe to drop charges. He is lucky he got home before they shake him.'

'Charges?' I trembled. 'What charges?'

G waved me away. 'That was idle threat, like as test. I hope there will be charges, for those what steal from us. But for that we wait. Meantime I talk with Mr X.'

'X?' I blinked back vacantly.

'That boss,' he said impatiently. 'Mr Big! In wars, he was a partner of Arkan. Then he did turn to side of Djindjic for revolution. You know whole whitewash story, stinky circumstance. Now he is power in that business club of Democrats.'

I couldn't keep up. He forged ahead.

'You know what that guy asked me, man? He say is your money in a grave! Seriously, he sees whole world his way. Now he wants that we make festival next year. Just not on island. And we would first sign business to him. We keep percentage.'

'And why would we want to do that?'

G shrugged. 'What choice we have? That lawyer already told me my mistake. I didn't make a dialogue with mafia. If I did, we could avoid this kind of threats.'

'I thought you said the police had made the threats...'

His forehead scrunched in frustration. 'You do realize minister of police is friend with gangsters?'

'Maybe,' I said. 'But he was locking them up by the hundred when Djindjic got shot...'

G cut me off. 'My friend, is hard for you to see perhaps, but here is liars and thieves on top of structure. Everyone I talk to agree. We have powerful enemies. Even prime minister deputy is crying, like we wanna convert his island onto drug beach, without him getting proper cut.'

'*His* island?'

'You remember that story we hear about investors? Well, seems fantasy was real. City was supposed to take island from Zemun, because foreigner planned to invest over period of years. But first they need to clear out jurisdiction.'

'And?' I said, none the wiser.

G pressed on. 'So you know who own island before? Guy I met! The Mr Big. He was in Radicals party, close with mayor in Zemun. But now those conservatives run there council, and X did join to Democrats instead, tight on circuit with minister of police.'

He reminded me of interviewing diplomats. They'd act like cryptic references were obvious, so you had to imply that you got it while fishing for details. If you asked too many questions, they'd dry up. My partner, by contrast, needed no encouragement.

'So they had problem with us on island all through summer, and with option to extend for next year. It was dispute on that contract from first day. Zemun did want to give to us three years. Always was same game, buying time.'

'Sorry, when?'

'Since first meeting! Now city wanna make privatization on account of French guys, what did plan to invest their millions into aqua park. Of course, would be payola there for everyone, and investor already paid down some deposit. So city and X need island back and quick. But council doesn't wanna give. They give to us.'

'Why us?'

'To push him back! We were perfect for them - big festival dragging support from even police. But when Djindjic died they all did start regrouping. Police don't like that army works with hipsters. So there was extra problem just right there. For them, only thing in common was destroy us.'

'Who?'

'Politicians!' he said brusquely. 'Like I thought, was only when ambassador speak they decide not to ruin festival completely. Instead they let us do but crush financially, you know, like they discredit so we never can come back.'

My head hurt. 'How exactly?'

'Since May, our local partners undermine us,' G said. 'And for that I'm pretty sure they take their share. Certainly they help to bring security, what let in thousands on cheap money every night. They organize black supply of drinks with our sponsors. And they even had support of apparatchik. You know that Otpor guy, what orchestrate war with woman from bird protection club? And he is close friend of prime minister vice, who gave green light to target us direct. They hug you close to knife you hard in back.'

'I don't understand,' I said. 'We weren't a threat.'

My partner pulled up a chair and sat down opposite. When he spoke, his voice was half an octave lower.

'Just by *existing* we are threat, don't you see?' he said. 'Because we *do* something for city when they don't. And you should hear what police and gangsters now are saying. Those kids who work for you they also talk. One newspaper says I am number one salesman of ecstasy on Balkans, with partner washing cash for Croat mafia. And you, Raoul, you are renegade British spy.'

For all I knew, that's really what we were.

'Let me tell you I don't plan on backing up,' G went on. 'I had few of personal signals fight is worth it. I was walking down crowdy street where kids were screaming long live ECHO, bring us more of drum and bass. S'aright man, some people understand.'

'I'm glad to hear it,' I said. 'I don't think I do.'

'That's great!' G grinned. 'Already you came close on understanding.'

'Eh?'

'Reality on Balkans is surreal,' he said. 'You think you understand, I guess you don't. You stop that search of thinking, you sense truth.'

I exhaled slowly. 'So you're saying our partners robbed us with security, on behalf of some gangsters, an investor and the government?'

'It is much worse!' G said. 'You forget B92. Legendary fighter of crimes was on same side this time, since we scrambled plans with EXIT. They are the ones what broadcast word against us. And both are American toy, we know that. Effectively we fight with CIA!'

My eyes rolled shut. 'We're in a conspiracy theory.'

'You can call whatever you want, but facts are facts,' he said. 'Mafia here work close with who has power, and Americans and Brits they support that, to build up Serbs as stable Balkan leader. Yes, mafia is very stable and healthy in Serbia. And on top of that one-eye pyramid is dollar. Jah Rastafari ten million times!'

It was hard not to join in his laughter, but I couldn't. Whatever G said, we weren't just simple victims. 'Surely we're still partly to blame,' I said.

'Like how you mean?' he snapped.

'Well,' I said, abandoning my caution, 'we've been trying to exploit politicians since we started. If you knew all the risks, then why not manage them better?'

My partner ran his hands through his hair. He took at least a minute to reply.

'And how you think we do that here?' he said quietly. 'You think you even master of yourself? We had to work with what we find. What else we do? Whole action was just spice on wrong cooked brew.'

I persisted. 'Yes, but we're the ones who chose to light the fire.'

He chuckled wryly. 'And who it is you think did choose that action?'

'You've lost me,' I said.

He stood again and stared me in the face. 'You know if *you* lose me, you maybe learn to choose. But most of things we find in life choose *us*. We all tied on one big chain of caused effects. How much of that you think we can control? Like few percent? You should investigate yourself. I think you find you don't control your thoughts. And then you see you don't do actions. Most things you think you choosing is reaction.'

I stared back aghast. 'Are you denying we have any responsibility?'

G was wheeling round me like a hawk, his hands flashing tracers. 'No!' he shouted. 'All are to blame, for everything, but still it doesn't mean we should have guilt. You look inside yourself, my friend. I think you see. Maybe you learn to forgive.'

I braced myself and rose to have it out. 'You can't have it both ways,' I said. 'If we're free to choose, we have to face the consequences. I'm not predestined to jump out the window, but I'm free to choose to do that if I want.'

G stopped and smiled. 'I don't think is such great idea.'

'Perhaps,' I said. 'But without free will, we might as well be dead.'

'My friend, you wanna be free, you should stop running.' G was backing his way to the door. I kept my distance.

'If you accept shit as it is, you are OK,' G said. 'There's no escape. And that is why I feel my conscience clear. We show we not afraid of living dead. Fear is energy man, like Buddha coming in to knock your heart. You know, I sometimes feel too sensitive for world. But I will try to do few more good things, and hope that out of my ashes and dust some tiny sparkle join to highest light. For now though, I am gonna let you rest. I think you need, Jah bless. You relax man, stay cool and be good!'

With that he swirled out of my flat and down the stairs.

When I was sure he'd reached the corridor below, I tiptoed to the door and peered outside. I knew he'd be waiting for the lift. It stopped a level short of my apartment, but I could hear its steady creaking from the shaft. At least I usually could, but this time there was silence. I heard a powerful finger press the button twice. I crept to the banister. My partner's voice rebounded up the stairwell.

'Elevator is broken man!' he shouted. 'I think is problem with a fuse. Wiring in this city is fucked up. I'm gonna call for you repair guy.'

My heart shot up my throat and hit my skull. It was all I could do not to leap for the fuse box at once. I crouched there breathing deeper than a bellows, convinced he'd hear me soon unless I moved, which would surely be noisier.

His leather soles resumed their loud descent.

Paralyzed, I waited several minutes. Then I grabbed the bag of drugs and dashed indoors. I couldn't really say who scared me more: the smuggler whose narcotics I'd made off with, the police who'd lock me up if they discovered them, or the trickster Balkan mystic they belonged to. If doing so weren't patently insane, I'd have flushed the parcel's contents down the toilet. Instead, I rolled a joint and panicked more.

REVELATION

I wanted to find out the truth, but it seemed inconceivable. I felt ignorant, and couldn't trust a soul. In any case, who really knew? Even if the facts could be agreed, people would frame their stories differently. The universe unfolds inside our heads. Whatever we say reality is, it can't be. Language doesn't begin to come to grips with it. Believing is seeing: the mind can convince itself of anything. We merely have to ignore the awkward proof. Little wonder journalists are fucked.

Of course, I only had a single source. I ought to have interviewed everyone, including our multiple creditors and the police. This didn't seem wise. We owed vast amounts of money to powerful Serbs, and I was an attractive Western whipping boy. Although I mightn't have the cash to clear our debts, my home was hiding someone else's drugs. So I worked on the precautionary principle, and got the fuck out of there.

My departure was swiftly arranged without much fuss. I hired an agent to ship all my stuff to a warehouse in London. My personal destination was oblivion. I'd retreat to the middle of nowhere, and do nothing.

Once the movers had boxed up my flat, I bought a ticket to Amsterdam, paying cash. Before departing, I called on G at his apartment, and handed him the remnants of our stash. What I'd taken was a write-off, like my fee. The rest was his to dispose of as he pleased. My partner simply nodded at me and smiled.

'You realize that you can't run from yourself?' he said.

I couldn't mask my indignation. 'Who says I'm running?'

He shrugged. 'I just try to offer you spiritual advice.'

Yeah, fuck you too, I thought. 'Fair point,' I said. 'It feels like time I built a chrysalis.'

'There is no chrysalis!' G laughed. 'That is whole point.'

I left my partner to himself, and hailed a taxi. When the plane took off, a burden started lifting.

Whatever G might think, I had to change. I felt stuck in adolescence, craving mentors, but no one could teach me how to be myself. My ceaseless search for gurus was deluded, and heeding them had knocked me off my path.

It had never been my dream to run a festival. I did it for the challenge. I was desperate to show I was capable of anything, but nothing could bear the weight of expectations. Whatever people said, it wasn't good enough. If they praised what was clearly flawed, they must be liars. And if they criticized my efforts, I felt crushed. Beyond looking good, I'd lost sight of what I wanted. I barely felt connected to my instincts. Identities are epic works of fiction, and mine had been unraveling for months.

Whose crazed ideas had colonized my mind? The thought of changing Serbia was ludicrous. And yet, as Kurt Vonnegut put it, 'There is no good reason good can't triumph over evil, if only angels will get organized along the lines of the mafia.'

So who were the mafia that thwarted us? A proper cartel like the Zemun clan? Or our security goons, their political friends and businessmen who told them what to do? Or were the villains little more than common crooks? The operator type, like A and B? Opportunists, like J and G? Even me? I didn't know what to believe, or who was who. The only sane response was paranoia.

G manhandled details like a bra strap. Whoever ripped us off, we'd helped them do it. And if we'd strengthened all the forces we'd been fighting, did it matter that we didn't really mean to? We might as well parrot Rumsfeld's line on Baghdad, when American troops waltzed in to guard the oil ministry, and pinned the resulting carnage on 'dead-enders', from the ranks of an Iraqi army they'd demobilized. All the looting and killing was 'stuff' that simply 'happens'.

I smelled the usual Balkan bullshit: enemies are always to blame, and everything's put down to undermining. Western meddling globalized this mindset. Since NATO was so blatantly self-serving, its critics spied a capitalist plot, to demonize Serbs and carve up Yugoslavia. By the logic of reverse propaganda, there weren't any concentration camps, the Muslims bombed themselves, and the mass executions at Srebrenica were faked. Skeptics took fiction on faith. Was I being told to do the same?

I was torn between denial and liability, the same dilemma afflicting Serbs in general. Few agreed they shared collective guilt, unlike the liberal *New York Times*, which was still printing stories that asked 'Are Germans Nazis?' Don't be absurd. There's no such thing as evil genes. Indifference is as ubiquitous as the herd instinct. It's as banal as taking 'the President's plans' as read. And the awful truth was far too grim to countenance: perhaps I was as flawed as those I loathed.

If there's really a giant conspiracy, it's everywhere. Everyone's complicit in stupidity. I'd chucked all my toys out the pram and deferred to G. I scarcely cared if my partner took advantage. I'd done the same. He'd helped to shock me into action. Without him, I'd have been stuck at *The New York Times*, still seething at their spinelessness and mine, and drinking myself to sleep to stay employed.

Whatever the rights and wrongs, we'd run a festival. And somehow I'd now got away unscathed. I knew this meant I ought to feel relieved, even pleased. But I could only process the outcome analytically: every thought was supplanted by its opposite. What couldn't be wholly good was really bad, and the tyranny of reason led to madness.

Thankfully, I planned to switch my brain off.

I didn't stay long in Amsterdam. I headed straight for my favorite coffee shop at the Spui, and ordered €1,500 of finest Moroccan. Since this was roughly twenty times the legal limit, I had to wait more than an hour to pick it up. The rule of law is rarely what it seems. Dispensing with the usual precautions, I packed my hash down the front of a purpose-bought pair of sports briefs, and boarded an express train to Paris.

To distance myself from distractions, and Belgrade, I was borrowing a farmhouse in France. In return for repainting the walls, I could live there for free. The time to face my demons had arrived. I'd been avoiding this since flipping out on acid. Back then I read a book on meditation. It was titled *Experience Beyond Thinking*, but it failed to provide experience without practice. I'd filed it away with my diarized 'Notes To Self', which I composed with disconcerting repetition. According to one such entry, 'the aim is to focus on the present rather than worrying about the future,' and to 'work at stress management without relying solely on cannabis.' So much for that, like the postscript: 'CARE LESS HOW PEOPLE SEE YOU (AND SAY WHAT YOU MEAN)!'

Unless I learned to live with how I was, I'd persist in wild attempts to save the world, in fruitless pursuit of salvation from myself. If I observed how the process worked, I might stop feeding it. I couldn't keep investing in my fantasies. The answer wasn't to find a nice illusion. There wasn't an answer at all; that was the problem. My Indian inspiration had misled me. I thought *charas* was the essence of enlightenment. But as Tolstoy confessed: 'One can only live while one is intoxicated with life.' And 'as soon as one is sober it is impossible not to see that it is all a fraud.'

I had to stop depending on a crutch. I'd smoke less dope each day until I gave up. And in the meantime, I'd start work on letting go, by writing up a memoir of the Balkans. The result would be a gradual shift in consciousness, diminishing anxiety and anger, and cultivating greater loving kindness. Or so my Buddhist book implied. All I wanted was to realize what was in me. Whatever else life threw at me, I'd handle it. I'd have to. I was on my own at last.

The quietness at the farmhouse was alarming. The only animals in evidence were birds. Fields of flaxen crops rolled down to a stream, and blended into thickets in the distance. Every other building looked deserted. The days dragged on interminably, then blurred.

Writing proved much harder than expected. Like where do you start? When to stop? What to cut? How much of it could put you six feet under? My character drove me on towards the edge. If I didn't rewrite it soon, I'd push me over.

To focus on the task, I kept a journal. 'There is no getting there,' I warned myself, 'no solving eternal mysteries. That is truth. Everything else is illusion. Were it not for mysteries we'd be robots.' I sounded like G. He'd corrupted my hard drive.

'The truth can't be explained,' I tried explaining. 'It has to be felt. And it can't be propagandized, because it is experience. It can never be fully attained, for perfection is elusive. Yet it's the only pursuit to which it's worth devoting your life.'

That produced a warm swollen glow. It wore off fast. 'Nothing can be fixed,' I moped. 'I fear that once again I've been proved to be an asshole.'

As long as I kept smoking, I felt great. But as soon as I tried cutting down, the world turned bleak. 'What is the point of writing?' I wrote. 'Being trivial frightens me. I am not a visionary, just curious and restless, exploring the world to try and make sense of life. But cutting myself off from others won't help much. So I'm back where I started.'

Like me, the bar got higher by the day. 'If there's a purpose it must surely be this,' I decided: 'to awaken in others a sense of basking in the aura of magic that transcends the humdrum.' I dreamed my voice was Hamlet singing Beethoven.

This mash-up was drawn from the text of *The Glass Bead Game*. Its master player taught me all his tricks. 'My life,' the narrator wrote, while he renounced it, 'ought to be a perpetual transcending, a progression from stage to stage; I wanted to pass from one area after the next, leaving each behind, as music moves on from theme to theme, from tempo to tempo, playing each out to the end, completing each and leaving it behind, never tiring, never sleeping, forever wakeful, forever in the present.'

I skinned up and prepared to get serious, tomorrow. I'd crank out a one-draft wonder of a book, and wouldn't go to bed until the end.

Day One [cue Geordie accent]: the inmate is in the diary room, keeping it Raoul.

He's wearing a smoking jacket, disguised as a toweled bathrobe. Hip-hop howls from the stereo by the window. The ashtray on the desk is overflowing. He's been working on a manuscript all day. He's calling it *Confessions of a Failed Spy*. That's as far as he's got. He keeps checking email.

'Raoul, I have a problem,' some nut writes. 'Life is too short. I either work too much or not enough. I am not satisfied. Sometimes I believe the only way to learn is to observe. Other times I think it's to participate. I dream of making films, writing books and feeding the poor, but there is so little time. Lately I feel happy doing very little, but I'm afraid I will fail. I am conflicted and want to be at peace. Am I normal?'

'Dear not enough or too much,' we reply. 'What's normal then? For each and every fraction, there's an equally opposite reaction, so what goes down comes up and failure is just another experience to learn from. All you need is love. Love, Raoul.'

If you have a problem, if no one else can help, and if you can find us, maybe you can hire... Raoul Djukanovic. Charlatans need followers to feed on. Maybe you can buy them an identity. Heads G wins, and tails I lose. Say yes, Raoul!

My frontal lobes are bleeding THC.

Day Two: the lunatic is on the grass. Hash. Whatever. Thirty-six hours in, my head explodes. Blueprint's been blasting on auto-repeat all day.

'...*I waltz in and bless this ceremony with an exercise in exorcism. First I rock the rhythm, then I spit a venomous open-mic sermon for the trite vermin that had a hard time learnin' how to properly prepare for the final frontier. We're here...*'

We're skulking in the most secluded room. Raoul's scrawl has filled the notebooks on the floor. Our rap's now been renamed *The Mob Ate My Homework*. News blares on mute in the corner. My laptop on the desk is wired to porn. Round midnight, the CD mixer flips to Shadow: '*From listening to records I just knew what to do...*'

All of the windows are locked, their shutters drawn. I'm cross-legged and butt-naked, bending double. We're slouching towards a beastly Second Coming. Its disembodied goat's head hangs in the doorway. Some Shady tunes are screaming through the static.

'*It's the return of the...*' Ah, wait, no way, you're kidding.

'*He didn't just say what I think he did, did he?*' Who? What? When? Eminem?

'*Here we go again, we're out of our medicine, out of our minds, and we want in yours, let us in!*' Begone, you fiendish queen! I'm not your type!

'*So what's the difference between us? We can start at the penis. Or we can scream I Just Don't Give a Fuck and see who means it!*' AAAAAAAAGGGHHH!

Raoul flops his cock across the table. I want... I want... detachment from desire! Sever the dirty Great Chain of Being! Kill the prick! Cut its throat! Spill his blood!

'*You raise the blade, you make the change...*'

I can't. I'm too weak. I pass out.

Day Three: the Redeemer's in the house! Thank fucking Christ... Some cunt's bugged all these rooms with hidden cameras. You can't fool me. I heard the whirring. Camp X-Ray, innit? OK, so what do you spooks need to hear to set me free?

That's right, oh best beloved in Hell's Kitchen. They screwed us up for one of those moral inventories. So here we are on the couch, like right about *now*! Yes, it's time for watch and learn with the fucked soul brother! Will the mate of Beelzebub's grandson come on down!

Oh sorry, *please allow me to introduce myself...* I'm a man of unhealthy tastes. Raoul Djukanovic, Prince of Discs, your orally fixated rational egotist! So you saw us crack one off to chicks with dicks? Judge not lest you be judged, eh? Turn on, tune in, black out and drop your load. Hey whoops, there goes Dick Alpert out my backside. And Mallett's Mallet is a word association game in which you mustn't pause mustn't hesitate or repeat a word or say a word I don't like otherwise you get a bash on the head like this, and that one *hurt*!

Thank you for joining the real Reformation, live on reality TV! Listen to those voices, barmy army. The United Kingdom of Heaven is within! Suffer and your heart gets stronger, see? Or would sir enjoy another few hours on the rack?

And now for something completely different: news. It's everyone's fault. The whole damned mind-fuck. Hey kids, just say no. Switch off and do something less boring instead. Oh, you know that already, do you? Well, fuck you! And fuck me too. We're all projections of a flashback. And like the English say, we can always make do.

Now go back to bed America, here's another six billion channels of mental monkeys. I'm a hallucinating hack, and you've been great!

Day Four: *sleep nil (bugger), calories ditto (but two vats of Volvic), cumulative hash consumption 28g (the big O!), breakdowns 1 (boohoo!), breakthroughs ∞ (hurrah!).*

Psychotic, you say? Aren't we all? Trapped inside our funny little tunnels. Out in the big wide world, it's all connected. Hello Mum, I'm a plasma ball! The machine elves stuck electrodes on my balls. We're all one endless moment making time. You just have to learn to read the signs. And call things by their names, it's very important.

Oh, thank Bog I sank in quicksand in the Balkans! When his droogs drop in to off me, I'll be back. I'm the one who's always witnessing. I'm love.

So spread the goddamn word and share Good News!

Who to call? An American journalist in London! We've been playing this sordid game since university. Typical hack, he answers right away.

'Giiimp!' he says, through the ringing in my ears. 'What's up dawg?'

I get to business. 'Woodward calling Bernstein!' I scream. 'It's time to prove we're not all the president's men!'

Pin-drop silence. He needs details.

'The world's being held to ransom by gangsta rappers. And you and me are going to expose them.'

Another pause. I titter awkwardly.

'I've been playing *2001* on constant loop... Eminem is really George Bush. And Dre is his Dr Strangelove boss Dick Cheney. They *representin' for the gangstas all across the world... hit my boys off with jobs, no more living hard...'*

Surely he can hear the voices too? *Sorry Doc, but I been crazy, there's no way that you can save me, it's okay, go invade Cheney.*

Sounds pretty crystal clear to me!

'They're fronting for the Neoconz With Attitude. The codename for POTUS is Dubya Money. They've hijacked the Empire to play hold 'em in God's Casino. You know oil, the Middle East? Fucking End Times?'

I mean how blatant can they get? *This is the millennium of aftermath, it ain't gonn' be nothin' after that, so give me one more crack at Iraq and fuck rap, you can have it back!*

My friend keeps trying to talk. I shout him down.

'So we'll rent a big flatbed truck, OK, and park the fucker up behind Times Square. You can wear the Bush mask, and I'll be

Dick. Just like *Point Break*, but we don't rob banks. We're going to exorcise *The New York Times*, with a fat pair of speakers. Live on every network in the country! We'll blast the quisling fucks from Hell's Kitchen!'

'Hey!' he interrupts at last. 'Slow down!'

'Only once I write a different future. We've got to change the American way of life. They say it's non-negotiable. We're screwed.'

'Are you OK?' He sounds suspicious, like that clicking on the line.

'Oh *sure*,' I say, sarcastically. 'I only met the devil and worked out my karma.'

I swear he's typing while he talks. 'Are you still in France?'

'Purgatory,' I tell him. 'All that shit we pulled? Well someone has to pay. And no one can, and everybody hates us.'

He'll understand my angst, I'm sure. He's Jewish.

'Listen,' I explain. 'I've seen the light. I get it now. We're all Jews! We always were of course. It began in Africa. So we're all eternal victims till we *choose*. But I can't, you see, because I'm the *king* of the Jews. So now you'll have to kill me.'

This shuts him up for a good ten seconds.

'Daniel,' he says, 'it's OK. I'm coming to get you.'

We can't get away from the Word. It runs our lives. I realize far too late I've sealed my fate. If only I'd learned to read the signs beforehand. Someone's put a chip inside my head. It's always tuned to *them* instead of me.

I'm lying in a heap and it's night when I hear their voices. He's brought an accomplice. They've got keys. The other guy's a friend of the owner. He lives nearby. The bastard must have had me in his crosshairs. Now they've come here to get me!

How could I be so blind? They're CIA, or NSA, or worse. My so-called friend's been all over the War On Terror! He's some false-flag Mossad freelance on the make! Now hey, I know it was mean to hustle Wiesel. Poor old Elie stuck in Auschwitz. I'm just double-O death wish in his farmhouse. And that's why faithful Felix wants to silence me! Every word I've said is on *their* tapes. And lo, it came to pass, Israeli commandos in American uniforms, precisely as the Mad Professor said.

I will strike down upon thee with great vengeance and furious anger those who attempt to poison and destroy my brothers. And you will know my name is the Lord when I lay my vengeance upon you.

Ezekiel. The prophet's cut my legs off. I fall to the floor with a thump as they storm the building.

'Who *are* you?' I protest. 'Who do you work for? And where's John Travolta?'

One of them passes a blanket to cover me up. The other offers tea from the kitchen. He must think I'm mental. I've not washed up a thing since I arrived.

'No way!' I shake my head. 'You're trying to poison me!'

But wherever I crawl, they're standing right beside me.

I burst into tears.

Nothing lasts. The next thing I know, I'm wriggling in the bedroom. A swarthy doctor holds me down. They've agreed among themselves what he's administering. I've been told to lie there on my front. He lifts the duvet, needle poised: I'm at the sharp end.

I try begging. 'I may be a hopeless deviant,' I scream, 'but no man's fucked me in the shitter. So before you go and kill me with that thing of yours, how about you let me feel your balls?'

It's all no use. He's emptying his fluid in my buttocks. A tranquilizing stupor floods my system. As the spirit of resistance ebbs, I yell farewell: *'Da bog da ti konj krvavim kurcem jebu sestru na majcinom grobu!'* By the will of God, may a horse with a bloody cock fuck your sister on your mother's grave!

I slowly submit. There's no one to fight except myself. There aren't even any Gods to intervene. It's always up to us to start again. Surrender to divinity within! Some day, I'll find the humility to try, and the patience to transcend our limitations. But first I must return to the void, where the love to redeem another life lies dormant.

I feel no pain when my body drifts below me, nailed to the mattress in exhaustion. All things black and white soon fade to grey. There's nothing to do in the end but laugh or cry. As the aperture shrinks on existence, its darkness and the light become as one.

http://www.roughguidedarkside.com

Contemporary culture has eliminated both the concept of the
public and the figure of the intellectual. Former public spaces –
both physical and cultural – are now either derelict or colonized
by advertising. A cretinous anti-intellectualism presides,
cheerled by expensively educated hacks in the pay of
multinational corporations who reassure their bored readers
that there is no need to rouse themselves from their interpassive
stupor. The informal censorship internalized and propagated by
the cultural workers of late capitalism generates a banal
conformity that the propaganda chiefs of Stalinism could only
ever have dreamt of imposing. Zer0 Books knows that another
kind of discourse – intellectual without being academic, popular
without being populist – is not only possible: it is already
flourishing, in the regions beyond the striplit malls of so-called
mass media and the neurotically bureaucratic halls of the
academy. Zer0 is committed to the idea of publishing as a
making public of the intellectual. It is convinced that in
the unthinking, blandly consensual culture in which we live,
critical and engaged theoretical reflection is more important
than ever before.